THIS SWEET PLACE

ISLAND LIVING AND OTHER ADVENTURES

by

Aileen Vincent-Barwood

with illustrations by

Allen Vincent-Barwood

Published by
Media Publishing

1998

*For my husband, Allen Vincent-Barwood, with
thanks for fifty-two years of patience, friendship
and devotion*

*and for Linda, Nan and Posy, a special circle of
friends never to be forgotten*

ISBN 976-8170-07-7

Designed and printed by Media Publishing Ltd,
31 Shirley Park Avenue, PO Box N-9240, Nassau, Bahamas
Tel: 242 325 8210; Fax: 242 325 8065;
e-mail: media@100jamz.com

*"I've traveled round and about
but I always long to come back to
this sweet place."*

**Will Nixon
Farmer's Hill,
Exuma
(1917 - 1997)**

1

Astronauts, looking down on the Bahamas from space, have called them "the most beautiful islands on earth." On vacation to the Bahamas in 1981 we found the island of Great Exuma. In 1984 we bought a small house there, and since 1986 we have been spending our winters there. Living on Exuma has been rewarding, energizing, but not always easy.

There are myriad reasons why people want to live on an island. Some hope to find eternal youth, some are searching for the last remaining peaceable kingdom, for some it is an escape.

To many, islands are like dream-worlds. They haunt our waking moments with images of freedom and an idyllic life. They fill our days with longings and our nights with visions. We think: some day we will go there, some day we will, perhaps, dwell there and know all the things of the world we are meant to know – such things as where we are headed, what will be there when we get there, our reason for being on this difficult voyage across planet earth, and what it all means.

Historically, islands of warmth and beauty have provoked mixed emotions in the Western mind; we are both fascinated and repelled by the thought of their laid-back style, light-hearted revelry, overripe charm and dangerous sensuality. Some visitors have been known to succumb on sight to the promise of such indulgences and settle in forever.

The most northern Bahama island, Walker's Cay, lies about 100 miles across the Gulf Stream from Fort Pierce, Florida; from there the Bahama Islands are scattered south over 500 miles of turquoise sea to Inagua Island on the edge of the Caribbean.

Exuma, lying midway in the chain, about 140 miles south of the capital, Nassau, had everything we wanted: escape from the cold northern winters at the very top of New York State; proximity — only a day's flight — to the U.S. and family; a warm climate; gentle, friendly people; a place where we could free ourselves as much as possible from the consumer society and live simply; a place of informality and casual living where we could live in harmony with nature and our surroundings. The more we thought about it the more we believed a home there offered the retirement lifestyle we'd been looking for.

Life there, we figured, would be easy, productive and fun. All day long we'd wear only a bathing suit or at most, a loose-fitting shift or shirt, and no underwear. We'd eat our meals looking out on a garden of riotous blooms and at night lie on the deck and watch the stars. With luck we'd never again have to think about fashion, technology, heating bills, TV violence or trendy psychology. In this lovely spot we'd be free of the distractions and annoyances of modern urban living, for by definition, paradise has certain qualities: it is peaceful, serene, beautiful, and filled with happy people.

We weren't well-heeled or mad enough to fling caution to the tradewinds, cut all ties, immediately sell our stateside home, auction off all belongings, and move on down — though some quite sane and reasonable people do just that. Even so, after we got home to northern New York, bought the house, and met up with some detractors, we began to have doubts about our sanity. Some of their advice was well-meant, some merely gratuitous.

In the knowledgeable and seasoned manner of practical people everywhere — bankers, insurance agents, realtors — and a few friends, relatives, and other self-appointed advisors — we were cautioned about the dangers of living on a remote island, in a foreign country, among a race of people not our own.

"Think of the difficulties of living with few amenities, few services, and where the entertainments of modern living don't exist," said one friend.

Said another, "you're 62 and 65, where will you find the medical help you're bound to need?"

A banker was mildly disapproving when he realized we were not looking at the house as an investment, but as a place to enjoy a warm, peaceful, unhurried life.

A friend asked, "what will you do without TV, discos, libraries, museums, restaurants, and the theater?" And, said one man who had never left U.S. shores, "beware the tropics! Everybody knows torrid islands breed loose morals and lazy ways. You'll soon get bored, start drinking too much rum at lunchtime, sleep away the afternoons and end up 'going tropo'.

Warned another, "you can't read *all* the time you know." A good ole buddy commented, "but it's so far away! How will I ever be able to visit you?" We felt that was something best left to him to figure out.

Though these prognostications sounded dire, in the course of our respective jobs — educator and journalist — we'd lived in remote foreign places before — Ethiopia, Lebanon, Sierra Leone, Saudi Arabia, and Boston — and we'd managed to stay healthy, we hadn't started drinking the local booze, sleeping away the afternoons, walking around in native cloth tied sarong-style under the armpits, or developed a taste for baked beans and scrod. So it seemed unlikely we would succumb to the enticements of "going native" or that, impelled by our "original" (meaning shiftless) nature, we would end up spending the day lying in a hammock under the seagrape tree sipping potent rum drinks.

But as we stood shivering on the front deck of our new home the first day we learned our first lesson: island life is not endlessly blissful, sunny and warm...

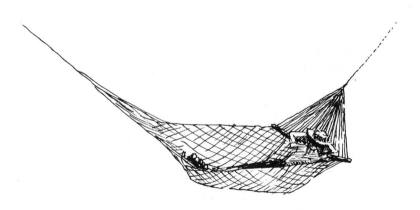

2

The day started out fine, bright, breezy and warm, the temperature around 75⁰F. Except for a rising wind it appeared perfect. The sun was high in a blue sky, the wind cooled the air nicely and the sea was a palette of greens and blues. In the garden exotic blooms bowed and nodded in the breeze and the palm trees swayed. We could see clear to the horizon and beyond.

But as we were about to learn, island skies can turn dark with the suddenness of a star winking out. Grey clouds were already moving in to shroud the sun, the wind shifted to the north and picked up, whitecaps appeared on the sea.

It appeared we had overlooked a number of factors, one being the fickleness of the island's November weather. It was an oversight we were soon to regret.

Within two or three hours the wind increased, sending white-crested waves crashing onto the beach beyond the house. Waves frothed around a small offshore island. Windows rattled and doors slammed. The fronds of the palm trees whipped about madly.

Unknown to a couple of new homeowners (and landlubbers) out in the Atlantic a storm was heading our way...

Our first big blow. That didn't sound bad. In fact, it might be exciting. An initiation to island living, an aspect of paradise that as former tourists here we had yet to experience. Time we learned about living on an island. But if it was a hurricane...

I got out the phone book. Though the house had no phone for some obscure reason a phone book went with the furniture. Under the heading HURRICANES it informed me that a hurricane "is a revolving storm of tropical origin accompanied by winds of 75 mph or more. The official hurricane season," it continued, "begins June 1 and ends November 30 but natural disasters can and do occur at any time of the year." Since it was only November 4 this was hardly a comforting thought.

Before a hurricane struck we were instructed to cover all windows and doors with plywood or hurricane shutters and put away all objects which could be blown around by wind and might create potentially destructive weapons. To equalize the pressure difference between the inside and outside of the house, and to prevent the windows and doors from being torn away, we were to open a window or door on the side of the house opposite the wind — but not to forget to close it when the winds shifted direction... a logical act, it seemed to me, and one you could hardly avoid remembering.

If the hurricane's eye, or vortex, passed directly over us there would be a brief lull in the winds lasting from several minutes to half an hour or more. Bearing in mind that the wind would return suddenly from the opposite side, and with even greater force, we were to remain in the house, or shelter, and at no time go to the beach — which, under the circumstances, seemed a highly unlikely venture.

Was a hurricane really on its way? Since the house was without phone, radio, or TV, and our neighbors were few and widespread (and we didn't yet know any of them anyway) we had no way of finding out.

Within the next hour it grew noticeably cooler. The skies continued to darken but for a moment a stack of creamy clouds, lit from behind and burnished by an invisible sun, glowed like rosy flesh — then a wall of grey cumulus clouds quickly moved in and the sunlight vanished. An eerie silence descended. A strange luminous light etched the landscape and bathed the sky in a metallic glow. The sea, now leaden grey, moved sluggishly and looked oily, as if something ominous was stirring in its depths and was struggling to surface. Thunder rumbled and lightning zig-zagged across the sky.

Following that, everything stilled. Every tree, every leaf, every branch, twig, and blade of grass, every blossom, remained motionless, waiting. No birds flew, no lizards scampered, no insects crawled. It feels as if a giant mouth had sucked up all the air and might never return it.

We, too, waited...

Though all one family, the islands of the Bahamas differ physically; some are large like Abaco and Andros in the north, small like Little Exuma, San Salvador and Spanish Wells, sophisticated and glitzy like Paradise Island and Grand Bahama Island with their casinos and smart hotels, and less developed like Cat and Crooked Island.

Within the mix there are pine forests, limestone caves, long stretches of satiny white beaches, the third largest barrier reef in the world, miles of uninhabited land, and small settlements where life goes on much as it did a century ago.

From the beginning what we loved about Exuma was its simplicity. Coming from the U.S. mainland, we found the color-washed unpretentious homes, the straight-forward-talking people, their civility and politeness, refreshing. The clear sea-light drenched everything in a most extraordinary beauty. A battered blue fishing boat, a front door painted orange, the seamed, dignified face of an elderly Bahamian woman, an old rock wall — all seemed to assume a significance beyond their actual existence.

The Bahamian islands themselves seemed more than just a collection of tiny specks on a vast ocean; rather, they were the embodiment of innumerable legends, their many inlets and bays suggesting their history of smugglers and pirates, storm-tossed ships, slaves and squalls and three-rigged schooners. When walking the shores where more than half a millennium ago Columbus reportedly landed, history and myth became one. When walking the unpaved lanes where cotton plants still bloomed, a link was made to those early American Loyalists who believed they could reproduce here the gracious plantation life of South Carolina, Georgia, and Florida.

We had found our island house in 1984 while on a drive with an expatriate American. As we passed a long hedge of casuarina pines lining a road near the sea, he'd slowed down and pointed above the trees. "You oughta buy that place," he said. "it's for sale for a ridiculous price. Rumor has it that the owner wants the renters out because they are into drug-dealing."

More out of curiosity as to how drug dealers lived than anything else, we got out to inspect it.

It was a square wooden house painted yellow. We walked uphill over a rough stone path lined with neglected shrubs and bushes and climbed two steps to a front deck. From there we looked out over treetops to an ocean view that stretched to the horizon.

The house was (more or less) furnished, there was a good well, a not-so-good well pump, and it was properly oriented to the prevailing (easterly) tradewinds. At the southeast corner was a good-sized seagrape tree; when taller and more filled out it would provide shade for an outdoor terrace where, presumably, one could sit and sip rum punches.

In the neglected garden two lime trees filled the air with lime green light, and there were several palm trees, a papaya, an orchid tree and various other trees we couldn't identify. Other bushes grew around the house and hung on — but barely — to the back of the lot, which sloped steeply and was mostly layered limestone. Opening off this rocky backyard was a workshop underneath the back part of the house. Things not favorable at this juncture were at least bearable and could be made better.

Best of all, a minute's walk down the road were 500 yards of totally unused, white sand beach, secluded, clean, and fringed with wild sea grasses. We took off our sandals and walked bare-foot and dreaming along the shore, remarking excitedly about the champagne air, the gentle tradewinds, the cloudless skies, the color of the water: luminous silver in the shallows, turquoise beyond the beach, jade green farther out, sapphire blue merging into deep purple on the horizon. The surf creamed around our feet. The air was warmed honey. Though we had come with no expectation of buying a house, we knew we wanted to live here. We wanted to see if we really could live simply.

We didn't know if we'd be any good at island living but we reckoned that, like anything else, the art of living on a small, isolated island among a different race of people could be learned.

It might take time and effort, would undoubtedly entail

some economic and psychological adjustments, but we were optimistic that with determination and luck it could be done. We would avoid the harsh winters of northern New York and maybe we'd even discover our retirement years could be fulfilling. Living here would mean setting ourselves apart in isolation from the rest of the world — the words isle and isolation derive from the same root, after all — were we ready for that? It would mean we'd have to learn to live with less but weren't we seeking voluntary simplicity?

The thing to remember, we told ourselves — recalling our fifteen years spent in developing countries — was that changing a lifestyle, though sometimes difficult, usually increased our energy and self-confidence. It tended to make us more alert and aware, it shaped new ideas, and restored our spontaneity and creativity.

And so, with great expectations, we decided to buy the house — and thus stepped into an ongoing adventure that changed our lives in ways neither of us could have foreseen...

3

Benjamin Disraeli once said *"the secret of success in life is to prepare for opportunity when it comes"*, so heeding this maxim, early next morning we tracked down the real estate agent, a large and formidable Bahamian woman with a stern eye. My husband remained cautious. "I'm told the renters are — were— ah — um — involved in drugs."

"Nonsense." She fixed us with a steely eye. "A bit wild perhaps, but basically good kids."

"That slash in the bedroom door looks suspiciously like a knife slash," my husband persisted, then pointing to a round hole in the thin wood paneling of the living room, "and that looks to me like a bullet hole."

"Just mice."

"Mice!"

She steered a course for the kitchen. "Look here. A dishwasher. One of very few on the island."

"Does it work?"

"Of course!" Keen as a crane driver, she threw a latch.

For a moment, nothing. Then a loud grinding burst forth followed by whirring and churning. A greasy wet sludge spurted into the sink and stayed there. The drain was plugged.

When asked if the plumbing still worked she acted as if island sovereignty had been impugned. "Of course it works," she replied huffily and opening the cupboard doors beneath the sink wiggled the drain pipe. It came apart where the trap had rusted through and dumped onto the bottom of the cupboard a thick, seedy greenish mess. It smelled foul.

My husband scooped up some, rubbed it between his fingers, and sniffed. "Marijuana seeds."

"To move on," she said, and hustled us into the back, or second bedroom. The windows here overlooked the south — or hot side — of the house and a large rain lake which she identified as Grog Pond. Beyond that rose a line of dense forested hills on the south side of the island, the side famous for its bone-fishing flats.

Below the house, at the foot of the hill, a few cars travelled the Queen's Highway, the island's main artery. A two-lane road, it starts at the north end of Great Exuma and runs south the length of the island (thirty-seven miles) to its sister island of Little Exuma. Here it crosses a narrow causeway linking the two islands. A little farther on it crosses the Tropic of Cancer *en route* to the end of Little Exuma, thus putting that island in the true tropics.

Everything about the house suggested warm weather living. From the slowly-turning ceiling fans and the many louvred windows to the sliding glass patio doors that led to the front deck, it invited nature in. With all doors and windows open from November to May there was bound to be a wonderful sense of being warm both outdoors and in.

Drug dealers apart, it was irresistible and affordable — $50,000 U.S. money. By the time we got on the plane to fly home the following day we had reviewed our savings, given in to a wild impulse, and made a down payment. It was only after the plane took off that we looked at one another and said "What have we done?"

Not to worry, we had bought a piece of paradise...

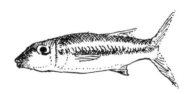

...and now, on our first morning there, the giant mouth finally let out its breath with a vengeance. A gust of wind shook the earth and then — the rain! A torrential downpour slashed at the windows and obscured the sea, a blast of thunder and a barb, of lightning put out the lights, turned off the fridge, stopped the stove, and left us groping around in the dark for candles. I opened a drawer beside the sink, found two candle stubs, dripped some wax into two saucers, and stuck them in it.

Wind howled around the roof shingles, moaned through the attic and shook the windowpanes. In just ten minutes the temperature dropped eighteen degrees, from 77°F to 59°F. We began looking for more clothes to put on.

These were few. Anticipating that winter clothing would be a thing of the past, we had given away to friends our heavy sweaters, cosy sweats, long robes and warm jackets, sympathising because they wouldn't be swimming on Christmas Day. To clothe us in our new tropical home we had arrived with the bare minimum: cotton nightwear, several changes of bathing suits, a light cotton sweater apiece, two light cotton shirts and shorts apiece, a pair of slacks, three changes of sneakers and sandals, two loose shifts and a few tee shirts. For formal occasions I'd brought two cotton sundresses. Now we layered on our extra tee shirts, our cotton sweaters, our tennis socks, and put on our one pair of slacks over our shorts. It wasn't enough to combat the clammy chill that penetrated through to our bones.

How was it possible to be so chilled? Exuma is little more than 23 degrees above the equator, near enough, surely, that "chilly" must be a relative term, since such delightfully warm places as Hawaii and Bajas California are on the same latitude. Didn't this mean it would never get really cold here? Havana, after all, was just 50 miles over the western horizon. I'd never heard of Cubans complaining about the cold.

The strong north wind continued to howl. We put on our cotton dressing gowns. Impossible as it seemed in this climate, the house suddenly felt as chilly as a late autumn day back in northern New York. Thermal underwear or, lacking that, an electric blanket to crawl under was needed. That night's dinner loomed as an impossible feat.

Still, this was, after all, our first meal in our new home, so if for no other reason than that of bravado, some effort, some defining gesture, was required. Stumbling around in the near dark we managed to set the table with the plastic cutlery and glasses, the napkins and condiments. For a festive note I put the two candles on the table where they flickered crazily in drafts from around the windows and doors. Obviously this was not a house for gale force living and could well be named (if we ever got to that point) Wuthering Heights.

Wrapped in the cotton blankets off the beds, we found ourselves doing what we had rejoicingly said we'd never have to do again in winter: huddle. We huddled around the table in the flickering light to eat our first candlelit dinner in our new semi-tropical home — a romantic meal of cold canned tuna, crackers, pickles, tomatoes and warm beer.

Though the house had a phone book and information on hurricanes it had no blankets, so that night we huddled in damp-ish beds wearing slacks and cotton sweaters, shivering under every covering we could find — including an ancient pair of musty acid-green drapes.

Does disappointment inevitably lie in wait for those who go journeying in search of paradise and find reality? At this point the longing for the simpler life seemed based on the fantasy that island-dwellers in warm climates lived like sugar barons lolling about palatial haciendas during the day and glorifying the sensual life all through the night — a lunatic perspective if ever I'd heard one. It was hard to believe that to escape a cold northern climate we had instead committed ourselves to huddling in layers of clothing on this not-so-tropical island.

It was a long night and in the morning — stiff, chilled and grumpy — we looked out on grey skies and a churning sea.

Obviously, since we were now committed to spending our winters on Exuma, the thing to do as quickly as possible was to learn how to live here. We would have to learn about cold fronts coming through, about how to stay warm and dry when they do, about shells and stars and plants and flowers, about getting to know our fellow islanders, about shopping and eating and passing the time.

I found myself hoping it was all do-able.

4

In search of blankets and groceries we drove to George Town, never guessing we'd meet an adventurer and hear a salty tale.

If you discount the short side-street leading to the government dock and beyond that, to Regatta Point, the island's small capital has but one main street. The town is an unstructured collection of haphazardly-painted blue, yellow and pink houses that straggle in an untidy fashion down both sides of the street and eventually curve around a small saltwater lake called Victoria Pond.

Though it seems to lack any formal street pattern, the town was actually laid out over 200 years ago by the British colonists who emigrated here from Florida, Georgia and the Carolinas after the American Revolution. They named it George Town, after George III of England, the king to whom they had chosen to remain loyal. Bringing their animals, the contents of their plantation houses, and their black slaves, they came to rebuild their lives and their plantations and grow cotton.

Most of this small island capital (pop. 900 or so,) overlooks Elizabeth Harbour, the largest harbor in the Bahamas and the country's uncontested yachting center. Opposite the town, a long barrier island named Stocking Island protects the town from storms and offers several hurricane "holes" where yachts can seek refuge in rough weather.

But the best part of George Town is that always, and unexpectedly, whenever you turn a corner, look out a window, or glance up from what you're doing you glimpse the shimmering, glistening turquoise sea. It polishes the town with an extraordinary light of incredible clarity.

Since neither of the two boutiques we entered sold blankets, we left our rented car beside the *Peace and Plenty Inn* and walked on down the main street, stopping first at the pink and white government building to check the post office — just in case there was mail from home; when you live far from home and family, mail assumes an inordinate importance to your health and well-being. It was too soon; it took a week to ten days to get a letter from the States.

On past the post office, in the middle of town, we passed a colorful scene. Sitting under three enormous fig trees that formed a canopy of dense shade, four or five Bahamian women sat plaiting straw wares. From lines strung around their small booths and between tree branches, straw baskets, hats, pocketbooks and place mats, along with strings of shell jewelry, scarves, tee shirts, and various other colorful articles swung gaily in the sea breeze. Opposite these "straw ladies," the people-watchers lounged on a low stone wall in front of the small library, laughing and gossiping with passers-by. On the hill behind them school children out on recess from the primary school ran and yelled in the dusty schoolyard. A few steps farther on we came upon Regatta Park, a fenced area of grass with a bandstand which we later learned was where outdoor concerts, games and civic events took place year round.

Exuma Supplies, a store located just behind the park, carried blankets. It was an old-fashioned emporium with merchandise crowding the floor and stacked to the ceiling. Mrs. Bowe, the wife of the owner, was a polite woman who was sympathetic to our need for extra warmth and eager to help. Yes, they carried blankets. Now, if she could just find them...

After pulling stuff out of numerous shelves she eventually discovered two pink, twin-size, nylon blankets which, at that point, seemed too light to keep us warm enough. Heavy wool, or perhaps an eiderdown comforter seemed called for. Sorry, the nylon was all she had until the mailboat came the following week. If we wanted her to order wool blankets from Nassau...

We took the pink nylon blankets, having learned a valuable lesson: If it didn't come on the weekly mailboat last week you don't need it until the boat comes next week.

Back at the *P&P* we put the blankets in the car and went into the inn for breakfast.

The *P&P*, as islanders call it, is the island's main hostelry and the place where, sooner or later, everyone in George Town heads to find out what's going on, who's in town, and the latest gossip, some of which may actually be true. It is named after the trading ship that brought Englishman Denys Rolle's 300 slaves to Exuma in 1783 where he established a 2,500 acre cotton plantation (which later failed.)

Today the Inn is owned by American Stan Benjamin. It is centrally located, overlooks the harbor, has an offhand ambiance, and in the old slave quarters there is a funky bar run by the island's best-known bartender, Lermon "Doc" Rolle.

The rain had stopped, the sun was out, and the north wind had abated so we sat outside at a table by the pool and ordered breakfast — with lots of hot coffee. Seated at the next table was a silver-haired man with a gold ring in his ear wearing a slightly grubby but rakish yachting cap, who was drinking rum. In the casual way of the islands he introduced himself as Captain Pete Balloil and we started up a conversation.

Historically in the Bahamas there has been a racial mix: Seminole Indians from Florida, pirates, freebooters, Spanish explorers, an early English group of settlers known as the Eleutheran Adventurers, the Loyalists from America's Revolutionary War and their black slaves, and, since the 1950's, tourists from all over the world. Adding to the mix more recently is a new kind of modern adventurer — the cruising boater.

Captain Balloil was one of these. He looked to be in his late fifties and was sinewy, bearded, deeply tanned, and had a profligate air about him. "I'm an Englishman," he told us. "At fifteen I ran away from home, joined the British Army, parachuted into Malaya at age eighteen, fought in the streets of Kuala Lumpur, and by twenty had killed a man in Korea." He swirled the rum around in his glass and, holding it up, peered through the amber liquid at the blue sky. "In time I rose to be an army captain, and for the next twenty years I lived a hard-drinking, soldiering life." He took a long swig.

"Then I went home. I love my country and I guess I'd die for what England stands for," he mused, "but I'm no killer. I love the world and all that's in it." He paused and looked out over the harbor and the boats at anchor, "but when I got home I found I couldn't stand the stuffiness and dullness of English life. The narrow-mindedness. The antiquated thinking about class and religion. About immigrants and race." His laugh was dry and hard. "So I took all my pension, came to the islands, and bought me a boat — see that black-hulled ketch out there?"

He pointed to a graceful sailboat riding at anchor in the harbor just off the *P&P* dock — "that's my boat. The *Buccaneer*. A beauty, isn't she. I love her like a wife. See this?" He flexed a forearm with a tattoo of the *Bucc* etched in dark blue.

"Well, about ten years ago the *Bucc* and I started a charter boat service outa Nassau." He took another swig. "I thought, boy, is this the life for me. Was I wrong."

Again his bright blue eyes went to his boat, one of several hundred in the harbor which, by this time of year, was filling up with boats. Because the harbor is the largest boat basin in the Upper Caribbean — so large in fact that during World War II the U.S. Navy used it as a southern navigational aid station — it is a favorite spot for yachters to spend the winter. By early March every year well over 350 boaters escaping northern winters are anchored there for three months or more. By mid-March there may well be over 400 boats bobbing and tossing out there.

Cap'n Pete, as he asked us to call him, leaned back, a rather worn and faded twentieth century adventurer in a jaunty cap who would probably have been more at home in the seventeenth century wearing a pirate's scarlet headscarf. He continued spinning his yarn:

"Turns out charter captain is a dog's job," he said morosely. "Let me give you an example..."

He chartered to a honeymoon couple, the second marriage for both, the bride, a high school English teacher, still not too sure she was married to the right man — a New York stockbroker. Both appeared bright, intelligent, friendly.

"His instructions to me," Cap'n Pete said, "were to stock the boat well with champagne, booze and steaks, so I did, figuring this is going to be one pleasant trip." He shook his head. "Wrong. The guy arrives aboard with a gun — God knows how he got it into the country — and as soon as he's on board he starts drinking. That night I have to put him to bed. His bride was less than enchanted. I figure it's probably stress from the wedding and next day he'll be over it. Wrong again."

From then on the climate onboard — if not the seas — got

stormy. The husband began drinking early in the morning and once tanked up would begin to accuse his new wife of having an affair with Pete Balloil. Her teary denials only made things worse; the more she denied it the more he accused her. On their third night out he tried to beat her up, and might have shot her if Pete hadn't intervened and grabbed the gun.

"That did it," he said. "This was not only my boat it was my home and I wasn't about to have this guy turn my home into a maniac asylum. I locked up the gun, locked up the booze, turned the boat around, and headed full ahead back to Nassau. He didn't like it, but she was visibly relieved."

Cap'n Pete swirled the last of the rum in his glass. "He never did pay me for all the food and booze but I didn't care. I figured it was worth it for learning the best lesson of my life: getting away from it all does not solve anybody's problems. It can make them worse. Last week I took down my charter sign and sailed away for good from that business."

He lifted his yachting cap, resettled it on his curly silver hair, and became philosophic. "Y'know," — he watched a wad of cloud drift by — "I believe that in some inexplicable way, how I choose to live really does *matter*. Too often these days, those, like me, who decide to follow their heart's desire are considered radical and irresponsible because their decision flies in the face of expected behavior." He shook his head. "In our conformist society we're often made to feel we have to conform to a life dictated by others: by family or friends, or by society's idea of what is appropriate. I don't go for that..."

He stared out at The *Bucc*, rocking on the water. "Sometimes politicians, economists, sociologists, or the media have sketched our lives long before we're able to do so for ourselves, and by the time we're able to ask, 'is this what I want? Or need? Or desire?' it's too late. They've destroyed our sense that life is an ongoing adventure."

"But the heart knows something the brain doesn't," he said, nodding reflectively. "The heart knows about dreams, intuitions, fantasies, and longings, and that anyone who embarks on an adventure stays young at heart."

With this thought he reset his cap and tugged at his gold earring. "I believe how I choose to live *does* matter. It matters that I realize I'm not a killer but a lover — a lover of the sea and the sky and the earth and all that's in it."

When we asked what he planned to do next he said with a grin, "oh, I'm not worried," and tipped his soiled white cap in gallant acknowledgement of the two women tourists sitting at a table on the far side of the pool. Blond, roasted to a turn, arrayed in blinding white bikinis, they had been giggling and eyeing him for the past half hour. He released his lopsided grin on them and they fluttered their eyelashes in return. His responding laugh was a rusty chortle.

"Something'll turn up," he said, lifting his glass to them in a jaunty salute.

5

S hopping for food on the island presented numerous problems, not the least of which was that it was time-consuming, demanded patience, and required a willingness to walk or drive from one place to another.

It seemed only fair to split our grocery shopping between the two main grocery stores in George Town, Darville's Market and John Marshall's, but that decision, plus the mailboat schedule, (arriving George Town every Wednesday morning, unloading that afternoon, the goods reaching the shelves by noon Thursday) made shopping a game of hunt and find. Overall, the rule was: "if it didn't come on the mailboat we ain' got it. An' if we ain' got it you don' need it."

Until Thursday afternoon each week, when the mailboat was fully unloaded, there was little on the shelves and never a wide choice at best. Everything cost at least three times Stateside prices. This was not surprising, though, because whether it arrived direct from Miami on one of the monthly freighters — the MV *Lady Rosalind, The Cavalier,* or the *Sea Hauler,* or by mailboat from Nassau aboard *The Grand Master,* all goods underwent a lot of loading and unloading — a labor-intensive and costly business which the customers ultimately paid for.

For our first major grocery shopping foray we went to John Marshall's, (he is seldom referred to only as John,) whom we had become acquainted with during a vacation several years earlier. A tall, handsome, greying Bahamian with a quiet reserved air and great dignity, he was Chief Warden of the Vestry at St. Andrews, George Town's Anglican Church, and was considered one of the island's most honorable men. With the help of his wife Veronica and his four children, he had expanded his original grocery business to include a gas station, a liquor store, a luncheonette, and alongside his store, a twelve room motel which he called *Marshall's Guest House.*

We had met him on our second trip to Exuma. Just prior to that trip, my husband had completed a three year stint for the U.S. government in Saudi Arabia, and we had arrived in New York's Kennedy airport flush with cash, and in the midst of a late April sleet storm. The temperature was just below freezing and was expected to stay that way for at least the next two days before warming up to about 45 degrees. On a whim, and without having any reservations, we decided to go to Exuma.

We crossed to the other side of the airport and caught a US Air flight to Nassau, planning to catch a Bahamasair flight on to Exuma the same day.

En route Nassau, a Bahamian businessman sitting next to my husband told him we had no hope of finding a room anywhere on Exuma — even if we were successful getting a seat on the plane to George Town. Hadn't we remembered, this was the time of the annual Out Island Regatta? And that the sailing world was converging on George Town? The island would be chock-a-block with visitors. Why, people booked a year ahead for this event!

As he'd predicted, there were no seats on the Exuma plane. Had we been sensible, we would have stayed in Nassau but our minds were fixed on Exuma. We hurried out to Nassau's Potter's Cay and — just barely — caught the mailboat, which at the time, was the old *Exuma Pride*, a former Norwegian ferryboat. The overnight trip was rough but at dawn we saw schools and schools of flying fish.

When we arrived on Exuma — still comparative strangers to the island — we were amazed to find the main street of this sleepy little island filled with cars. In George Town, as we remembered, eight cars usually constituted a traffic tie-up; now there was not only gridlock in a place which had no stoplights, but a total traffic stoppage.

It was a happy crowd that milled around the streets. Laughing, eating, dancing, buying, selling, talking, or just sitting on the library wall to watch other people go by, they made an ordinary weekday seem like a weekend. The yachting crowd — plus a lot of the rest of the world it seemed — had arrived in George Town for the races.

With the typical optimism of American travelers who believe that "no rooms available" can't possibly mean them, we inquired first at John Marshall's to ask if there were any rooms in his guest house. Sorry, no rooms available. But we were welcome to leave our two suitcases in his charge while we looked elsewhere. Surely, we thought, there would be somewhere we could lay our heads for the night. Come to that, the weather was balmy, we could always sleep on a beach somewhere couldn't we?

We spent the afternoon walking around to the five small hotels the island then boasted. Everything had been booked for months. "Book now for next year," one hotel receptionist said. There was not a room to be had nor a bed available anywhere. Private homes were filled up, and anyway, we knew no one from whom we could beg floorspace. Even if sleeping on the beach were lawful, the mosquitoes and no-see-ums would make it unbearable.

Around six o'clock, tired and disconsolate, we were back at John Marshall's sitting on the cement wall outside the store. We'd exhausted every possibility and our chances of having a place to even lie down looked bleak. Testily, I asked my husband what we were going to do next, and when he suggested we might try to contact someone with deckspace on his boat — and wouldn't it be fun to sleep out under the stars? — I attempted to reply enthusiastically but with no visible sign of success.

At that moment John Marshall came out of his store and started locking up for the day. He spotted us and said in his quiet way, "are you having trouble finding a room?" We said we were.

"Well, if you wouldn't mind," he said, "I have a small store-room at the back where you could stay. It's clean and dry and I could move in two cots for you. You could eat breakfast in the dining room." We were only too glad to accept, and the room, though bare, was, as he'd said, clean and dry. At the end of the week, when presented with the bill, we saw he'd charged us only for the breakfasts. We wanted to pay for the room but he said, "I was glad to be of help to you."

That was the first — but not the last — of the many kindnesses we were to receive from a Bahamian, and on that day long before we moved to the island, it helped confirm that this might be a good place to live.

Now, back again at John Marshall's as householders stocking up an empty larder, our purchases were many. We loaded our baskets with, among other things, laundry detergent, rice, flour, sugar, bread, milk, tea, cereal, potatoes, raisins, toilet paper, cookies, butter, coffee, mayo, tomato paste, salt, pepper, spaghetti, soups, oatmeal, tins of peaches, pineapple, and fruit cocktail, three kinds of jam, and frozen chicken, frozen hamburger, and frozen mutton chops. The bill came to $134.94.

The only thing cheaper than in the States was the over-the-counter drugs such as aspirin and cold remedies which we didn't need. When asked why they were cheaper John Marshall said the drug companies charge what the traffic will bear. "And they know that here in this country most people don't have much money." We noticed he didn't say people here are poor; only that they didn't have much money — a proud distinction which we took to mean that Bahamians consider themselves rich in ways other than monetarily.

With old-fashioned courtesy John Marshall loaded our purchases into our shopping bags then said he had just received some Australian cheddar and would cut us a piece if we wanted to try some. We did. So from a wheel of cheese on a marble slab he cut off a goodly portion for us to taste. We nodded. He cut a wedge, weighed it, and wrapped it in greased paper. His son Michael helped us carry the bags to the car, all the while discussing his favorite subject — NBA basketball and the superior ball-handling of Michael Jordan. Did we know that great star is Bahamian-born? We didn't. We discussed the merits of the Bulls vs. the Celtics.

Ten miles west of George Town, and just two miles from our house, in the small settlement of Mount Thompson is the Government Packing House, an agricultural facility to which the up-island farmers take their produce for shipment to George Town, and thence to Nassau by mailboat. Some of the produce is kept to sell locally. Since there were few fresh vegetables at the two grocery stores, on the way home we stopped there.

The building was a large metal warehouse, open at both ends. High up in the girders three large fans stirred the humid air. Four women sat on upturned pails sorting grapefruit and oranges into cardboard shipping boxes. A bosomy woman in a bright print dress and headscarf got up and approached us with an orange in either hand. Could we buy fresh vegetables here? we asked. "No problem," she answered, beaming as she handed us each an orange. "They're sweet," she said. "You can eat them now. I just washed them under the tap." Her name, she told us, was Ora Lee Martin. She was stately, graceful and beautiful, with cheeks the color of russet apples.

She introduced us to the three other women: Birdie Mae Musgrove, Kerlene Nixon, and Valerie Ferguson. We shook hands formally then inquired about produce availability. It ran like this (depending on the rains, of course): tomatoes and squash from late November to March. Cabbage in February and March. Sweet peppers January to May, potatoes March through May, watermelon in January and February, and bananas, papayas, grapefruit and hot peppers year round.

We were disappointed by the paucity of tropical fruits but were told the guavas, sapodilla, pineapple, and mangoes were summer fruits, ripe when we were back in the States. We would not, however, lack vegetables.

Or onions! By March, Kerlene assured us, there would be lots of onions. Spring onions, red onions, Spanish onions, sweet white onions. Exuma, as it turned out, exported onions by the sackfuls and was unique in that it grew onions in sand. It is known as the "onion island" and has an onion emblazoned on the island's blue and gold flag.

Mentally I considered this bonanza of onions. I could already taste pickled onions, glazed onions, boiled onions, onions for salads and soups, and wonderful French onion soup with Swiss cheese and crusty bread. Onion lovers ourselves, we did, however, wonder if an island displaying an onion emblem on its flag would be attractive to prospective tourists. Might they not think the island would smell of onions rather than exotic blooms?

Still, the onion is a member of the lily family, a respected heraldic symbol, and often used to keep vampires at bay. Maybe the onion abundance would also serve to ward off pestiferous flying insects, of which there seemed to be many at sunrise and sunset.

In Farmer's Hill, the small sun-washed settlement of about 100 people three miles further along the Queen's Highway, there were two more grocery stores: a faded sign above the door of a one-room emporium informed all and sundry that this was Christine's Friendly Store. The other store, a small ma-and-pa place, was Louis Rolle's Supermarket. These stores, two auto repair shops and the area's Bahamas Telephone office, made up the commercial aspect of the settlement.

More spectacularly, though, there was, scooped out of the nearby shore, a long curve of bay called The Bight. One of the most beautiful beaches on the island, it was a half-moon of white sand, a quarter of a mile long, and fringed with tall, feathery casuarina trees swaying in an onshore breeze.

Who cared if it took all day to get the food for the week — or that groceries cost three times what they did at home? You could shop at stores that lay under the palm trees, watch the sea shift colors while you waited for your change, meet and talk to hospitable people on the way out, and at the end of the day jump into the wide green sea.

6

We started meeting some of the winter residents and found them to be a mixed bag. Some became friends almost immediately; others remained on the periphery of our lives. All — particularly the women — had stories to tell about learning to live on the island. Some of the stories were heartening; others weren't.

Although island existence seemed to free and replenish the male winter residents, it could, and often did, wreak havoc on their wives. Rather than restoring her with feelings of psychic replenishment, the life of a foreign woman on the island often turned out to be monotonous and unrewarding.

The wife of one former homeowner, a long-stemmed showgirl from Miami, didn't bother to hide her dislike and did not mince words. On her first visit to her new home, so the story goes, she looked around the house and island, saw no evidence of TV, telephone, shopping malls, nightclubs, or smart watering holes and said plaintively, "what's to do?"

She might have also added that there was no movie theater, golf course, galleries or museums — only four unkempt tennis courts, one hardware store, three liquor stores, one proper hair salon, one dry cleaner, just three small variety stores, two gift boutiques for tourists, five small hotels, and no MacDonalds, Burger King, Kentucky Fried Chicken, Pizza Hut or Baskin Robbins.

Her solution was simple. "Sell it!" she said, and never came back.

In the States, wives often complain that a retired husband is unable to raise the will or the strength to take out the garbage or put up the screens. Once he "retired" to an island idyll, however, and started building, or fixing up a home in paradise, his wife usually found he willingly developed the muscles of his back and stomach by lifting and hauling everything from concrete blocks and bags of cement to outboard motors and buckets of topsoil.

In general, the men viewed island life as a kind of updated frontier living and appeared to enjoy a place where everything was not speckless, clean and painfully tidy — a place where they didn't have to get dressed up and could go around all day in shorts, tee shirt, or brief bathing trunks (which, despite the tan, was not the most flattering attire for those who failed to press weights and work out after age 55.)

Whereas I was having some difficulty getting adjusted, for my husband, finding purpose in our new way of life was not a problem. Like many of the foreign men he found the move to the island brought out his hidden "Robinson Crusoe" qualities. With great gusto he rose every morning at six, swam, ran up the beach and back, showered at his outdoor shower, prepared our breakfast, ate hungrily, and spent most of the day in his workshop building and fixing.

He liked living close to the sea and being able to run in and out of it at any time. He reveled in the simple pleasures of his new life, his brief attire, his growing knowledge of shells and fish and plants, the birds in the garden, snorkeling and diving and beachcombing. Vast was his enjoyment when he worked up a heavy sweat at some labor or other and could then strip down and stand naked in the outdoor shower gazing out over Grog Pond, soaping up and rinsing off while he watched the planes fly into the airport on the south side. He said he'd never felt better in his life. It was as if he and the other men were living out a deep-seated primal desire to wear nothing but a loincloth and carve out a new civilization by the sweat of their brow. Sighed a Canadian wife, "my husband is talking of growing a beard and letting his hair grow to shoulder length." She rolled her eyes. "Next it'll be a gold ring in his ear." She sighed again. "He thinks he's thirty-two again, not sixty-two — but that's okay as long as he doesn't run off with some young thing of twenty-two."

An American advertising executive, then in his seventies, owner of a handsome island house, fled to the island because, he said, the U.S. had too many rules and regulations, too many laws and social conventions, and too much greed. He maintained the U.S. had too much of everything, including too much money and too much sex. Coming from someone who boasted he'd once thoroughly enjoyed both, and could now count his wealth in millions, he appeared to be speaking from the point of view of the sinner who'd tasted it all, had now got religion, and thought everyone should live like a priest or a nun.

Christine Rolle, however, (*Christine's Friendly Store* in Farmer's Hill,) loved her home island and couldn't imagine living anywhere else.

"Morning," she said, coming up the front path one morning, wearing one of her madly reckless hats, a black yachtsman's cap set at a jaunty angle and tied with a scarlet bandanna. Slight, wiry and lean as a whip, she wore on top of her workshirt a length of rope over one shoulder, a nail pouch around her waist, and in her right hand carried a hammer and an axe.

"Got to fix the steps on my rental Rondette," she said, "wonder if you could lend me some strong pliers. Wouldn't mind if you'd lend your pry-bar, too, if you've got one." Her grin was good-natured and infectious. Chris, we soon learned, was a self-styled businesswoman, one of the island's hardest working and most enterprising. Not only did she own and drive Taxi 25 — which on certain days became a tour bus — she owned several rental houses, the grocery store in Farmer's Hill, and a stone supply business for which she herself cracked the rock for foundation fill. And oh yes, she'd published a pamphlet about bush medicine, about which she had wide knowledge; she also looked after an elderly "auntie," and a nephew.

And, as we were about to learn, with the right borrowed tools there were few maintenance jobs that could faze Chris.

She took the tools, waved cheerily, and headed back down the path. "I'll bring 'em right back," she called over her shoulder and did.

* * *

It was December and Bahamians complained of the cold and wore flannel shirts, sweaters, heavy jackets, and wool caps. (I am willing to swear that one morning a Bahamian child bearing a message arrived at our door wearing mitts and a woolen ski mask—something which, for obvious reasons, I did not mention in my letters to friends back home.)

One bright sunny morning my husband, a man undaunted by virtually every kind of challenge, a man who was always seeking new skills to conquer, announced with a happy gleam in his eye that he thought the house should have a wing added.

He wanted to "open up" our square box of a house by knocking out the northwest side to make a large new dining room that would have wide windows in all three of its exterior walls and could be used not only as a dining room, which we didn't now have, but as a room in which we could pursue all kinds of hobbies. Underneath it he would excavate into the limestone and build a third bedroom which would open at ground level onto the front garden. We could call the upstairs room the Great Room, the downstairs one the Garden Room.

It sounded rather grandiose and like a lot of work, nor did it fit my concept of a simpler life. To me the house was fine the way it was. It was a modest house, to be sure, but it was bright and pleasant, filled with sun and shade at the right times, and the small deck at the front had a view of sea and sky.

For what was, after all, a beach house, I felt the decor was best kept simple and casual—inside walls painted white so they made a tapestry of sun and shadows, color accents provided by bright wall-hangings, throw cushions and chair covers, treasures from the beach—sea fans, shells, driftwood, glass floats, fishing buoys and bunches of sea grasses, all beautiful and free.

Traveling the globe as we had in our careers, I had never been one for a lot of possessions and at this point in our lives could only see us ridding ourselves of possessions, rather than gathering more like some barnacled barge heaving itself toward a distant shore.

From the beginning I'd seen the island as a metaphor for a simple life, a way of demonstrating to ourselves the possibility of creating a life of meaning from simple things. Of using the beauty of the landscape, the gentle easy-goingness of the islanders, the peaceful days and quiet nights, to sustain ourselves.

This house, I felt, needed to be only a small simple place, a dwelling at one with the elements, one that reflected our wish to live on the earth lightly. Why not leave it as it was structurally and decorate with paint, paper, colorful textiles and found objects?

Yes, okay, my husband replied, but wouldn't it be nice to have a little more deck space with a wider vista of the sea? A larger dining area? He could paint there, I could write. There'd be some interesting nooks and crannies to sit and read in, or just dream in. More light and air. Windows that would let in the breezes. A terrific view of the sea on two sides. And downstairs another bedroom and bath for family and visitors.

His words were aimed at seducing me but I could see that he was eager to be busy with something. To be constructive. To fill his days. And, as so often happened in our long (forty-two) years of marriage, his plans succeeded in sparking off visions in my head. I could feel the cool breezes blowing through the house, stirring long sheer curtains that would drift slowly in and out, lifting and falling as if the house itself was breathing...

I saw guests holding drinks on an expanded deck and candlelit parties in a Great Room overlooking the sea...

"The first step," my husband said when I was hooked and was murmuring these visions to him, (as he knew I would,) "is to push out the northwest wall"... he went on making plans, sketching out drawings, considering such a pursuit enormous fun.

But surely he didn't intend to do all this work himself? Of course not.

And so we met Mr. Hymenious Flowers and Stanley Ferguson, two Bahamian men who were to become more than our co-builders. They became our friends.

7

In a city you can live all your life, get to know only a handful of the total population, become friends with a few of those, ignore all the others, and if you choose, live in almost total anonymity. On a small island with a population of about 3,500 souls, the people inevitably become a part of your life and you of theirs.

Up and down the island, from one end to the other, the islanders know what everyone is doing. They know when someone is born, dies, marries, or is sick. They know the names of a person's parents and grandparents, and which island they came from. They know when we foreigners "reach" (arrive) and when we plan to leave, if and when we plan to sell, or build, and probably a lot more than most of us are aware of.

The U.S. might have a new president, or a million people may become refugees in some far off war, and though most would know of the event from their TV or newspaper, it would not be considered of vital importance. But let an islander buy a house, a car, or a boat, build a wall or dig a well — or think about putting an addition on their house — that's news. Everyone knows about it in a flash.

Mr. Hymenious Flowers knew, somehow, that we were planning an addition. One morning he arrived at our house from Farmer's Hill on his old bicycle. "Heard you were going to build on," he said. "Came to offer my services." His small wiry frame was outfitted for construction work in a plaid cotton shirt, green plastic tractor cap with MIAMI HEAT written on it, faded blue jeans and a pair of heavy work boots. His face was lined and weathered, his hair well peppered with white, and his grin ingratiating. He had about him a pleasant old-fashioned scent of patchouli aftershave.

His eyes, while still holding a twinkle, were partly dimmed by more than seventy years of sun and hard work and would probably have caused an optometrist to prescribe magnifying glasses. But he wore no glasses and made every effort to show he needed none. There was a cheerful friendliness to him we found irresistible and my husband wanted from the first to hire him.

But he felt the need to warn the old gentleman that it would be hard work and require a pretty agile and strong man. Mr. Flowers assured us he was very fit and strong. Hadn't we first met him in Farmer's Hill when he was nailing down the roof shingles on his daughter Zelma's house?

Well, yes, we had, but -

If we were worried that he wasn't spry enough, then he recommended for the really heavy work that we hire Stanley Ferguson from the nearby settlement called The Forest. A good man. Strong. Honest. Hard-working. Stanley was like another son to him. During World War II they had cut cane and picked fruit together on contract in Florida and up and down the east coast of the U.S. On this whole island we wouldn't find a better man than Stanley Ferguson. We were going to need him so why didn't he go right now and alert Stanley.

The next day Stanley Ferguson arrived, moving quickly up the garden walk with a jaunty stride. A lean dark Bahamian in his late fifties, he had a ready smile and a laugh that served to cover his occasional stammer. Right away we could see he was a man at peace with himself, made obvious by his direct glance, the sureness of his voice, and his confident manner. We sensed in him a man who, all his life, had been determinedly independent, who thought his own thoughts and formed his own opinions. To be sure, this was a lot to determine at an initial meeting, but then, sometimes first meetings are the most revealing and, as in this case, displayed the character traits we confirmed later.

"Mr. Flowers said you were building on."

My husband nodded and asked if he was a carpenter.

No, but he was an experienced painter, could use a hammer, and was a hard worker. A quick study. He could learn whatever my husband wanted him to do. Mr. Flowers could vouch for that. Mr. Flowers was like a father to him and he guaranteed they'd work well together.

My husband hired him and the next day the three men set to work to change the house, a step that though we didn't know it at the time, was to change our lives as well. Over the years to come we were to meet many talented Bahamian men and women — nurses, teachers, lawyers, doctors, businessmen and women, athletes and journalists — but it was these two modest, unassuming men who taught us most about how to live on this island.

As the construction work progressed some tool, some compound, some vital piece of wood or hardware was inevitably lacking. Since the island's only building supply store was ten miles away on the outskirts of George Town, this meant that I, as chief gofer on the site, had to make numerous trips to *Darville Lumber Company*. Driving back and forth on these errands I learned a great deal about the island way of life.

Because there is no public transport, a long held island custom is to share rides with walkers. Driving in one day I passed a little girl of nine or so walking. She was dressed prettily in a plain blue pinafore and white blouse, her hair neatly braided in corn rows and tied with blue bows. She walked purposefully, head up, looking neither left nor right.

About to stop, I checked the rear-view mirror and saw she had been picked up by a panel truck, one that earlier I'd seen pick up an elderly woman.

In town I completed some errands and headed for the bank where I found a long line-up in front of the counter. Idly, I picked up a discarded *Tribune*, one of Nassau's newspapers, founded in 1913. Mincing no words, the editorial by Mrs. Carron, the publisher and editor-in-chief, criticized the government and the prime minister for a variety of misdemeanors. In the letters-to-the-editor column readers vented their views — irate as well as laudatory — on a range of topics, including an elected official, the Ministry of Tourism, the Water and Sewerage Corporation, the hotel worker's union, and the commissioner of police. Each letter was signed, and as a former newspaper editor I was impressed by the candor and by this irrefutable evidence of a free press.

The line ahead of me at the bank moved forward. I looked up to see the little girl in blue trying to pull open the bank's heavy glass door. It was too much for her tiny weight so big J.R. Rolle, the gas man, opened it for her. She thanked him politely through the space where she once had two front teeth and looking serious and determined, entered the bank.

Unaware, or unheeding of the line, she ducked under the barrier rope and arrived at the counter when I did. I stepped aside. Because she was too short to see over it, or be seen beneath it, I pointed her out to the cashier. The woman leaned over and said, "hello, Shareena. Mummy send you? Who do you want to see?"

"Mr. Floyd, please ma'am." She dug into the pocket of her blue pinafore, produced a folded note, and handed it up. The cashier took it to the manager in his glass-walled office. He read it, motioned young Shareena in, wrote on her note, added several papers from his desk, sealed it all in an envelope, and returned it to her. She nodded politely and left.

We met at the door. I pulled it open and asked, "how old are you Shareena?"

"Nine, ma'am." Self-possessed and unsmiling, intent on the responsibility of her errand, she put her small weight against the door and politely motioned me, as her elder, to exit ahead of her. I watched as she started her seven mile trip back, as certain as she must have been that she would not have to walk all the way home. That a nine-year-old child, as well as her parents, could feel completely safe accepting a ride from strangers, once again notched up my opinion of the island.

The three men worked well together. Often, as I worked in the house, I could hear them laughing and joking outside. In prevailing white male fashion, my husband wore only a battered painter's cap and a pair of cutoff jeans. Mr. Flowers, on the other hand, was always dressed for serious work in his work shirt, jeans, heavy boots, and trusty MIAMI HEAT plastic cap. He, the mannerly veteran, took an obvious delight in the work itself. "Work is good," he would say. "I hope to work until the day the Good Lord takes me home."

Stanley, the conservative member of the trio, wore long grey pants, grey tee shirt, and sneakers. No hat. He was more into making the hard work fun. "Stanley, you got the framing square?" my husband might call down from his perch on the scaffolding. Stanley, calling up from his hammering would reply, "Vince, I goin' to frame this ss-s-sea view in it," and he'd hold up the tool as if framing a picture.

The men were having a good time. They looked forward each day to resuming their work, joshing each other over lunch at a small table my husband had knocked together and put on the deck, chivvying Vince out of his postprandial nap and urging him to "get on with the job."

For me, things were not going so smoothly or well.

8

Not all winter residents were sanguine about life on the island and you wondered why they stayed. By now we had met the L's. I encountered them at the post office one morning and, as usual, they were complaining. If it wasn't about the cost of things, it was the flight from Nassau, the condition of the roads, the increase in traffic, the litter, the delay in trash pick-up, the inconsistency of electric power. Mostly it was a general sourness about the island and its people.

The L's said things like: "I don't understand these people. They don't think like us, don't work like us. Don't hold the same values." At every opportunity Mr. L. eagerly provided a catalogue of Bahamian differences and shortcomings.

As we stood in front of the Post Office in the morning sun under a beautiful azure sky studded with fat white clouds Mr. L. complained loud and long about the inefficiency of the postal clerks. Flaring disapproving nostrils at me he said, "I don't know why *these people* can't learn how to sort mail. How do they expect to run a country efficiently if they can't even sort mail correctly? I'm telling you, the country is not like it was before they got their independence. Things worked when the British were in charge."

Mrs. L. chimed in. "We forfeited a lot when we moved here for the winters 20 years ago. We left a modern and efficient community to come live in this Third World country and help the economy. They might show us a little gratitude." I was tempted to ask why they stayed if they found it so disagreeable but was not given time to voice my question. Mrs. L. — always adept at telling you something you already knew, or didn't want to know, said — "and did you know they're not going to fix the roads 'til next *July*! Lot of good that'll do us. We'll be gone in May."

She was also an old hand at spreading gossip. Leaning forward she whispered, "have you heard about T.? He's going back to Arizona and leaving his wife here. I guess he won't put up with her affairs any longer. They say he was verging on a heart attack! Poor man. It'll be her fault if he has a stroke."

In normally good health themselves, they felt constrained to worry about a host of possible ills for themselves and others. Strokes, heart attacks, emphysema, skin cancer, gastroenteritis, gall bladder, severe sunburn, dehydration, strep throat, rape, muggings, theft, break-ins, osteoporosis, broken bones, Asian flu and periodontal disease — at least one of these, and possibly more than one was, in their opinion, likely to carry us all off before our time.

No use pointing out that there was emergency medical care at the two small government clinics on the island, each of which had a fully qualified East Indian doctor. And that there was also the wonderful Bahamian nurse-midwife — Lydia Rolle — whom many considered more able than many doctors. And, if needed, there was more advanced care after a forty-five minute flight to Nassau, or two hours to Miami.

But the L's preferred to worry about what would happen to them if they got "really" sick. I long ago realized they enjoyed their doleful whining and there was no use arguing with them, so, (somewhat meanly I admit,) I asked Mr. L. what appeared to me the obvious question. "Why do you stay here if you dislike it?" "If we leave now I'll never realize a return on my investment in the house," he responded grumpily. "The real estate market's soft. I'd lose money if I sell now. All these years here would be worth squat."

"I told you in 1983 we should've sold and put our money in a Money Market Fund. Or a nice safe CD," his wife said crossly.

"Have to run," I said, eager to make my escape. But before I could get away Mrs. L. leaned in my direction. Because she has a sly look and a certain way of imparting confidential information, I knew I was about to hear a juicy piece of gossip.

She whispered. "I hear a woman on the island was mugged. They say no one is safe. Of course, no one will testify or even talk. They'll never speak up about anything because they're all related. I don't know why we think they have a democracy!"

In fact, I found the mugging story hard to believe and said

so. "I'm certain anyone could walk the streets of George Town at 3 a.m. and be perfectly safe. I'd do it without a qualm."

"Not me," she said huffily. "And you just wait. Rising crime is going to keep us all prisoners in our homes at night. This place is not a haven from crime, you know."

In one way, she was right. The island was not totally crime free. It does have some of the usual ills of the human condition: theft, prostitution, marital spats, misuse of alcohol and drugs, child abuse and break-and-enter — but only three murders in the past ten years, and those, we were told, were drug-related. As usual, Mrs. L. was exaggerating, something she was prone to do about everything.

Violence, we'd often noticed, isn't a natural act for most human beings wherever they live. It's a product of deprivation, despair, and a feeling of "I have not." A Bahamian lawyer we met this year, and were later to become friends with, put it succinctly: "I blame a lot of Bahamian violence on American TV. Oh sure, we're responsible for our own actions, but the idea that I'm a "have-not" is induced — in the U.S. and overseas — by America's mass advertising. It works hard to convince people their lives lack many things, and that their greatest value to their society is to buy more and more things. People's value to the country's economy, the ads imply, is not as a good citizen, a responsible adult, or a moral person, but as a consumer. American TV, magazines, newspapers and advertising — all of which now circle the globe — tell us this so often we Bahamians have come to believe it too. And so, like you, we are becoming a consumer society. And our value to the country will soon rest on this fact. Consume, because it helps spur the economy! If you don't, you are slowing down progress! It's all nonsense."

Whether he was right or not, whether this affected crime or not, was hard to tell, but it was easy to perceive that those Exumians who were removed from most of that advertising, worked their land, tended their neighbors and family, cared for their children, and created a good, if modest, life, did not lead a meaningless life but instead, created a life full of significance for themselves and others.

In another respect, though, Mrs. L. was totally wrong. The Bahamas is without doubt among the more enlightened Third

World democracies. It has a freely-elected parliamentary system, an outspoken loyal opposition, a long-established judicial system based on British law, and freedom of speech. A country has a lot going for it when citizens feel free to sign letters to the editor expressing their dissatisfaction of the society.

And any place where old ladies and nine-year-old girls feel safe hitchhiking has to be accorded respect.

* * *

It was nearing Christmas and I couldn't bear to think of again spending the holiday so far from family and old friends in upstate New York. But neither did I feel we could spend the money to go home. Nor did I particularly relish the prospect of below zero weather, either, or snowbound days, frosted windshields, icy roads, and winter winds roaring down from Canada, but all of a sudden I was feeling homesick and trapped on this island...

9

Sometimes, when you go to live in a foreign country, there comes a time when you realize you are the foreign one, when you know that you are outside your own country and therefore, somewhere outside your own skin. You begin to wonder who you are.

All of a sudden I felt this strongly. One morning, for no reason I could discern, I awakened and wondered: what am I doing here? Will I ever feel truly at home here? Will I ever feel I belong among the islanders?

The island's history is rife with stories of impermanence. Many before us, including those displaced English Loyalists from America who came after the Revolutionary War and lived here for a while then, when their cotton crops failed, moved on to Nassau. And Lord John Rolle, Denys Rolle's son. He sailed away to England leaving his name, and 2,300 acres of cotton plantation land (after the crops had failed) to his 350 slaves.

Over the centuries since then, others had built homes then left, or anchored a while then sailed away. Permanence does not necessarily imply joy, of course, nor impermanence disappointment, but humankind likes to have some sense of place. Of belonging. Of purpose. On a remote island in the sun the days can seem not only pointless and endless, but purposeless.

So all was not well with me. Despite the pleasant weather it was difficult to adjust. My days were extraordinarily long and quiet, as if time was overabundant and had to be used before I drowned in it. After years of cold, slow-starting, North Country winter mornings, each island sunrise hit like a jolt of new energy. With island mornings so clear and bright and warm I jumped out of bed feeling the day must not be wasted.

An early morning walk along the wooded back roads took an hour. Because the house was simple and spare the household chores took a minimum of time and were usually completed by eight a.m. Writing filled up my morning but by noon I'd had enough of that.

The sun by now was too fierce to be on the beach without damaging the skin, so hatted, oiled and sun-blocked, I either worked half-heartedly in the rockbound garden at the back of the house, read a book on the deck, or stared at the sea and thought what passes for deep thoughts: what need of family or familiar things around when you have paradise?

Endlessly watching the emerald sea, noting how the colors shifted and merged, how the passing clouds cast shadows on the water, how jade mixed with turquoise and changed into amazing combinations of greens, was interesting but enervating. Watching sailboats go by on their way "down" to Nassau, or "up" to George Town was boring, watching the tiny hummingbirds whir and the mockingbirds scolding one another was pleasant but indulged in too often, tended to soften the brain.

So I sat, all the while telling myself: this is the life. Believe it, this is the life. And don't ask: what are we doing here? That's not pertinent. We're in paradise.

Inaction and empty hours can pole-axe a type A individual. We need to be "doing" something. For thirty-five years, while my husband worked in a variety of overseas and U.S. educational posts, I'd worked as a foreign correspondent in the Middle East and Africa, occasionally as a teacher of English, and in the U.S. as a journalist, a columnist, a teacher of journalism, a newspaper editor, and a freelance magazine writer. But now, when I had what I said I'd always wanted — all the time and quiet to write the important stuff — the well was dry. What can you say about paradise? It's perfect. With days, weeks, months of idyllic weather merging so seamlessly into one another it's hard to know which month or day of the week it is. And there seemed to be nothing important or relevant to write about. I'd long been a "news junkie" and these days I felt out of touch with the world. Sometimes I felt like a piano out of tune. Certainly I was out of sync with everyone around me. Often, when we were sitting in the living room in the evening and I looked around the house it appeared slightly out of focus, as if I was viewing it without my glasses. It wasn't the house or the island, they were where they were meant to be. I was the one that didn't fit.

On occasion now the island seemed alien. In town, looking out the windows of the Bank of Nova Scotia at Kidd Cove, watching the visiting yachts bob at anchor, as I'd done many times before, the scene would suddenly get gauzy and shift out of focus, as if the light glancing off the water was dazzling my brain.

Sometimes the palm trees alongside the road would blur and shimmer around the edges, and for a split second I'd wonder where I was, and why, and then I'd slip back into place. Staring at an empty sea after a while gets tedious. Days of perpetually sunny weather become wearying; grey skies and days misty with rain suddenly become appealing. A time of rest and quiet is good while living a fast-paced life but as a full-time lifestyle it can be depressing. Americans are not geared to idleness or contemplation. Consequently, even in paradise it is possible for us to be wearied by *ennui*, surfeited with beauty and harried by guilt for not enjoying it more.

Lunch — mostly fruit — took no preparation and little time to eat. The early afternoon sun was still too hot to be on the beach so I would try to write until around three p.m. Then reluctantly I would nap, only to awaken, groggy and sweating, around four. Then I got up, drank some iced tea, and stared out the windows. If the sea wasn't too rough or the waves too high, we went for a swim. Dinner took little time to prepare, and eat, so now the evening stretched endlessly ahead. And — may the gods of the intellectual elite strike me down — I thought longingly of four or five glorious hours of nightly TV!

My husband's days were filled with building and fixing, plumbing and finishing, swimming and diving, experimenting with a variety of things he hoped to make; in comparison my days yawned emptily. Housekeeping chores were few and, to me, have always seemed futile.

At work on a number of articles and stories on my computer I was constantly frustrated by erratic electricity, the lack of a phone or a good library, and an inability to do research or fact-checking. My husband could not imagine the terrible boredom that filled my days. Aldous Huxley defined utopia as an island; obviously he never lived on one.

As my edginess grew I saw the strain on my face every morning when I combed my hair. Long silences now came between me and my husband. Our talk revolved around trivia and in the evenings, once the dishes were done, we sank into our chairs like strangers in a hotel lobby, an unsettling quiet between us.

The time after dinner dragged. When not entertaining guests or visiting friends — infrequent pastimes since we knew hardly anyone on the island and Exumians don't often entertain winter residents — it was difficult to know what to do until bedtime.

We read a lot. As if fortifying myself against possible famine, I brought home a dozen books at a time from the small George Town library. Night after night I swallowed a whole book in a single gulp. But as our friend warned, you can't read *all* the time and around eight o'clock, sleepy with boredom, I was ready for bed. It was then I discovered that adults who nap in the afternoon, go to bed at eight o'clock, and are asleep by ten, are awake by three.

Wide-eyed and sleepless, then, with the hot stars blazing outside the windows, I would lie and think of northern New York, the North Country. It would have wooded mountains draped in snow, deep clear lakes, rushing rivers and by now would have frost patterns on the windows. People would be cross-country skiing over snowy fields, visiting well-stocked libraries... reading the Sunday New York Times beside a roaring fireplace, listening to National Public Radio... talking to one another...

Serious doubts began to haunt me. Were all those detractors back home right? Could I, an American from the progressive mainland, be content on a Third World island, warm and beautiful as it was? As gentle and hospitable as the islanders were, could I settle into a country not my own, amid people not my own? A country where the comforts and conveniences I'd come to accept as a given were no longer a given? Could I, in the long run, stand so much togetherness with my husband?

There's no doubt in my mind that lives are best spent pushing off from comfort and complacency into adventure and mystery.

But at this point the evidence against my making such a hopeful launch into that mystery appeared monumental.

Was paradise a bust then, if the dwellers therein weren't busy every moment?

In desperation one morning I drove to George Town to offer my services to the small library which was run by volunteer winter residents, some well into their seventies. All were in good health; no vacancies were expected soon. They'd let me know if anyone died.

I thought about family — daughter, son, grandchildren, and yearned to see them. Shouldn't we be home tending to them? I considered flying back to the States. It would be expensive, and knock an unexpected hole in our retirement budget, but maybe, just for a while? Christmas was coming...

Because of the expense we stayed put for Christmas, even though I was sure — since we knew no one — it would be among the loneliest I'd ever spent. I sat on the beach, staring at the sea, working hard at not feeling sorry for myself, increasingly filled with longing for the Christmases of my childhood. In a world of constant and rapid change those Christmases had long abided and endured. I cherished the pattern set in those youthful days, for it was closely related to the spirit of the season. It had three major delights: anticipation, gift-giving, and a family-centered ritual.

Christmas morning on Exuma we awoke to find the usual brilliantly sunny day and the light dancing across the waves. Spectacular, of course, but there was no gathering around a Christmas tree, no turkey dinner to prepare or eat, no friends to drop by, no cousins and aunts and uncles. After breakfast my husband and I exchanged gifts; a special planing tool for my husband, and for me, a new toaster from Darville's.

I considered how we could celebrate the day. A trip to the beach to look for shells? A ride to George Town? It didn't seem much like Christmas festivity.

But in mid-afternoon, Stanley and his wife, Miss Corinne, came to "hail us." Stanley looked handsome in a white shirt, maroon tie, brown trousers and checked sports jacket. Miss Corinne was festively dressed in a blue dress with long sleeves and a matching blue hat and veil. Delighted to see them, we invited them in and Bahamian fashion, offered coffee or tea.

Over tea, Stanley said they'd come straight from their Baptist Church service. Miss Corinne, very shy, smiled and murmured that they'd come to give us a present. From its resting place in her lap, she offered me two foil-covered plastic plates. I lifted the foil on one. "We call it Benny Cake," Stanley explained. "It's coconut candy. Corrine made it herself. The other is sesame seed candy. She made that too." We tasted both, commenting on how much we liked both, but particularly the coconut candy. Miss Corrine explained the process: grate fresh coconut into chips, roast them, simmer them in butter and sugar until the sugar thickens, then spoon them onto a buttered plate to harden.

High density cholesterol aside, they were delicious and we were moved by their generosity.

About four Stanley and Corrine left. Half an hour later Mr. Flowers came with his old friend and neighbor Will Nixon to "hail" us on Christmas Day. They stayed for a beer and a good long chat.

Feeling inordinately better after they left, I set the table with a pink cloth, red candles, and a blue bowl of scarlet bougainvillea. We ate a Christmas dinner of fresh snapper, boiled potatoes, canned peas and a salad of island tomatoes sprinkled with fresh sweet basil from the garden. Dessert was my favorite: vanilla ice cream. To go with it we opened a bottle of George Town's best (and only) champagne. With my heart only pining a little now, we raised our glasses in a toast to the season.

Just before sunset my husband suggested we go for a walk on the beach. In the fading light the surf foamed and bubbled around our bare feet, the dunes, soaring high and lonely between us and the land behind, were rose-colored. Golden sea oats streamed backwards in a steady sea breeze. The water was clear as glass, so clear we could see the rippled patterns of sand in the shallows, the tiny shells left by the tide.

The air was warm as a cloak around my shoulders. Sandpipers darted in and out of the surf, sand crabs scuttled into their holes, and above us the deepening sky was streaked with pale green and lit by one lone and brilliant evening star. It was beautiful. Beautiful and peaceful and serene. And lonely.

We inhaled deeply at precisely the same moment and looked up at each other.

"Merry Christmas." My husband took my hand.

"Merry Christmas," I replied, looking down at the sand so he wouldn't see my foolish homesick tears.

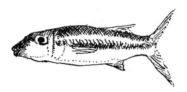

May, and time to go back to the States. We investigated the possibility of flying to the States and returning as passengers with a car on the MV *Lady Rosalind*, one of the freighters that plied between Miami and the islands on a more-or-less monthly schedule.

At the government dock in George Town we talked to her captain, Eddings Taylor, a taciturn black Bahamian of stalwart size. We said we'd like to take passage with him for ourselves and a car when he sailed from Miami to the island in a couple of months or so. He eyed us without any visible enthusiasm for the idea of having us as passengers, compressed his lips, looked over our heads and across the harbor, and finally said he never took passengers, just freight. "I'm not set up to be a cruise ship," he said, as if accusing us of some breach of good taste in even asking him for a passage.

We told him we'd traveled on a freighter once before, three weeks up the Red Sea, through the Med, and across the Atlantic to Boston. We knew how to stay out of the way and promised not to be any trouble. Would he at least think about it?

He might. But we were not to count on it. "Call my Miami office," he said over his shoulder as he walked away.

We decided such a loose arrangement did not bode well for our chances and went to Plan B. This was to fly back to the island in October, buy a car in Nassau, and ship it down on the mailboat.

Still, Captain Taylor hadn't given an outright no. If during the summer in the U.S. we called his Miami office weekly... and kept calling until he got tired of saying no and said yes... .

10

To be aboard a ship at sea is not unlike living on an island. There is a certain richness to days exposed to the weather, a heightened aliveness in being surrounded by an endless expanse of water. It's a bit like living in two worlds — on solid land but afloat at the same time — both of which sharpen the senses.

In early December it was time to head back to the island. We decided to take a chance and try to return aboard Captain Taylor's *Lady Rosalind* — if he would have us. On faith, we drove our newly-acquired, and overloaded Chevy Cavalier Wagon from northern New York to Miami. Here, after a two-hour search through the industrial area we eventually found Captain Taylor's *Bahama Shipping Company* on the banks of the Miami River.

We still didn't know whether or not he'd grant us a berth on *The Roz*. Numerous phone calls to him during the summer were answered by a secretary, who continued to say Captain Taylor had made no decision. Now we were here to confront him dockside.

We found him, large and sweating in jeans and a stained tee shirt, supervising the loading of his ship. When called by one of the men, he stopped work reluctantly, wiped his brow, came over to us, and glowered. We smiled engagingly.

"We called all summer but couldn't get you. So we decided to just drive on down," my husband said.

Captain Taylor frowned, looked displeased. "As I told you before, I carry cargo, not passengers," he said gruffly, "but I'll ship your car over to Exuma."

"We're both in excellent health," I said.

There was a long pause while he looked us over carefully, and saw (I guess) two, only slightly rusty seniors, who appeared sturdy enough and in sufficient good health to withstand the rigors of a trip on *The Roz.*

"Well —." He rubbed a hand across his sweat-soaked tee shirt. "Okay, then. You can sign on as crew. That way my insurance will cover you. Go to the office and tell them you're sailing with me." With no trace of a smile he looked at me and said, "you can be the cook."

I was pretty sure he was joking, but then, as we headed across the cluttered yard to a trailer set on cinder blocks to complete the paperwork, he called after us, "I hope you know how to cook mutton souse." Mutton souse! I didn't even know what it was! And could barely manage roast turkey.

"And *I* hope," I muttered to my husband, signing my name to some sort of fine-print contract, "Captain Taylor isn't serious. You know I can't cook." As my husband well knew, I've never been much of a cook and the thought I might have to do it on shipboard was, as far as I was concerned, profoundly ominous, not just for me but also for the crew.

If Captain Taylor wasn't just joking — something that, given his sober mien, seemed highly unlikely — I predicted the instant mutiny of his crew. Resignedly I slapped on my anti-seasick patch, thinking, along with Walt Whitman's prose from *Leaves of Grass*, *"The old ship is not in a state to make many voyages, but the flag is still at the mast and I am still at the wheel."* Or in the galley.

Throughout the hot afternoon we sat in the shipyard on a variety of crates and boxes to watch the ship being loaded. Eventually, our Chevy, heavy with blankets and warm clothes (because I no longer took chances on Exuma's winter weather,) swung high into the air. With great dexterity the crane driver placed it neatly on the aft deck, nesting it as precisely as you please amid a welter of boxes, bales, refrigerated containers, and three other cars. One of these, a brand new, white, Mercedes luxury sedan, (or, as the Bahamians would say, "a new-brand Mercedes,") with white wall tires, wire wheels, state-of-the-art stereo, and smoked glass windows, was destined for Rock Sound, on the island of Eleuthera.

It was early evening by the time we finally went aboard. Captain Taylor and his crew tended to their deck jobs with the concentration of experienced seamen. In this world of seagoing work we, the only passengers, the ones for whom the captain had made a special allowance, were the interlopers; the rich white people who could afford to make the trip for fun and pleasure. They ignored us.

As freighters go, *The Roz* was small, just 3,000 tons. She had one passenger deck with four staterooms, each with upper and lower bunk, a porthole and two chairs. At the end of the passageway was the "head," with toilet, washbasin and shower, small but well-polished, tidy, and spotlessly clean.

Fortunately for me, I soon discovered there was a cook already onboard, a lad named Roberto, who looked too young to do more than fry eggs. Captain Taylor had sent him to one of the four passenger-deck staterooms to move out the two resident crew officers, and move us in. I didn't ask where they were sent to sleep but guessed the crew's quarters below decks. Later, when I apologized for taking their beds they just shrugged. But weren't we crew too? Somewhere there was a paper to prove it.

Unlike a Princess Line cruise, with its ever-smiling stewards and beaming waiters, on *The Roz* it was hard to tell whether or not we were welcome. I suspected we were not, which meant the crossing to Nassau and on to Exuma would be rough going.

Roberto, speaking Spanish rapidly the whole time, unfolded two clean white sheets and began making up the bunks. He didn't need my help. He plumped up two pillows. There were, however, no pillow cases or top sheets. Fortunately, before setting out for Miami, reckoning that if we did get a passage aboard, and that since *The Roz* didn't usually take passengers, probably wasn't prepared for them, and might lack extra bed linens, I had brought along two sheets and two pillowcases.

While helping make up the bunks I tried to talk, but our conversation was limited by his minimal English and my total lack of Spanish. Through sign language, however, I was able to learn that he was twenty-one years old, a Columbian, and had signed on as cook two years earlier in hopes he would someday make enough money to own his own fishing boat. "Then I will be rich, like American," he said, his eyes dreamy at the prospect. Like so many non-Americans we'd met in other parts of the world, he saw us as spoiled, rich, dollar-happy people who can go anywhere, buy anything, or do anything at any time. We may have the world's best advertising but we don't do a very good job selling ourselves as people who share the same dreams and some of the same problems as the rest of the world.

I unpacked our suitcases for the three-day voyage. One well-traveled friend who had circumnavigated the globe on all kinds of ships, including freighters, had insisted we pack swim suits and something fairly formal — a dinner dress, and jacket and slacks.

"Even on a freighter you may want to change for dinner," he said. Secretly, I had followed his advice, though now I was loathe to admit it. Dress for dinner with a surly Captain Taylor?

One look around *The Roz* had told me there would be no lazing by a swimming pool or dining at the captain's table; as a crew member my jeans and shirt would be proper attire for the entire cruise. (If I was not the cook, what would my crew job be? Whatever it was, congenital seasickness was sure to largely define it.)

Around five o'clock *The Roz* moved slowly away from the dock and started down the Miami River, pulled along by two little tugboats. We stood on deck in the growing dusk as she slipped along through the heart of the city. The tugs, with the expertise of two sturdy seeing-eye dogs, guided the freighter under three lift bridges, past fancy hotels and apartment buildings, past high-rise office complexes — all of them brightly lit and decorated for Christmas.

One skyscraper in particular stood out, its exterior sheathed from top to bottom in a luminous blue light. Scattered across its azure skin were ten or twelve enormous lacy white snowflake designs, each the size of a large satellite dish; they looked as if they were plastered there by a storm of giant snowflakes. An offshore breeze blew the smell of the city toward us: exhaust fumes, cooking odors, hot asphalt and dust mingled with the salty, fishy smell of the sea beneath our ship.

From out in Biscayne Bay the Christmas-lit buildings illuminated Miami, making of it a fantasy city that appeared to float magically above the dark waters of the bay, a twentieth century miracle of lights and shapes, of color and form, a superb example of modern urban landscape design. It was beautiful and as *The Roz* pulled farther and farther away from the festive lights and into the ocean's darkness I almost panicked.

Six days away another Christmas loomed and my heart was still back there, on the U.S. mainland, with family, and friends, and the familiar lights and decorations and gaudy cheerfulness that make up an American Christmas.

I leaned over the rail as the magical city receded. But, I told myself, we'd lived overseas enough years — about seventeen — that I no longer demanded snow and sleigh bells. A Christmas Eve spent in Bethlehem years ago had shown me that Christ was born in a cave, not a wooden stable, and there were palm trees, not evergreens, in that early Christmas scene. The western Christmas, as well as early Christianity itself, was, after all, based on much earlier Pagan rituals, their purpose not to separate us from divinity but to reconnect us to it, and find it within us and within everything around us.

I decided right then I'd try to view this holiday season as a challenge to know myself, the real self hidden behind all the tinsel and gaiety, the frantic rushing about, the last minute bustle, the cooking and the shopping and the entertaining. This year, though not eager to return to Paradise for another Christmas, I was determined to rise to the challenge.

My husband, on the other hand, was eager to get back — whatever the season — to his island house-building. To him it was the culmination of a dream, long-held during his years in academia. Everyone, I thought, has many talents asleep inside that need only be awakened. My husband's broad capable hands could do more than push a pen, drive a car, take out the garbage, write a check, wash dishes, open a book, or turn on the TV — things that, until now, he had done for most of his life.

Being able to explore new talents on the island kept him alive in the joy of self-discovery. Three-quarters of the way through his life he was tasting a totally new way of living. I could not, nor would I try, to dissuade him from that. Maybe with luck and perseverance the same would happen to me this second winter of our sojourn on the island.

The Roz reached a floating dock and was tied up alongside long enough to bid goodbye to the two little tug boats. The breeze freshened with the fresh tang of the open sea, the ship begin to roll, and I hoped my seasick patch would be effective.

11

Our first night aboard was hot and rough, with gusty winds and choppy seas. Even with the aid of the anti-seasick patch I slept fitfully in my lower berth and when the call for breakfast came at 6 a.m. I passed on it. The smell of bacon and eggs and fried potatoes floating up from below decks made even the thought of food unappealing. Some ship's cook I'd make!

My husband, the former Navy man, was well-rested and ravenous. He hurried below.

A few minutes later Roberto tapped at my door with coffee and a boiled egg. Pushing these at me, he nodded and patted his stomach. "Good, good. You eat, *si?*"

To avert hurt feelings I thanked him and took the tray. But even the coffee was more than I could manage. I dumped it out the porthole, threw the boiled egg after it, and too late recalled that aboard ship there's something about throwing stuff to the lee of the wind. I could only hope the stuff sailed away from — not into — the men working on *The Roz's* decks. Could Captain Taylor be more annoyed than he already was?

By noon I was able to get my sea legs and figured I might try a bite of lunch. Hanging on tightly to the slim stair railing I negotiated the steep ladder-like steps which led down to the "lounge" — *The Roz's* all-purpose main room on the main deck. It had an open galley along one side from which Roberto was serving Bahamian food: fried fish, peas and rice, and cole slaw. Apologetically, knowing I was imposing on a vessel where we were really not welcome, I whispered to Roberto (out of the hearing of Captain Taylor) "could I please have some toast and tea?" He smiled, nodded eagerly, and busy as he was feeding the crew, he willingly set about accommodating my special request. Before it came I saw Captain Taylor leave and heaved a sigh of relief that he wouldn't see me eat specially ordered comfort food.

Meals aboard *The* Roz were eaten at a plastic-covered wooden table alongside the galley with whomever of the seven member crew was off-duty. If Captain Taylor arrived from the bridge there was some brief conversation. Very brief. He wasn't so much unfriendly as impregnable. How he felt about "foreigners" aboard his ship was still unknown to us.

Once, feeling the heavy silence around the table, I daringly asked if he was from the Bahamas Out Islands, or was born in Nassau. He put down his fork, regarded me silently for a moment, then said gruffly, "born in Nassau, where my Daddy taught me to sail when I was eight. You might say I'm part Bahamian, part failed Episcopalian, and part Viking."

He chewed his fried chicken for a while then added, almost as an afterthought, that he "knew all the islands well and loved his *Lady Roz*." For the first day out that was the extent of our communication. Was he sorry he'd taken us aboard and wanted no more to do with us than was absolutely necessary? We had, after all, displaced two of his crew members from their bunks, possibly jeopardized his insurance coverage, disrupted his cook's routine, and I had invaded his all-male kingdom.

Later that morning the ship headed into a downtown Nassau dock at the foot of Bay Street. Two berths over, the superstructures of three, giant, white cruise ships soared into the air; from our lowdown perspective they looked like enormous floating apartment buildings. Red and green plastic garlands, multicolored lanterns, and artificial Christmas trees strung with lights dressed the decks. From the stern of one, loudspeakers boomed forth a jazzy rendition of *Rudolph The Red-Nosed Reindeer.*

From an earlier experience we knew that when sailing aboard a cruise ship like that the food is elaborate and plentiful, the accommodations luxurious, the amenities numerous, and the service extensive, but it doesn't feel as if you are at sea; rather it's more like being residents in a high-tech city on floats. From decks that high above the water the sea is as impersonal as the earth's surface seen from a plane. No one aboard is a part of the sea. The crew works on steel decks or are safely enclosed within a steel hull. It is a man-made segment of land set adrift; you see much but understand little of the sea and its moods.

How different *The Roz*. Small, close to the water, she made me feel one with the sea, aware of it every moment, awake, asleep even seasick. All senses were on alert, you heard all the sounds — the hiss of the sea under the bow, the swish as it rushed along the hull, the creaking and groaning of the cables and the stays. On deck the salt spray stung your eyes and the salt air filled your nostrils with a smell as pungent as spice. It's not virtual reality, it's a real sea experience, queasy stomach and all. Despite Captain Taylor's cool demeanor, I found it preferable to be aboard *The Roz*.

Perhaps it's nothing but a romantic fantasy, but I felt it was a privilege to be aboard a freighter like *The Roz*, to be with men who constantly brave the ocean, who actually faced the elements without a lot of sophisticated technology and fancy airs. Listening to them speak, watching them perform their various shipboard duties, you are as close to the true spirit of seagoing men as it's possible to get these days.

I also felt privileged to be where I was at the age I was, and recalled the farewell made famous by TV's Star Trek: *Live long and prosper.* It is a suitable motto for any one of us, and defies the ageism that is one of the most severe biases of our youth-oriented, beauty-crazed, fitness-obsessed, glamor-ridden American culture. In 1880 life expectancy in America was 47, today it is 78 and the normal American life-span has grown longer in this century than in the previous 2000 years. But if you read the papers, look at the ads, watch TV or go to the movies, in the U.S. anyone over 50 is considered to be plummeting downhill fast with no hope of recovery before the Grim Reaper strikes. Nowadays retirement kills more people than hard work.

These days the truth is that thousands of sixty, seventy and eighty-year-olds are creating lives that are exciting and rewarding because they have been able — either through good genes, careful planning, disciplined saving, or determined optimism — to keep alive their passion and enthusiasm. Remaining healthy as we age is, of course, the luck of the draw — and no doubt about it, our generation has been lucky — but today's seniors have also earned their old age by ignoring the advertisers and nay-sayers and by saving, working hard and striving to stay well.

And here we were, ages sixty-four and sixty-eight, aboard *The Roz*. Now *this* was luck! I was reminded of something I read in high school about going on voyages: *When you set out on the voyage to Ithaca, pray that your journey may be long, full of adventures, full of knowledge.* It is from a piece called *Ithaca* by the Greek poet Kavafis, and suited me to a T.

Furthermore, had we not been aboard, we would have missed the next morning's spectacular show when we sailed into Rock Sound, Eleuthera, to off-load the "new-brand Mercedes".

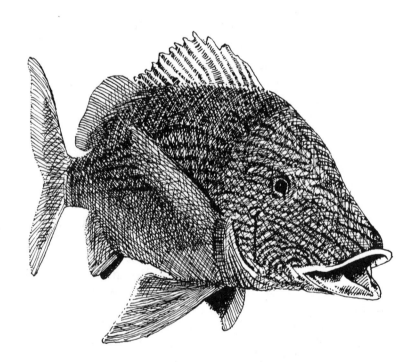

12

Of course, all journeys end but you never know what you'll find until you get there.

To our surprise next morning Captain Taylor sent down word inviting us to the bridge so we would have a good view of the off-loading of the cargo. We hung over the rail outside the wheelhouse and watched as a the crew readied the cargo for the ship's lift-crane.

Because there was no jetty at Rock Sound, Captain Taylor had eased *The Roz* alongside a stone wall that served the community as a landing stage. After snugging it close with ropes, the craneman, directed by several crewmen, began off-loading various crates and boxes, swinging them over the side and lowering them to the ground. Half an hour passed, with all going well, then suddenly there was a loud CRANK!, some alarming clanging noises, and the crane clattered to a halt.

Breakdown.

Captain Taylor swore and shoved his captain's cap to the back of his head. The crew went below for lunch. We joined them for fried grouper, peas and rice and cole slaw. No one talked about the crane or what was to be done to finish off-loading, but just before he left to go back to the bridge Captain Taylor said, "tide's going out." The crew got up and went out.

We got back to the bridge in time to see the "new brand" supercharged, white Mercedes luxury sedan, with wire wheels and state-of-the-art stereo equipment, the finest model out of the factory, being readied for off-loading without the crane lift.

I could see it would be a dicey proceeding, especially for the Mercedes, but also for the crewmen charged with the job of unloading her. No one seemed very worried, though, about the risk to car and human limbs — in the islands, it appeared, no one worries about such things — except, in this case, the

Mercedes' owner. He stood on the ground looking up, frowning, looking worried.

After much discussion and arm-waving aboard *The Roz* a solution as to how the car was to be removed from the deck was arrived at: the crew moved around the other cars on deck, including our Chevy, to start clearing space. With some planks they then made a wooden ramp from the deck up to the opening on the ship's gunnel, which was at least four feet higher than the deck. A similar board ramp was installed to run from the gunnel down to the ground ten feet below. The Mercedes was to be driven up and over this makeshift ramp/drawbridge and down the steep, 45 degree ramp, to the ground.

Upon being told this, the owner, a tall Bahamian in a spiffy white suit and dark tie, who looked like either a prosperous businessman or a Mafia don, objected loudly. He called and waved and shouted, flinging his arms about like a windmill. But since he couldn't get onboard nobody paid him the slightest attention.

The crew readied for action.

We leaned on the rail outside the wheelhouse to watch what we — and the others — must have known could only end in disaster. In this matter Captain Taylor, swigging at a bottle of Pepsi, was allowing his crew complete autonomy. "They're experienced," he said, shrugging, "they know their job. No problem." As if unleashing them on the unloading of the Mercedes qualified as an everyday experience. Or maybe it was.

All afternoon the intriguing drama unfolded. First, our Chevy suburban was moved, then it and two other cars were jockeyed back and forth around the deck, like those Chinese puzzles where you move the lettered squares around a box to get them in a proper sequence. The aim here, however, was to clear a long pathway the width of the deck so as to give the Mercedes enough room to make a good run at the makeshift gangplank — which one could only hope was lined up accurately. Otherwise...

Captain Taylor fretted about the tide. It was past high tide now; if he couldn't move his *Roz* soon she'd miss the tide and we would have to lay over another night. This would add another full day to the trip, more crew pay, more food eaten; in other words, for this trip a loss of revenue. Captain Taylor, it was obvious, was not a happy sailor.

Finally, the last crate and frozen food carrier was rearranged and around four o'clock, a pathway on deck was cleared. The Chief Mate, a lanky Bahamian named Jake, climbed into the Mercedes, started the motor, gunned it, and screeched the gears. Dockside, the Mercedes owner winced, loosened his tie, fanned himself with his white hat, and shook his head as if in disbelief of what was about to take place. Then too stressed to watch, he turned his back and walked away. It was a good move on his part because from where we stood there was every likelihood that his new car was going to drop over the side of the ship and plunge nose down onto the stone wall.

Slowly, amid a great deal of shouting and instruction, Jake bravely inched the Mercedes across the deck and up to the ramp. At this point everything appeared to be going well. Jake had obviously mastered the gear system, and the gas pedal, and the sleek new car was inching slowly and smoothly up the wooden ramp, with Jake in control.

Apparently, though, no one had yet thought of what to do about the fact that the two ramps, one inside the ship and the steeper one leading down to the ground, were not smoothly joined where they met on the gunnel. Here the jerry-rigged planks failed to meet by a good four inches.

Jake inched the gleaming car slowly, slowly... up... up... up the first ramp. He reached the fulcrum point atop the gunnel — the point where the jerry-rigged planks had a yawning gap — and the Mercedes, unable because of its weight and the height difference in the ramps to get over the ridge, stalled.

It teetered there alarmingly, rocked back and forth a bit, the ramp planks creaking and groaning under the weight. From the audience onshore, dead silence.

The owner, unable to stay away, held his head in his hands.

In the driver's seat, Jake gripped the wheel and looked down at the jetty. Now the onshore audience and the crew members started shouting instructions. Jake turned from his study of the jetty and looked up at Captain Taylor, who nodded encouragement. Jake visibly relaxed, took a deep breath, and ignoring the shouts and calls from the now-frantic owner, revved the motor, rocked the car back and forth a few times, and with sheer guts, risking life and limb, gunned it up and over the gunnel and down the ramp, braking in a cloud of dust at the owner's feet.

A cheer flew up from the crowd.

Everyone shouted hurrahs — the crew, the spectators on the dock who must have gathered to see what they were sure would be a disaster, the people floating nearby in fishing boats — everyone, that is, except the owner. Arms akimbo, he gazed down at his new car, its "new-brand" paint glistening in the sun, its chrome shining, its whitewall tires agleam — its white underside stove in.

He patted its hood, stroked its smoked glass windows, and tried the doors, none of which would open. He then stood back, looked at it, shook his head, and frowned. Finally, his anger surfacing, he aimed a kick at the front right tire in a frenzy of frustration — before walking away without another word.

Captain Taylor was not in the least distressed; he was more annoyed about his broken cargo crane. My husband asked if the car owner could claim on his insurance. "Hell no," he said, pulling his peaked cap down over his forehead. "Drug money bought that car. He doesn't even want people to know he has it. Serves him right."

(How the owner had intended to hide a white Mercedes on a skinny island 25 miles long with only one road, to this day remains a mystery.)

By now it was dusk and Captain Taylor was right; the Mercedes Affair had caused him to miss the tide and meant we had to lay over for the night to await the next morning's incoming tide. That evening Captain Taylor invited us to share his supper of freshly-caught grouper he'd bought at Rock Sound.

Something had obviously changed; for some reason we were unaware of, we had been granted acceptance. Even the crew was friendlier — though it was not evident what we had done to deserve this.

Over the meal and the mugs of hot black coffee that followed, feeling like characters out of a Joseph Conrad novel, we sat and listened as Captain Taylor and the crew spun yarns of adventure and growing up in the islands. They spoke of boyhoods spent sailing Bahama waters, of hair-raising adventures in storms at sea; of rum-runners and brushes with the law and loneliness and longing and wives and sweethearts who were unfaithful. Even if, as a Bahamian friend suggested later, the sea stories were somewhat embellished, that evening aboard *The Roz* would forever stand out in my mind as a memorable experience.

Around midnight, as we got up to leave I said, "thank you for a wonderful evening, Captain Taylor," and when he, nodding curtly, replied "call me Cap'n Eddy," it was like winning a lottery.

As dawn broke the next morning we headed for George Town on a bright calm day with huge cumulus clouds scudding overhead and a brisk wind pushing us southwards. On board only two days, it seemed as if time had ceased to exist. Providing I didn't have to cook I felt I could go on forever like this, ploughing through the sea and sailing along under a cornflower sky.

A few miles northwest of George Town, when nearing the small settlement of Farmer's Hill, Cap'n Eddy again invited us topside. "See if you can see your house," he said, handing me his binoculars. I pressed them against my face waiting for it to appear. At first, because I'd never before seen it from out at sea, I couldn't find it. I swung the binoculars in an arc, searching, looking for landmarks. The house wasn't there and I had a momentary pang when I considered the idea that it might have been blown down in a hurricane. But surely we would have been notified...?

With relief I spotted it, sitting atop its little hill, its wide windows reflecting the afternoon sun. Seeing it from the sea, as though we were tourists, gave me a different perspective. For the first time I could look at it objectively.

If I had been a tourist passing, I thought, what would I be thinking now, seeing that pretty pink house sitting up there on its hill, a scarlet bougainvillea tumbling from its garage roof, palm trees shading its deck, and a long scoop of white beach edging the nearby shore?

I would think the people who live there got the luck of the draw...

In the wheelhouse Cap'n Eddy tuned in his portable radio

to ZNS, the Nassau radio station, which at this time of year played continuous Christmas carols. Everyone — the crew, even taciturn Cap'n Eddy — began to sing along. And that's how it was as we motored slowly into George Town's Elizabeth Harbour on a crest of *Silent Night, Holy Night,* singing and waving to the sailboats at anchor. They were decorated for Christmas, with colored lights glittering from the rigging, and they, too, were tuned to Radio ZNS and as *The Roz* steamed slowly into the Government Dock the boaters waved and called up to us, "Merry Christmas! Merry Christmas!"

And there, beaming as we disembarked, waiting for us in his Olds Cutlass, a welcoming smile on his face, was Stanley Ferguson. He and my husband bear-hugged. Then Stanley turned to me, and taking both my hands in his work-roughened ones, pumped them up and down in welcome. He said, "I've come to drive you and Wince home."

En route, we got the latest island news: R. had disappeared, drug dealers were suspected; P. had built a new house; N's wife had left him for another man, and Will Nixon, father of five, grandfather of seven, had married Mr. Flowers' daughter, Zelma, thirty years his junior and mother of six. The bride and groom were blissful, the six children delighted to have a father around the house. Mr. Flowers, who lives directly across the road from them, is, according to Stanley, exuberant.

During the summer, when I thought of returning to the island, and our life here, I had been threatened by an overwhelming sense of depression. But now that we were here, and I saw the friendly familiar faces on the dock, the late afternoon sun glancing off the blue and pink and yellow houses, the haphazard town lying among the palm trees, and the glorious turquoise sea all around, to my surprise nothing of the sort happened.

Instead I experienced a kind of rebirth, and with it came the original feeling of lightness and joy I'd experienced upon seeing Exuma for the first time from a plane, lying long and luxuriant against its peacock sea, the sunlight dancing off the water, the immensity of ocean spreading out in all directions.

13

Many years ago I left behind my traditional religious beliefs for a more holistic and spiritual faith, one with personal meaning and intent, one that perceived all existence as interconnected and sacred. I nonetheless enjoyed some traditional celebrations and on Exuma preparations were being made for Christmas.

In George Town's main square strings of colored lights outlined the pink Government building and decorated a tree in Regatta Park. The little stores had lights in the windows as did the Bank of Nova Scotia and the Baptist Church. Father Keith Cartwright had exuberantly draped the Anglican parsonage and its garden in flashing red, green and blue lights. One mean-minded critic said it made the place look like a particularly hazardous construction site but as Stanley sagely observed, "every country has its scrooge!"

One advantage I could see this Christmas would be a fortunate lack of Christmas frenzy. With only three variety stores there would be no last minute buying spree, and with only two grocery stores, no mountains of food to buy, no hectic preparation of it, and no bloated nap afterward to mar the day's pleasure; without TV, newspapers, or magazines we would not be bombarded by advertising hype or insulted by endless commercials.

And, we learned we were not without friends. The morning of Christmas Eve Zelma and Will Nixon arrived to invite us to be their guests at that evening's special service at the Church of God The Prophecy in Farmer's Hill. There'd be music and Zelma's Christmas play would make its debut. Will would pick us up.

The night was full of moon. Will arrived at seven in his blue van. It was decorated inside with red and green bunting, and from the mirror hung a glass angel with spun silver wings that twirled to the Christmas music on the tape deck. At the door of the small cinder block church Mr. Flowers greeted us and though we whisperingly told him we preferred to sit inconspicuously at the rear he insisted upon ushering us to the front row. With everyone nearby smiling at us and nodding acceptance we sat down on one of the hard wooden benches facing a raised platform.

The smiling welcome made me reflect on a passage from the book *Stark's History of, and Guide to, the Bahamas*, published in 1891, in which the author quotes Mr. L.D. Powles' book *Land of The Pink Pearl*. Powles wrote about the reception on Harbour Island in the late 1800's of *"five coloured men who determined to test the right of the authorities of the Methodist church to prevent a colored man from entering the chapel by the same door as a white man."*

"With this in view," Powles wrote, *"they walked quietly in at the white man's door and up the aisle. The service was discontinued until they were turned out; they were prosecuted the next day before the resident justice, who convicted them of brawling, and fined them twenty shillings each, with the alternative of imprisonment."* How different, I thought, was our reception in this church.

A warm breeze blew in the open windows and doors, an air of jollity hung in the air as people talked, gossiped and hailed friends. Children wriggled excitedly as the church filled. People sat on metal chairs in the aisles, on the floor in front of the stage, or hung in the windows. Drifting out from backstage (behind a folding screen) we could hear shuffling and whispering and muffled laughter as the actors got ready. Zelma's loud "sshshhshhing!" could also be heard.

Star of the show was Zelma's twelve-year-old son Kivi, who appeared dressed in trousers, an oversize sports-coat and a grey fedora that rested on his ears. He represented, we soon learned, a husband and father who had turned to drink and had forgotten not only the day but the whole meaning of Christmas. By his actions and words he showed his family he was unloving, selfish and indifferent to their welfare.

But the Christmas message was that he was not irredeemable. By their small acts of kindness and love, he was re-taught the lesson of Christmas by his wife and children, played by Zelma's other children and their friends. When the play ended the actors took their kudos calmly, and when Kivi pulled the grey fedora down over his face the church filled with laughter.

Next we sang Christmas carols, the deep rich voices of the congregation and choir joyfully belting out the familiar words to *O Come All Ye Faithful, It Came Upon a Midnight Clear* and *Silent Night*. As our songs rose above us — everyone clapping in sheer pleasure to the music — I became caught up in the sound and carried away by the energy and enthusiasm I felt around me. When a woman choir member solemnly sang O Holy Night in a vibrant contralto, I was deeply moved by her rich voice, and though I had left traditional religion and its roots behind, my eyes filled with tears.

Reverend Curtis gave a sermon about the giving of oneself, which made many nod and murmur agreement. Elderly members dozed in the shadows, infants slept inertly on generous laps, and children wandered about, leaned against a parent's knee, and whispered to each other. The little girls, flitting from pew to pew in their pastel colored skirts and perky hairribbons resembled a bevy of butterflies.

Outside, as the "good nights" and "Merry Christmases" were said, people shook hands formally, or hugged, or stood around reluctant to leave. Stars blazed down, the Christmas moon rode the sky, voices floated up and away into the warm darkness. I could see that though their lives may lack materially, Exumians were immeasurably strengthened by their religious faith.

Christmas morning we awoke to the usual, brilliantly sunny day and the light dancing across the sea. I felt a slight melancholy that there would be no gathering around a Christmas tree with family, no turkey dinner, no friends to drop by, no cousins and aunts and uncles. After breakfast we exchanged gifts; for my husband a book from *The Sandpiper*, for me, a beautiful box carved by my husband.

In the evening Will Nixon and Zelma came with some Johnny Cake that Zelma had made, and brought with them Mr. Flowers, who gave us a bag of sugar apples from his garden; later Christine arrived to "gift" us with some bananas and fresh green peppers. The thought that they weren't just "gifting" us because we were going to "gift" them in return, or because it was a charitable thing to do, but because we had come to their island as strangers, "people from away" as Bahamians put it, and this was a giving season, made their simple generosity over-whelming. What a different Christmas from last year, I reflected at the end of the day; then I had felt a stranger, alone and with-out a community around me. Now I felt accepted and included.

* * *

Junkanoo, the annual parade starting before dawn the day after Christmas (known here as Boxing Day) was a big part of the holiday. Contestants vied for prizes for best costume, best music, best group and best dance. Competition was keen and groups in Nassau spent up to a year and a lot of money fashion-ing their costumes and floats. On Exuma it was a more modest celebration and less costly but as eagerly attended. We were told not to miss it, that we would find it an unusual event. Getting up at 4 a.m. was unusual enough but an auto accident made it more so.

No one seemed to know exactly where the tradition of Junkanoo started; local myth said it was the mid-nineteenth cen-tury in Jamaica. As legend has it, a former African chief, a cap-tured slave named John Canoe, was homesick for his people. Missing his former prestige and status, he made for himself a bright cloak of colorful scraps of material which he secretly wore to keep his spirits up and retain his royal status.

Came the Christmas when his white master was away, and John Canoe held his own celebration. Donning his "coat of many colors" he summoned his fellow slaves to join him in the re-membered chanting and dancing of their former lives in Africa. They, in turn, named the celebration after him; John Canoe, aka Junkanoo.

While it was still dark we joined scores of Exumians and tourists in the early morning streets of George Town. Amid the prancing and dancing, drinking and revelry, singing and shout-ing, we cavorted along main street with young men and women in elaborate costumes and masks made from paper, feathers, plas-ter of Paris and *papier-mâché*.

Some costumes were theme-inspired — Arawak Indians, Mother Earth, Our Fair Island Home. Some were meant to scare — monsters, dragons, dinosaurs, ghosts. Others were religious — St. Peter, The Virgin Mary, or Peace on Earth — and one or two were meant to impress with their intricate construction — a sailing ship, Raptures of the Deep, Flora and Fauna of the Bahamas. Hovering over all and strengthening the air was a strong smell of rum.

Along with everyone else not in costume we brought up the rear of the parade behind the last float, clapping and singing at the top of our lungs. A young man sporting a devil's mask and a large *papier-mâché* bottle atop his head leapt in front of us.

"Who are you?" we asked.

"The Spirit of Devil Rum." He threw back his head and laughed hugely. Flinging an arm around our shoulders he drew us along with the mob. The decibel level by now had risen to deafening so seven o'clock found us partly deaf, eating breakfast at the *P&P*, and longing for sleep.

On the way home we noticed that the combination of drink and dance has had an alarming effect on some Exumians. One who had overindulged in rum and was revved-up with exercise, was driving home tempted by the thrill of passing us on a blind hill. Another wove back and forth across the two-lane Queen's Highway, veering off to the side from time to time, all the while honking madly for us to get out of the way.

One car didn't make it home, stopped cold by an electric pole. As we rounded a curve just below the Packing House we saw a badly smashed red car listing drunkenly to one side. My husband slowed, stopped. "D'you s'pose it just happened?" I asked. For some reason I whispered, perhaps because my heart was pounding so hard. I felt ill at the thought of what might have happened to the occupants.

Hurriedly he got out and ran over to the car, leaned down, and peered in. My husband responded well in situations like this; I was not so sanguine. I imagined fire. An explosion. Heart attacks. I hoped the occupants had already gotten help.

There was no ambulance on the island. The sick and injured were transported to the government clinic, or the airport, in any available truck or car. There was a medivac helicopter service from Miami which could be summoned for cases needing treatment there; the alternative was a charter flight to Nassau for treatment at one of the two hospitals there.

My mind raced ahead. If there were injured where would we take them? It was a holiday, the government clinic in nearby

Steventon would be closed. Was the Steventon doctor on-island or off-island? Was the George Town doctor on-island or off-island? Could we safely carry anyone that far?

Then I remembered Nurse Lydia Rolle. She lived just a mile away and was as good as many doctors and, some said, better than most. An American friend on the island traveled for several years to a wide variety of Stateside doctors, none of whom could find what made her ill. Finally she went to Nurse Rolle who, after an examination, told her she had cancer and should take the next plane to the States. The diagnosis was correct.

At another time one of our house guests fell on jagged limestone and badly cut her hand. Nurse Rolle stitched it up; later a surgeon in the States examining it asked what surgeon had done the expert stitching job. I could drive and get Nurse Rolle; she would be sure to know what to do...

My husband straightened up, ran a hand over his face... Uh-oh, it must be bad news... I tried to quell my queasy feeling. He walked back...

"How many?" I expected the worst.

"Not a soul in the car. No blood nothing. Car's a write-off though. I can't believe anyone could have gotten out alive. Somebody must have already taken them away."

Next morning I mentioned it to Mr. Flowers and asked if he knew whose car it was and what happened. As I might have guessed, he did. By now everyone on the island probably knew. He said it was a man from Stuart Manor and gave me his name. He was alone in the car, and walked away without injury.

"That's amazing! Have you seen the car?"

"It's going to be there for a while," he said, "I'll see it later on." He nudged back his tractor cap, a grin on his face. I knew by this time it was a signal one of his jokes was coming.

"How many Exumians does it take to move a wrecked car off the road?" he asked.

"I don't know."

"Heh, heh, heh," he eyed me to make sure I knew it was a joke. "No one knows because it's never been done."

14

A profound knowledge of how to live simply and graciously in one's later years, and the simple elements of a successful old age, are qualities to be revered.

We were invited to a tea party that took place at Nigel and Edith Minns' home in George Town. The invitation card read: *The Pleasure of Your Company is Requested at 4 p.m....*

This charming Old World Bahamian couple were favorite friends. In their eighties, their values were old-fashioned, their conversation interesting and their ideas challenging. They lived in a cosy white cottage amid a carefully tended garden in which hibiscus, frangipani and oleander bushes mingled with guava, lime, orange, and sapodilla trees. The house was full of plants, flowers, books, and well-worn chintz-covered furniture, suggesting immediately that the people who lived here led a life of unassuming comfort and ease.

Miss Edith — tall, willowy, graceful — traced her family history back more than a century to the time when some English ancestors settled in the islands. She was born and raised on Long Island, 15 miles southeast of Exuma. Her grandfather, a landowner, was a man of substance, who acted as the local dentist, barber and — because he had "doctor books" — the island's doctor. Her mother, a teacher, died of jaundice when Edith was seven so she and her two sisters were raised by their grandparents. Visitors to the island were few and they led a sheltered life of housework, studies and reading, their books arriving regularly by mail boat from the Nassau Public Library.

Miss Edith was a fund of early island lore. One of her best stories was about her 1923 schooner trip to Nassau when the ship encountered a calm spell and they spent six days becalmed in Galliot Cut, ran out of water, and had to be rescued.

Nigel — thin, wiry, weathered — with a bounteous infiltration of Native American Indian in his Anglo-Bahamian blood, had nut brown skin and a thatch of snow-white hair above his handsome seamed face. Like a tough old sea captain, he had a lot of worthwhile knowledge and a quiet, salty way of sharing it. Exuma-born and raised, he, too, was a master storyteller and could spin yarns of a lifetime of adventures. He grew up without shoes, fixed up boats and sailed them, crewed aboard three-masted schooners, nearly drowned at sea 13 times, "planted" sponges on Andros, sponge-fished off the Abacos, and in his courting days, regularly sailed a little ketch across to the settlement of Sims, on Long Island, to visit Miss Edith.

They married, had four children, and eventually went to live in Nassau where both parents worked so the children could be educated up through college. When hard times arrived they returned to George Town to open a grocery business.

Their original store — now Exuma Market — was similar to the small stores that still exist in the island's small settlements and provide an education in island living. Redolent with the smell of coffee, rope, rubber boots and kerosene, these little stores — perhaps no more than one room — sell everything from fishing line to groceries, from aspirin and pain liniment to pails, lanterns and candles. The Minns' modernized store in George Town, run by their oldest son Godfrey, their youngest son Michael and his Canadian wife Sandy, carried, albeit on a small scale, everything found in a U.S. corner grocery.

On the day of their tea party twelve guests arrived to sample a proper English tea. Present was a Brit, a Canadian, two Germans, a Bahamian couple, and one other American couple besides us. The table was laid with a stiffly starched, white linen cloth, a low bowl of pink hibiscus blooms, and a set of cups and saucers and plates with tiny rosebuds on them. There were plates of thin cucumber or salmon sandwiches, and two kinds of cookies. Two cakes — one chocolate, one a lemon sponge — reposed above lace doilies on silver platters. Rosemary, one of the Minns' two daughters, was home from California where she lived and poured tea from a china pot. Miss Edith talked about native plants and trees and her gardening efforts.

Over Earl Grey tea and sandwiches the guests made polite conversation. Son Michael dropped in, drank a cup of tea, and departed to return to the store. Because most of the guests were non-Bahamians there were a lot of questions to Nigel about winds and weather, humidity and hurricanes. He knew everything about those things, especially hurricanes.

"In hurricane season — September to December — hurricanes come boiling up from the southeast," he said, "and can they wreak havoc! I remember the storm of '24. It was bad enough, but the one in '26 was far worse. We still lived in the house that's now the *Peace and Plenty Inn* and I can remember Poppa and I had to drill holes in the upper floors to let the water drain out. All through the night we could hear the sea crashing on the roof. People lost boats, roofs, farm animals — everything."

That was the hurricane that almost leveled George Town, he said, destroying most of the island's buildings and its records and archives, and demolishing many of the small settlements. But in the way of the islands in those days, rebuilding was a combined effort, with nearby islanders, sailing over to help.

Worse still for the Bahamian economy was the hurricane of '29. "That one was tragic for everyone," Nigel said, setting down his teacup and rubbing his white thatch with a gnarled hand. "I was in Nassau then. We had 125 mile per hour winds that blew four days without let-up. Brought down every power line in the city. But worse'n that, it wiped out the whole sponge-fishing fleet. Every single boat gone."

He looked out the window towards the sea, sighing heavily. "It was the end of an era. Sponge-fishing never came back the way it was before and the economy was devastated. Seems like the island is always subjected to outside forces beyond our control."

In the scented indolence of the tea party, conversation flowed easily. Sandwiches, cakes, cookies, tea, then chocolates disappeared as Miss Edith nodded and smiled graciously, appearing to talk to everyone. Periodically, Nigel gazed at her fondly. When a guest caught him doing it he said sheepishly, "she still amazes me with her beauty!" They'd been married over sixty years.

Nigel and Edith's simple but gracious life, their unaffected speech, their natural good manners and optimism in the face of adversity, their kindness to others, their contentment with life and each other, and their mutual devotion had just furthered my education in gracious living.

The work on the house continued. We lived in the midst of a construction site. Some days it had seemed as though there would never be an end to it, that my husband would never have enough of it; never have the house the way he wanted. He was not, I'd had to remind him, constructing a housing complex or the Taj Mahal, simply enlarging a rather modest home.

He was not offended (seldom is), "I know that," he said, "but for my sake it has to be done right. Besides, for me it's a joy." How could I argue with that?

Stanley and Mr. Flowers had gone to school, traveled to the States, and knew how to speak and write perfectly good English. Yet between themselves, when they thought we weren't listening, they often spoke an old Bahamian dialect referred to in the islands as Plain Bahamian.

"What you ger do now?" Mr. Flowers would ask Stanley, handing him the hammer. "I ger bound out dis werry stubborn nail," Stanley would reply, reversing the pronunciation of his "v's" and "w's". This reversal, I learned, was a mixture of the 18th Century Elizabethan English spoken on America's southern plantations in the 1700's and the pidgin English of the plantation's slaves. On the island of Abaco, it is said, you can still hear English as it was spoken by the Loyalists who fled there after the American Revolution.

"Hey, mon, you mussy giv dat ter me nex," Mr. Flowers might say to Stanley in fun, reaching for the hammer, "cuz I fixin' ter bound dis nail inter dis vinder frame." In Plain Bahamian the past tense is usually disregarded altogether. "We done go," is we went. "Well, I gorn outta here now. I done finish," Mr. Flowers would say to Stanley at the end of the day.

Verbs are made to be reversed with the subject, as in "where dey is?" "Who it is?" or "How much yer grapefruit is dis day?" Plurals of anything are seldom used. "I done bring um swee' potato, banan, and onion. You gwine want any of dem ting?"

"Ting" disregards the "th" in "thing" and makes it a mere "t". From this comes the even more useful "ting-um" — meaning *that thing*. It is very useful and can be used whenever any word can't be remembered. As in "hand me that — um — er — umm — *ting-um*."

Until I encountered it in a joking letter to the editor of the *Nassau Tribune* I didn't know Plain Bahamian was a written language. The letter, written by someone from Andros Island, commented on the Water Corporation's decision to take water from Andros and barge it to the thirsty people of Nassau. It was direct and to the point: *"we ain gat enough water now and they wan' take from we and send it South? They mussy flamming! (joking.) Say Mr. Water Corporation, who fooling who?"*

Because this vernacular dialect interested me I began saving and writing down the best samples. One day Mr. Flowers saw me doing this and asked, "why're you doing that?"

"Because I feel this old dialect is unique and should be recorded for posterity. Besides, I enjoy hearing it."

He eyed me. "I tell you, it's a mix of all those different people come to these islands. There be plenty, tang God." Mr. Flowers moved his green plastic MIAMI HEAT cap to the back of his head. Then giving me his knowing smile he made a favorite gesture among Bahamians when they are mocking themselves about thinking serious thoughts: he noisily sucked his teeth.

In print this gesture is written "suck teet" and often appears in the *Nassau Guardian* newspaper cartoons when Bahamians poke fun at Bahamians. One figure, usually a grossly exaggerated figure (often a politician,) says to another, "dis new law gwine be good for you," and the reply is, "I doan know. (Suck teet.) But I doubts it."

Mr. Flowers said, "some foreign people laugh at us. They think we're ignorant. Complain we're stupid. Think we don't know anything about anything."

"They're the ignorant ones."

He nodded. Reset his cap on his grey hair. Gave me one of his conspiratorial grins. "Dey mussy raise by poor folk. Dey mummy doan teach dem good manner and dey doan know when you a gues' in one man's house you mussy be polite." His faded eyes twinkled at his joke.

15

As with most things, life never turns out as expected. The constant conviviality among the three men meant the arduous work of digging and chipping into the soft limestone for the Garden Room foundation went smoothly, but was not without some difficulties. One that we all hated to face was that Mr. Flower's eyesight had failed more than he liked to admit.

But eventually the joists and flooring for the second floor add-on — actually an extension of the existing house — were done. This would be the new upstairs dining — or as it was grandly referred to in our conversations — the Great Room. When the time came the cathedral ceiling would be planked with tongue and groove pine and, to match the sea view, painted turquoise.

Outside, the roof was designed to overlap the roof of the original house. Because it was a good thirty feet from the ground, to work up there required no fear of heights and careful footing when walking the rafters and scaffolding. Anyone up there needed good eyesight, a fine sense of balance, and a lot of agility. Much to his chagrin, this grounded Mr. Flowers.

For it had become more and more apparent over the previous days that, though willing, Mr. Flowers was not only not very spry, he really did not see very well. Stanley and my husband had constantly to take care that he wasn't in danger.

At the end of the week, my husband, after much agonizing, told Mr. Flowers he wouldn't be needing him any more and laid him off. With consummate pride, the old gentleman said he quite understood. Wasn't he, after all, a builder himself? With a wave of his hand he rode off on his bicycle.

I looked up the road after him, Stanley gazed at his feet, my husband busied himself looking into his toolbox. None of us could look at one another. Already I missed the old gentleman. His dignity and gentle wit brought a sense of old-fashioned values to our days; without him the construction work would be just that: work. He'd had a way of imbuing it with a special grace.

It was time to take a break. We drove into George Town to the regular Friday night barbecue at the Two Turtles Inn where once again we learned that plans and promises usually turn out differently than we imagine.

The outdoor courtyard was crowded with "yachties." Lines of hungry people stood in front of the grills and the picnic tables were filling up. Eventually we got our hamburgers and beer and were looking for a place to sit when we heard a familiar voice.

"Come sit with us." It was Pete Balloil.

He was comfortably ensconced at one of the tables with a bottle of champagne and an arm around each of two comely young women. He sported clean white jeans, a white yachtsman cap, a white shirt with the sleeves rolled high and the neck open to the waist. Gleaming amid the manly chest hairs nestled several gold chains. We walked over to say hello

"Hey! Good to see you. Have some bubbly." He waved the bottle aloft. Not wanting to interrupt we said we were expecting friends. "Catch you later then." While kissing one woman he was caressing the other's thigh. Neither seemed to mind. Was half Pete Balloil's attention worth the full attention of any other man?

We sat down at a table with the island doctor and his wife. "By and large," he told us as we munched on our hamburgers, "the Bahamians are in pretty good health. Their teeth aren't great because they suck sugar cane from babyhood, but it's the boaters I see most. I treat the men for mashed fingers, rope burns and sunburn. I treat the kids for colds, broken bones and fungus diseases. And I treat the women for nerves."

"Don't I know it!" A leathery-looking woman in her late fifties returned to the table with her second glass of rum. "I'm one of them." She wanted to talk about being a boat wife.

As difficult as it was for some women to adjust to island life, it was even more difficult for some women, plucky and brave as they were, to adjust to living for months aboard a boat. Once on board, men were the captain of the ship. About this there could be no discussion. Command was from the top down; wives or women companions were the first mate.

"My duties," the boat wife said morosely, "aside from all the usual things I do on land — includes washing the dishes in a sink the size of a crash helmet, cleaning the cabin, making up the bunks, and cooking the meals on a stove so small that if you set three pots on it they bubble over into one another. Believe me, it's not a vacation!"

She paused, took a sip of her drink. "The stove is set on gimbels, a device used on boats to keep things like stoves and compasses level when the vessel is rolling and tossing. It's like trying to cook on a hot plate mounted on the backs of four ger-bils running in place."

She took another sip of rum. "My husband is a perfectly nice man ashore." She waved an arm in the general direction of a big barrel-chested man comparing sailing stories with other men at the end of the table, "but when he gets aboard his boat he turns into Captain Bligh." She paused, then added, "he barks orders at me as if he was Blackbeard the Pirate expecting me to leap alive. He won't accept that I don't have his physical strength."

The doctor commented that eventually the crew aboard HMS Bounty mutinied. Did she ever think of doing the same? She shook her head. "We have no other place to go. We sold the house."

Some men avoided the disillusioned wife syndrome by hiring on a boat mate when they hired the yacht. Young, nubile and comely of face and figure, the rented boat bunny, though initially willing often got a rude awakening. It came when she found she was expected to haul anchor, hoist sail, stow gear, cook on a stove mounted on gimbels, wash dishes, leap ashore and tie up, and at night lie on her back to view the stars.

"My husband promised me a life of adventure and travel." The boat wife contemplated her empty glass. "Adventure, hah!

All I get is lift that bale, tote that barge! And look at me! My skin is weathered as a walnut!"

Of course, not all boat wives feel this way. In fact, the majority seem to enjoy cruising as much as their husbands. They like the life of being on the go, of constantly seeing new places, meeting new people, and having new experiences.

* * *

With Mr. Flowers gone the work lost some of its fun. He was the brunt of some of Stanley's jokes but took it good-naturedly and responded with jokes of his own, all of which tended to make the days pass lightly. After his departure, however, the work moved ahead more quickly. The addition went higher and higher and any thoughts I'd had that we might at some future point decide to leave this house and this island grew increasingly remote.

My husband was enjoying himself immensely. After our many years of marriage I was still impressed by his concentration when working with his hands, or when building, creating or fixing something, far more content than when he was pursuing his lifelong profession of educational media expert.

Each morning he set to work on the house construction with eagerness and good will and stayed with it until he was finished. There was energy there, a sense that he'd found his center.

He should really have been an architect, or an engineer, but when he was growing up there was not money for such high pursuits. Like many thousands of others in the Great Depression, he began as a teacher and worked his way along to other jobs, another profession, a postgraduate degree. Now he was realizing his dream; he was architect, engineer and builder all in one.

Once the rafters were all in place Stanley climbed down and said it was time to wet the roof tree. Not one of the three of us said a thing but I knew we felt it wouldn't be right to celebrate such an important moment without Mr. Flowers. Wordlessly, the event was postponed.

* * *

79

Time for another break.

Fishing and swimming in Exuma's multi-hued water and sunning on the island's white sand beaches were considered by many yachters and tourists to be the most attractive aspect of coming to the Bahamas. But for those of us who resided here, there was another pleasure that entailed a less active agenda. Because you never knew what you'd find, a favorite activity was beachcombing. It was like getting something for nothing, a form of acceptable lawlessness that satisfies the urge to steal. Or like helping yourself at a vast outdoor garage sale.

The proper dress to go searching for these and other treasures (shells, seaweed for the garden, coral or driftwood) was an old pair of shorts, a straw hat, heavy work gloves, and a basket for the gleanings.

These came from unseen storms brewed far out in the Atlantic that cast up with the tide an endless supply of some quite amazing objects: usable lumber, glass floats from Portugal, long lengths of bamboo from who knows where, crates and boxes and driftwood. Then, from passing ships and yachts there came toys, half-filled bottles of suntan lotion, snorkeling gear, dented pots and pans, sunglasses, faded jeans, sunvisors, flashlights, baseball caps, and tee shirts with a wealth of messages.

Also strewn across the sand from distant storms were great heaps of seaweed, piles of leathery algae, turtle grasses bleached by the sun into long pale ribbons. And littering the sand from one end to the other, like globules of honey glowing in the sun, were tiny golden bladders of sargassum. These were fun to drape upon yourself and dance upon the sand. We used it on the gardens (an old Bahamian custom) and carried back armfuls for fertilizer.

Once we found a bottle. It was clear glass, had a screw top, and a piece of paper inside.

Tales of *Robinson Crusoe, Swiss Family Robinson* and *Kidnapped* immediately came to mind. I imagined: a map leading to buried loot, a message of distress from a floundering ship, a cry for help from someone alone and desperate and stranded on a tiny island and waiting to be rescued; suddenly they all became actual possibilities.

In 1972 our friend Blanche (Inchie) Frenning found a wine

bottle washed up on her beach with a message inside. Opening the left-hand screw top carefully, she pulled out and unfolded the still-dry roll of paper. Inside was a letter with an address, written in German, dated 1967, with the information that the bottle was dropped into the Baltic Sea. No loot, no distress signal, and no cry for help.

Instead, it merely asked — rather unromantically — for a reply as to where the bottle was found. Unable to reply in German, Inchie sent back a friendly note in English saying the bottle had been five years in transit and probably crossed the Atlantic on the north equatorial current, the same current that carried Christopher Columbus to the Bahamas. Though she waited a year she never got a reply.

A Canadian couple had better luck. Their bottled message was from a couple in Norway with whom, over time, they corresponded in English. The Canadians journeyed to Norway, where the foursome became good friends, then the Norwegians came to visit Exuma.

Maybe our bottle would be from some far-off land, from some exotic person who would invite us to stay in his castle — or her tent — and ride across his estate on a rare white stallion — or across the desert — on a milk white camel...

My husband picked up the bottle and we examined it. It was a crusted green, obviously a wine bottle, and had a cork jammed in it. It was not tight, just wedged in enough to keep the contents dry, but would require a proper corkscrew to open it. And yes, there was a note inside. My fantasies rampaged.

We took it back to the house and set it on the coffee table, speculating where it might be from, how long a journey it could have made, and what kind of person puts notes in bottles. I urged my husband to get on with the opening. With maddening deliberation he got the corkscrew from the kitchen drawer and began prying out the cork.

It came out easily. The letter unfolded in my eager hands.

We're four Americans on board "Runaway" a day and a half from George Town, Bahamas, on our way to the Out Island Regatta. If you find this bottle have a nice day.

The date was the day before yesterday.

It was a bitter disappointment, especially with the inane

wish to "have a nice day." Churlishly, I scribbled on the bottom of the note, *I had other plans!* and put it back in the bottle.

The next morning when my husband went to the beach for his early morning swim he pitched it back into the sea. The following morning it was back again. And the following morning. And the following morning.

Five times he flung it as far out as he could. On the sixth try it went on its way, probably caught up by the current that sweeps past the island on its way to merging with the northward-moving Gulf Stream. This would carry the bottle across the North Atlantic to the English coast where some other romantic would likely take it out of the sea. By now I was regretting my churlish addition to the note and wished I'd written a kinder reply to the fatuous greeting.

It is not possible to go beachwalking without getting an interest in shells. Inevitably, one spots something special and stoops to pick it up to examine it. Though no longer plentiful on the island's north shore beaches there are occasionally wonderful finds. It is tempting to take them home to add to a growing collection but ecologically, this is destructive. Left in place, the shells are pounded and ground down by the sea and ultimately help create beaches. Shells are so delicately and intricately formed, so exquisitely fashioned and colored, that I soon became enchanted and sent for a book — *Shells of the West Indies* — so I could start learning about them. I marveled at their incredible intricacy and colors, and to my ear their names sounded like exotic music, or a haunting prose poem of the sea:

Cowries, pectans, murex and mussels;
Cockleshells, clamshells, and tellins.
Augers, coquinas, butterflies and jingles,
Scallops, pink coffees and limpets;
Rice, Job's tears, clams and conch,
Umbobiums and small purple snails.

A Queen Helmet shell, (*Cassis madagascarensis* Lamark) discovered among the sea grass, was a real find. About five inches long, the outer surface was mottled cream and brown, with the areas between the dental ridges on the outer lip and the lower portion of the outer lip, dark chocolate brown. The inside was a creamy beige and the remainder of the shield and the outer lip were a beautiful, deep salmon pink. This one I was unable to resist and did take home to put in the sun to dry. Once dried, its mottled brown and cream crown revealed a feather design and its pearly insides gleamed a soft ivory below its dentured opening.

We restrained our eagerness to take the shells home and mainly left them where they were, but on occasion, we found some we could not resist. So, on a shelf of a bookcase we started a "museum shelf" of found objects which, along with the helmet shell, soon contained a large crawfish head, a green turtle head, a furled pink conch, and a collection of sand dollars and driftwood. It became a place of interest for everyone who visited, in particular the grandchildren.

Though we'd never seen one yet, a conch pearl would be a prized find. This tiny jewel was not part of the conch itself but was attached within the fleshy lip of the creature; jewelers considered it a rarity, as true a gem as the oyster's pearl. A large, rose-colored one reposed among Britain's crown jewels, a gift to Queen Elizabeth from the Commonwealth of the Bahamas as a symbol of these islands.

Eating or cooking conch, as the Bahamians do, was not something we did. The meat, with a texture akin to snails, was, to my mind, too rubbery and tasteless to warrant serious gastronomic attention. Bahamians, though, make it a major staple of their diet. Conch fritters, conch salad, boiled, fried and raw conch were all favorites, so when the Nassau newspapers announced that because of over-fishing and pollution there would be a declining conch harvest coming, it was a matter of great concern and one the government and the fishermen had to address soon.

One day when I was raving to a new American acquaintance about the beauty and delicacy of shells, she said, "well then, if you're interested in shells you must come and see the shellwork my husband and I do." Handcrafts are not a skill I have ever mastered, nor want to, so I thanked her politely but thought to myself: *shellwork!* and pictured huge piles of shells gathered indiscriminately to make shell-covered toilet paper rolls, ugly picture frames, tatty lampshades, cigar boxes, tacky wine bottles and other godawful bits of shell-encrusted bric-a-brac. Over the next few months she repeated her invitation but I consistently found a reason not to go and view her hobby.

As things turned out, it was a wrong decision... .

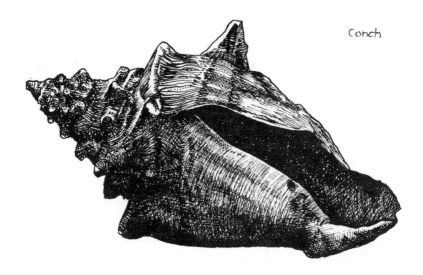

Conch

16

The following Monday Mr. Flowers was back. Would it be all right, he asked, if he came back to work? He'd be glad to work for nothing. Just wanted to be useful.

Even though the work was sure to be slowed, my husband put him back on the payroll. "But you're not to go up on the roof," he warned. "It's not safe for you."

"I'm not afraid of roofin'," Mr. Flowers grumbled to me as he carried tools, drinking water, or more nails up and down the ladder. "I'm a carpenter, not a water boy." I consoled him with the thought that once the roofing was done a great deal of indoor carpentry would be needed.

"Hmmph!" His dignity was offended. "They treat me like an old man. What do they think I'm gonna do? Fall down? Slide off that roof? I bin roofin' before they was spanked the first time. Besides, I got to be up there to help Stanley keep Vince awake after lunch. (Before going back to work each day my husband was in the habit of taking a short nap.)

Next day, in a brisk wind, Stanley and my husband were standing atop the roof rafters wrestling with one of the large plywood sheets. It was obvious they were having trouble managing it, and Mr. Flowers, eyeing this performance with disdain, muttered to me, "they should have me up there to help." It didn't seem to occur to him that one good gust of wind and his frail form would topple over like a rake handle.

The two men got three of the plywood sheets nailed down and had picked up a fourth when they were hit by a gust of wind. My husband staggered. To keep his balance he let go, but tottered. Stanley grabbed him, saving him from a fall, all the while still gripping a corner of the plywood. Before either of them could right themselves another gust shook the plywood and it flapped like a giant sail. Stanley hung on but nearly took off,

85

heading, I was certain, straight for Grog Pond.

Only by letting go was he able to keep his balance. The plywood clattered to the ground with a resounding crash. One corner was badly splintered. Mr. Flowers shook his head in disgust. "I tell you," he said, "they should've had me up there."

A few days later Mr. Flowers arrived in the back garden calling for me in his rusty voice. "Come quick! Put down that trowel and come quick!" I flew, believing something dire had happened... one of the men had fallen off the roof... one of them has been hit on the head... cut with a saw... punctured with a screw driver... .

"Break out the beer!" my husband called down from the roof. "We're a little late but now that we're all present we're going to finally raise the roof tree." He waved a long branch from a jumbay tree that Mr. Flowers — for purposes of good luck — brought that morning from a tree outside his house. Stanley and my husband nailed it to the roof peak and we all sent up a cheer. I served the cold beers out under the seagrape tree.

"That branch is special," Mr. Flowers informed us solemnly. "I cut it fresh this morning early."

"Go on, Mr. Flowers," Stanley teased, "that jumbay jes' like any old jumbay you cut every day for your creatures."

Mr. Flowers' creatures were a matter of great hilarity. Once when his old bicycle broke down he asked my husband to drive him into the bush to find his "creatures." They had broken free of their tether and wandered off.

Dubious that in all the surrounding bushland anything at all could be found, my husband nonetheless took him to the area where Mr. Flowers claimed he would find his creatures. They drove around for ten minutes or so on dirt roads in the dense bush and then, in the midst of a jungle of undergrowth, Mr. Flowers said, "stop here!"

My husband stopped the car.

Mr. Flowers opened the car door, leaned out, peered into the surrounding bush. All was quiet. Undismayed, he gave a loud "*yeah*!"

Within seconds his creatures — six goats — appeared, bleating and blatting at the sound of their master's voice. Ears flapping, muzzles lifting, feet prancing in a kind of demented dance, they shouldered one another aside trying to crowd into the car with him.

"You see?" Mr. Flowers said, fending them off, "they know me. They're glad to see me."

"They may be glad to see you," my husband said, laughing hard, "but they are not riding home with you."

Ever since, Stanley and my husband have teased Mr. Flowers about misplacing his goats. Stanley now called our Chevy the "Goatmobile," — a word designed to send all three men into gales of laughter.

With the roof tree raised, the plywood, roofing felt, and shingles soon followed. By May the new dining room was closed in up top, the large picture windows were in place, and suddenly the sea and sky moved into the house. The guest bedroom below — which we still euphemistically termed The Garden Room though there was no garden in any discernible proximity — was still open to the elements but would, everyone hoped, be finished in the next few months.

The men worked on; I prepared the daily lunches which we ate at a table on the deck. When the last of the house shingling was done, the walls sheathed in plywood, the wide picture windows installed, and the patio door to the deck in place, the Great Room began to reveal itself in all its cavernous size. The cathedral ceiling soared aloft, the two long windowseats stretched into an L-shaped bench beneath the picture windows, and the 360 square feet of floor space stared at me emptily. I wondered how we were going to fill it up. With customs duty added on furniture was expensive here, even more so if it was shipped from Miami.

"To fill this up you're gonna have to get a lot of furniture," Mr. Flowers said, gazing around, eyeing me closely. We were having a break for tea.

I glared at him. He had a way of reading my mind.

"No prob-lem," Stanley, as usual, was optimistic. "Vince will make it, won't you Vince?"

"If he has time." Mr. Flowers was watching me. "But we still gotta build the steps and close in that downstairs room. That'll take a while. Guess for now you'll have to leave it like it is."

He gave me an amused grin and held out his cup for more tea. Knowing he liked three teaspoons of sugar, to pay him back I gave him only one. He laughed. He'd made his point.

While Stanley and my husband painted the outside — Stanley comfortable on the high ladder, he said, because he'd spent many years as a migrant worker picking fruit in the U.S. — Mr. Flowers taped joints in the Great Room and I hand-sewed curtains and covered chair cushions. Periodically he would fling comments my way about how much sewing and furniture it was going to take to fill up the Great Room. I ignored the barbs. (Like cooking, sewing is not something I do well and if Rita Dupill, my neighbor, who eventually became my walking buddy, had not helped out several years later by covering the windowseat cushions I would not have finished until the turn of the century. Gleefully, Mr. Flowers has never let me forget this.)

With the first coat of outside paint completed a startling transformation took place. Everything shifted from the look of a construction site to the appearance of a romantic tropical pink house. It was time to name it.

Houses and their names play an important part in the life of the islanders, not for reasons of prestige or status, and not just as shelter, but as expressions of individuality and character. Under the spell of the island, freed from all the conservative ideas of what a house is supposed (by convention) to look like, the winter residents often toss aside all practical considerations and go wild.

Some build structures designed from some dazzling inner vision they have carried around within them for years, or perhaps from childhood: visions of treehouses, lean-to's, or tropical huts like Robinson Crusoe's; or, as in the case of Americans, maybe from grand palaces and smart designer homes seen in *Architectural Digest*.

Others, following their dream and throwing caution to the winds, build rooms around a central courtyard, even though it traps the heat, and when it rains means they can't reach one room from another without getting wet.

Or, like us, they perch atop a small hill to take advantage of the tradewinds and a spectacular view, even though there is greater hurricane danger, and the need to hike up a steep slope to bring in the groceries.

Or, they build so close to the beach their insurance must cover not only hurricanes and wind damage but surge (high wave) damage too. The yearly cost of this is so high you could heat a house in Alaska for ten winters.

With whimsical abandon island homeowners add wooden porches, gables, decks, patios, flying wing-shaped rooms, or wooden lattices, forgetting — or ignoring — that there are such problems as woodrot, high winds, termites, corrosion, constant salt spray, snakes, toads, lizards and thieves. They add on a rooftop room to a perfectly adequate house, forgetting the new roof must join perfectly with the old or it will leak.

For centuries the British have had the custom of naming these follies, though often the names they gave them were more fanciful than actual. Seaview and Orchard Cottage, The Abbey, or Greensward may have nothing to do with the sea, an orchard, a church or a beautiful lawn, but are more likely meant to convey the hopes and dreams of the inhabitant.

This custom of naming your home is prevalent on Exuma, too, brought, no doubt, by the British colonizers. Usually, though, the names were more realistic, even boring. On a drive up and down the island it was possible to find The Pink House, The Round House, Beach House, and Beach Garden. More imaginative are Jambo, HiHo, Sacre Bleu, MiDunDee, Toad Hall and Slack Tide.

"What shall we call our house?" I asked my husband upon arriving home from the library one day and seeing it sitting, newly pink, atop its wooded hill.

"Seaview?"

"Uninspiring."

"Hilltop House?" I gave him a pained look. "Rosey Cottage?"

"It's Bahama Pink."

"The Pink House then."

"Already taken."

"Barwooden House," Mr. Flowers offered.

I gave him a pained look too.

We couldn't decide.

Except for various cabinets and furniture, the Great Room

was by now mostly finished with built-ins made by my husband. It had a cathedral ceiling, four 4x6 foot fixed windows, a smaller louvred window for ventilation, large glass patio doors, and in one corner, stairs leading down to the Garden Room bedroom. From visiting Morocco, we were taken with Moorish architecture so my husband added carpentry details of arches and fretted panels, and I painted touches of Berber blue on furniture and cupboard doors.

When the time came to match the floor tiles of the original house with new ones for the Great Room, Darville's regretfully informed us floor tiles one-sixteenth of an inch thick were no longer made, having been superseded by one-eighth inch thick tiles; moreover, these, also, were not available in the original pattern.

What to do? My husband considered using ceramic tiles like those he laid in the downstairs Garden Room, but the Great Room floor was not built to carry so much weight. After several days of discussion my husband painted the plywood floor with a red deck enamel simulating terra cotta tiles. This looked attractive but appeared flat and uninteresting so he decided to give the floor the look of real tiles.

From a 12-inch square of plastic foam he cut out a king-sized rubber stamp with a design resembling one from some antique Turkish tiles we'd hung as a frieze against one wall. Using a darker terra cotta paint he applied the pattern to the painted plywood and a simulated tile floor was made.

The next morning, however, the paint having dried, the tile pattern had changed color and vanished into the background. Another batch of enamel was mixed, a shade lighter this time, and my husband painstakingly re-stenciled the whole floor. This time, the design stayed. Then, to make the squares look slightly irregular and more like handmade tiles, he next painted black lines around each one to simulate grouting. The result was amazing, and few people at first realized the floor was painted, not tiled.

Since the house by this time had a vaguely Moorish look with Turkish tiles, a Berber rug, and Moroccan blue accents we decided to name it *Cinnabar* — a romantic, vaguely exotic-sounding, but meaningless name. (Actually, it is a red ore mined to produce quicksilver, or mercury, and when powdered, is used to make a dark red pigment called vermilion.)

Partly because it bore a portion of our name, partly because we liked the terra cotta color and had used it lavishly to complement the Moroccan blue in the house, and partly because it has a vaguely exotic sound to it, it seemed appropriate. (The Cinnabar Coast perhaps? Whether there was such a place or not didn't matter; it still sounded like somewhere Blackbeard the Pirate might have roamed.)

Mostly I liked it because it sounded magical and spoke of the inexplicable enchantment we had found on Exuma.

My husband painted the word in red letters on a weathered board and hung it above the garage on the road. Mr. Flowers regarded it suspiciously. "Funny name. What's it mean?"

"It's an exotic-sounding name. Actually it's a red ore."

"The Red House. Funny name for a pink house." To this day he refers to it as The Red House. So much for being different.

Naming the house was a defining gesture. Painting the exterior, building some of the furniture, doing the interior decoration, creating a "tile" floor, and making our own cushions and curtains, made it ours and no one else's. Once we had become used to living in such an exotic-sounding place, it began, little by little, to feel like home.

17

The Bahamian economy is based almost entirely on custom duties, offshore banking and tourism. The prime attraction for most tourists is the incredible sea-blue, sea-green water. If they're not sailing across it, they want to be in it, fishing, diving, snorkeling or swimming and they expect to leap joyously into water that is as tepid and safe as their bathtub.

The idea that sharks are waiting is not good for tourism.

Because several lemon sharks and one hammerhead had been sighted in George Town's Elizabeth Harbour and in Kidd Cove, the small half-moon bay in front of John Marshall's, the topic of the day was sharks. Everyone agreed the sharks were too close in, suggesting that perhaps some sort of phenomenon was taking place in the undersea world of Exuma.

Few older Exumians have learned to swim, perhaps because they have lived all their lives with such an intimate knowledge of the sea they have learned to respect and fear what's in it, especially sharks.

The title "shark" actually comprises many species which are widely distributed but most numerous in true tropical waters. The most carnivorous of all fish, they can grow, as in the case of the whale shark, to as large as 50 feet. The ocean's top predators, sharks are sleek, swift creatures that cruise along slowly with slight flicks of the tail fin until they find their prey, then they torpedo toward it and attack with swift ferocity.

Sharks have a high-powered sensoring system. They can hear a struggling fish over a mile away, smell the scent of blood on the ocean currents, and detect at close range electrical fields given off by animals and humans. As far as anyone on Exuma knows, though, no one here has ever been attacked by a shark.

But Mr. Flowers believed in caution. He thought swimming was for fish and his advice was to stay out of the sea. Didn't we know? he asked. Sharks were always lurking just offshore. He'd never seen one but he knew they were out there, waiting. That's why he'd never learned to swim. Too dangerous.

"Nothing to worry about," my husband the ex-Canadian-Navy frogman argued, "swimming here is like moving in liquid sunlight. You can see hundreds of feet in all directions. Sharks usually attack only when they can't see clearly who you are."

Mr. Flowers remained dubious. "Wince, you expectin' that shark to recognize you an' swim up and say hello?" He cackled loudly at his own joke.

Mr. Flowers represented a rich source of island lore, some of which might be somewhat suspect but nonetheless more informed than my husband's opinions of these foreign waters. If Mr. Flowers thought sharks were out there waiting, they probably were.

Our family's first experience with the barracuda — was on our first trip to the islands in 1965 with the children, Scott and Jennifer, then ten and six. We had little money — my husband was doing post graduate work at Syracuse University at the time — but we had saved up for several years for this much-needed vacation and came especially to dive in the Thunderball Cave, one of the underwater sites used in the filming of the James Bond movie *Thunderball*.

The cave is under a small island about halfway down the Exuma chain. It is really no more than a limestone outcropping forty feet long and twenty feet across. It is wedge-shaped — like a piece of cake — and barren except for one wind-twisted tree. Early one morning, wearing snorkeling gear and following Roger, our Bahamian guide, the five of us tried to dive down to the cave entrance at the base of the island. A four-knot tide kept us from entering.

By mid-afternoon it was low tide and we were able to gulp air through our snorkels, dive down the four feet to the entrance, swim under a flying buttress of rock and around an inner barrier rock, and surface in a high cavern where the water was no more than three feet deep. We had entered a silent mysterious world flooded by sunlight.

Like miniature spotlights it poured down through tiny fissures in the rock ceiling, illuminating a beautiful underwater room. The jade green water, the spray of sunlight, the sea floor white as sugar, and a garden of lacy sea fans waving slowly in the current arrested us in wonder. Encrusted on the walls were minuscule barnacles, white and intricate as snowflakes.

In one interior wall was a window-like opening which led into an adjoining chamber. One by one we swam through the "window" and found another chamber also lit by chimneys of light from above. A tunnel, with an entrance hole black as the inside of a boot, led off from here. Despite my reluctance, we entered the blackness and swam slowly along it, the light gradually diminishing until we turned a corner and found ourselves in total darkness.

I could feel the darkness pressing on me like a tangible weight; suddenly I became aware of the mass of rock above me. Tons of it. I thought about all the sea creatures that hide in places like this. Close to panicking, I groped for my husband's hand, found it, and was given a reassuring squeeze. While comforting, it did little to allay my worry about the children, swimming just ahead between us and Roger, who was in the lead. What if...

It was easy for my imagination to get out of control and conjure up images of sharks, moray eels, manta rays and other unnamed monsters of the deep; as a result it was a struggle to remain calm and slow my panicky heart.

Though the total dark lasted about a minute in all, it seemed like five whole minutes before we entered another "room." Here, finally, we were once again bathed in sunlight; it lit the jade-green water, bounced off, and shimmered across the cave walls in ripples of light.

Revealed at one side was an exit gap in the cave wall. We swam out and up — and found ourselves amid a school of circling barracuda.

Roger yelled "dive!"

Grabbing air into our lungs we submerged, and quickly swam down the corridor back to the cave. En *route* Scott scraped his leg on a jagged piece of coral, a worry when sharks are around and apt to be attracted by blood in the water. My always active imagination now conjured up a dramatic scenario of the family being chased down the long dark corridor by a creature with the enormous mouth and cruel teeth of the shark in the movie *Jaws*

Without dallying, we swam through the second sunlit room, through the window into the first one, and were about to leave that when Jennifer suddenly pulled away from my hand. She dived down to the sand bottom to pick up some treasure she'd spotted.

It was a dive of no more than a few feet, and not dangerous, but by now I was eager to get the family out of the water and back into the boat. About to reach down and drag her up, I was spared the job when she suddenly popped up on her own. Grinning through her mask, she triumphantly held up a discarded flash bulb. I was annoyed and couldn't imagine why it was important. We swam on around the barrier rock at the cave entrance and up to the boat where we hauled ourselves aboard.

"Those were *sharks*!" I exploded to my husband.

"Barracuda." He removed his mask and snorkel and shook the water out of his brown hair. "Not terribly dangerous, especially in water this clear."

"Except," said Roger, whom I trusted knew island lore, "when they're swimming around you in a school like that."

Later in the day we climbed up to the top of the little island. Sitting under its lone tree, a venerable sea grape twisted and gnarled by years of wind and weather clinging God knows how to the rocky surface, the five of us ate a picnic supper. By turns laughing and bragging, we relived our dive.

The children were still excited; they hadn't been the least afraid. Their father had taught them to look upon life as an adventure and this, certainly, measured up to the definition. Adoring eyes on Roger, ten year-old Scott decided when he grew up he, too, wanted to be an underwater guide. For Jennifer, the highlight of the trip was more romantic. "Look!" She held up the treasured flash bulb. "James Bond really was here!"

18

The authority on Exuma's sharks, the person to consult, we were told, was Gloria The Shark Lady. She lived in a settlement called The Ferry, on the adjoining island of Little Exuma.

There was a time when, to get to Little Exuma, you had to cross the 250 yards of water between Great Exuma and Little Exuma by ferry, a flat-bottomed barge on a cable that was hauled back and forth by a ferryman who, often as not, had either gone fishing or was asleep in his little hut.

In 1966 a one-lane bridge was built so that now the two islands are joined. Just past the bridge, Gloria lived with her husband George, a displaced Scot. A sign in front of their four-roomed bungalow informed visitors the house was named *Tara*.

It was painted white, sat well back from the main road, and appeared to be floating on a sea of tropical plants and bushes. Bougainvillea, hibiscus, oleander, flame trees, and a host of other exotic blooms climbed, twisted and wrapped themselves around trees and anything that had managed to stay upright.

At the honk of our horn, and a loud "hallo-o-o" there came, bouncing down the path through this exotic jungle, a handsome barefooted woman wrapped in a blinding green sarong. Gold necklaces and earrings glinted against her tawny skin. Hair white as a dandelion clock framed a smiling face. Her vigor and rude good health made it hard to believe she was sixty plus, and not only knew about sharks but had caught dozens.

"Watch where you're puttin' your feet," she called back over a bare brown shoulder as we followed her up the path. "Those are shark's teeth." She stopped and pointed. "That one is a female hammerhead jaw. Know why they're best?"

She grinned and there was a devilish twinkle in her blue eyes. "Because, those suckers have the largest teeth." She let loose a whoop of laughter and headed on up the path. We'd already been told her tongue was as salty as a sailor's, her jokes bawdy.

She climbed five stone steps and opened a screen door, ushering us into the house, explaining that it used to be The Ferry's post office. The front room, now her shop, was a dusty jumble of everything from shark's teeth jewelry and shark's backbones, to antique furniture and old glass bottles. Plates hung on the walls and crossbeams, sprays of coral sprang forth from a broken jug on the floor, some of her husband's paintings rested against the walls, and pinned to a board were numerous yellowed newspaper clippings about Gloria's shark exploits.

The middle room was the bedroom. A big double bed, a piano in need of tuning, and dozens — no, a hundred or more — family photos decorated the walls from ceiling to floor. Jokingly we asked if it was difficult to sleep with all those familial eyes peering down at their bed.

"Doesn't bother me. Best room in the world to sleep in. The Tropic of Cancer runs smack-bang through the middle. And that's why," she wiggled her generous hips and gave one of her earthy chuckles, "I have such a good sex life." (Unaware that this imaginary line running around the globe had such a practical use, we pondered whether the Tropic of Cancer could be marketed to tourists as a potent attraction to those interested in improving their sex life.)

In the living room at the back of the house windows opened on three sides and brought in sunlight on an assortments of rugs, chairs, tables, sofas, daybeds, a TV, a VCR with dozens of tapes, and an enormous central table piled high with books, pots, vases, chandeliers, candlesticks, glassware, china dishes, and bowls of all sizes — the abode of a collector, or of someone who saw beauty in all things.

"Sit down, sit down." Gloria pushed some plump cushions out of the way and nested her own ample self into a pile of pillows on one of the sofas. "You can watch the last of the film with me." There was no need to ask which film. She flicked on the VCR.

Though it seemed an uncharacteristic entertainment for a woman who catches sharks, she'd watched *Gone With The Wind* over 100 times. "My life is about as far removed from sweet-talkin' Scarlett O'Hara's as pink lemonade from hard likker," she said, "but we're both independent women, and that's what I admire about her. That and her style."

After half an hour of GWTW, Rhett Butler delivered his famous last line about not giving a damn, a determined Scarlett sat on the steps of Tara vowing tomorrow would be a better day to think about her problems, and the movie ended. Gloria sighed. "Mon oh mon, I love that film," she said, settling back, prepared now to talk.

Gloria is a third generation Bahamian, the descendant of Irish- Scottish ancestors who risked their lives sailing to the Bahamas in the early 1800's to preach the Anglican faith. Her great-grandfather on her mother's side was an Anglican priest in Nassau who, at one point, bought land just south of The Ferry on which to raise sheep and cattle. Gloria was born there, grew up on a tiny, nearby island called Hog Cay, and was four years old when her father taught her to fish; she could already swim.

Gloria's tale, in her own words, follows the tradition of *South Pacific* and other romantic tales of the South Seas. At age sixteen, undoubtedly a beautiful honey-skinned maiden at the time, she met Edgar Lewless, an American engineer from Washington state on his way around the world in a yacht. During a stop in Exuma, smitten by the glorious teenage Gloria, he stayed on for months on end and eventually proposed.

Her father forbade a marriage until she was eighteen so they waited two years and were married in Haiti. They settled in Nassau and raised nine children. Widowed in her early fifties, Gloria married the Scot, George Patience. Several years later she discovered she had "healing hands." Through contact with the Nassau hotels she practised massage and physiotherapy on such rich and famous clients as Liz Taylor and Mike Todd, Sean Connery, Ava Gardner and Presidents Kennedy and Nixon.

"But for the poor and needy," she said, holding out her strong, tanned hands, "the treatment was always free."

Told in 1969 that she had diabetes, she and George "retired" to The Ferry for eight months of the year. During the other four months they traveled among their children's homes in Nassau, Canada and England. The diabetes disappeared. "But moving back here from Nassau was difficult," she now admits. "It was such a quiet life here and I was used to being busy. I knew I couldn't just sit in the sun and string beads. Like Scarlett, I'm an adventurer. I like a challenge! So I decided to catch sharks."

Her children, those now grown and living on Exuma, objected, but stubborn as usual, she refused to listen. "Even though I was afraid of sharks, I'd made up my mind," she said. "I have great respect for them, but once you make up your mind to handle them, and learn how to do it, it's like anything else. You can do it."

When hunting sharks she anchors her thirteen foot Boston Whaler about two miles offshore on the Atlantic (eastern) side of Little Exuma in four to five hundred feet of water. She secures her boat with a heavy anchor attached to a two-inch-thick chain hook with a three-inch curve to it. This is fastened to a buoy with a one-half-inch rope. "Even at that," she said, "a shark can straighten out one of those suckers easier'n wink."

She then sets out eight or ten lines bated with grouper, or other fish heads. Leaving the lines out overnight, she returns the next morning at dawn to land her catch. Though she once caught six in one day, her average is two, and she reckons that over the past 15 years she's caught around two thousand sharks.

Sharks ten feet and under she hauls into her boat, maneuvering them with a gaff — no small feat when you figure an eight footer can weigh up to six hundred pounds. If she uses her "attention getter," — a six foot steel bang stick with a .45 magnum bullet in the head — the shark soon becomes more willing. "And *that* is because I shot the flaming thing into its goddam brain."

The largest shark she's ever caught was an 18 foot tiger shark. "That bloody shark was no picnic," she admits. "I had the time of my life trying to pull that sucker in. He was stubborn — like me! — extremely strong, and very heavy. Fortunately my oldest grandson was with me and together we pulled him in and fastened the sucker alongside to tow him in. I tell you, I was pooped out and glad to get home that day!"

In the last couple of years this grandmother of nine and great-grandmother of six has met increasing opposition from the family, so while she will still clean them out for her son Jerry

Lewless, who still fishes, she "goes sharking" less frequently these days and usually takes someone with her.

To clean out a shark she first cuts off the shark's tail, decapitates it, takes out the spine and teeth (two rows, top and bottom,) and uses them to fashion the necklaces and pendants she sells in her shop and the jewelry stores in Nassau. Up there they cap the shark's teeth with gold or silver and fasten them to gold chains; tourists love them.

If she doesn't sell the meat she buries it as fertilizer for her garden — the secret behind her luxuriant bushes and profusion of blooms. She thinks it might make a product that would interest tourists. She could just imagine it: bags of fertilizer that tourists could take home to put on their gardens. "Though come to think of it," she said, pondering the idea, "it seems rather unlikely they'd want to carry back a load of decaying shark meat in their luggage!" She gave a whoop of laughter at the idea, "that's providing, of course, the U.S. customs would allow it into the country. Can't you just see it?"

"Actually, though," she said, "it'd be no problem, you know? It could be dried in the sun and minced up. Then it'll hardly smell at all. An' it'd be good ecology to recycle shark meat."

With visions of hammerheads and tiger sharks patrolling a few yards off the beach below our house, just waiting for us to enter the water, I asked, "what about sharks off our beach?"

Her reply was offhand and not too reassuring. "Hell, girl, you don't have to worry about sharks close in like that. Long as you don't thresh around like a windmill they're not likely to bother you. These waters are so clear they can see what you are." (My husband grinned, smug at being right.)

"Besides, they've got lots of other things to eat. They don't want your flesh."

Though she seldom mentioned it, Gloria, because of her courage and knowledge of sharks, has been sought out by famous explorers Jaques Yves Cousteau, Stan Waterman, and Dr. Eugenie Clark to advise them on various explorations. Several of the newspaper clippings in the front room told of these encounters but when asked about them, she shrugged a shoulder. "That's all in the past and not important," she said indifferently.

Gold necklaces and earrings swinging, she straightened up, stretched gracefully, and seductively moving her brown shoulders above her sarong-style garment said, "me and that Scarlett O'Hara, are two of a kind. Being brave, and independent, with a mind of your own — *that's* what's important."

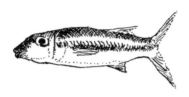

Sometimes you get one of those rare moments when all actions seem to come together and you realize it is good to be alive.

The next afternoon, Mr. Flowers' admonitions aside, we donned bathing suits and went to the beach to swim. If Gloria, who knew shark habits and at age sixty plus was brave enough to go shark fishing, I was brave enough to resume swimming. Even so, as I pulled my tee shirt over my head and took off my beach shoes and put them with my towel on the sand, my eyes scanned the water for a triangular shaped dorsal fin cutting through the water like a knife. The sun was low in the western sky, the breeze balmy; in front of me the turquoise sea beckoned. Sunlight danced on the surface.

This was no time to hesitate. Too much imagination can ruin the most determined intent. I paraphrased some inspiring thought, whose author I couldn't recall, but it went something like: in order to experience life more fully and move forward we need to at least attempt to do what we fear. I had been swimming here for over three years now and if I was to continue to enjoy island waters, and not spend the rest of my life sitting onshore and wondering what is out there waiting for me, I had to act now. I struggled to quell the unease just below my breastbone.

Tentatively I approached the surf and put my feet in the water. Wavelets warm as sunlight rippled around my ankles.

My husband, by now floating above the offshore reef, called me to come in. I waved to him. Stepped in up to my knees. It was deliciously warm. Carefully, ignoring all thoughts of what might lie beneath the water, keeping my head above water so I could keep an eye on what might be moving around me, I began to swim out to meet my husband.

Ahh-hhh. How could I have forgotten how wonderful the water felt against my skin — smooth as silk. I turned over. Stretched out on my back. Gazed up at the sky. Relaxed. Closed my eyes. I felt I was floating on the glass belly of Mother Nature herself, rising and falling with the gentle waves, breathing her in and out along with my own breath. For a brief moment I was nameless, genderless, and ageless, suffused with a feeling that I belonged to something greater than myself, aware that the world was more than I knew, more than I would ever know.

I opened my eyes. Gazed rapturously at the sky, the pile-up of clouds, the seabirds flying, the casuarina trees lining the white beach. I felt the water buoying me up, and the world seemed to expand until there was no end to its boundaries. Or to ours...

Crawfish (spiny lobster) season was still open so taking Gloria at her word, we looked for some. Supine, we lay on the sea peering down through twelve feet of water transparent as glass. So clear, in fact, that we could see the crawfish's delicate feelers twelve feet below. I floated — suspended, it seemed, on air.

Mindful that crawfish, as well as conch, were being fished out (or killed by using bleach) my husband speared only two. Hurrying them home, dripping and still partly alive, we plunged them into boiling water and twenty minutes later, ate the succulent pink and white flesh while standing outside on our deck, still in our bathing suits, the melted butter dripping down our chins to oil our bare chests. Never had food tasted so good.

19

Because of its "salubrious" climate, Englishman Peter Bruce, in his *Memoirs*, written in 1724, proposed the Bahamas as a health resort for British "sick and afflicted inhabitants." *"The Bahama Islands enjoy the most serene and temperate air in all America,"* he wrote, *"the heat of the sun being greatly allayed by refreshing breezes from the east, and the earth and air are cooled by constant dews which fall in the night, and by gentle showers which fall in their proper seasons, so they are free from the sultry heat of other settlements (colonies.)"*

But by April of the next year a drought had been on for eight months and the small rains, expected to start now, didn't come. It got hotter and drier by the day. Crops that couldn't be irrigated were dying in the fields, the supply of produce at the Packing House had diminished, the gardens thirsted, and though watered faithfully, the two orange trees in the back garden were dying. At considerable expense we'd bought the trees from a Nassau nursery our first year with high hopes that they would be the start of our own small citrus orchard. Those hopes now appeared dashed.

We began to worry about our well running dry and cut down on showers. On Exuma, unlike some of the other islands, there is a good supply of fresh water. It lies protected from the boiling sun in underground aquifers, constantly replenished each year (as long as everyone used it wisely,) by the filling rains.

Good soil, on the other hand, was at a premium — a fact the Loyalist settlers of the 1870's discovered too late. To their despair and subsequent loss, they found poor farming here; the sun was too hot, the topsoil sparse, the island's allotment of earth spread too thinly over its limestone base to permit roots to get a good grip on the soil. The seasonal rains — when they came — were so heavy they washed away the soil from the fields.

Because there was almost no topsoil on the limestone slope that passed for our back garden, my husband had excavated small "pockets" in the limestone and filled them with topsoil which he hauled from elsewhere at great trouble and effort. In these we planted the two orange trees, a sapodilla or "dilly" tree, several hibiscus bushes Nigel Minns had given us, and a guava tree from Miss Edith.

At the bottom of the garden where it more or less leveled out onto the flat was a coveted "banana hole," a deep natural well in the oolitic limestone that went down eight feet or more and had a pocket of rich soil trapped in the bottom. Around the island were thousands of such holes, fissures in the rock which had been worn away by centuries of rainwater beating on them. In many, as in ours, there grew a banana plant — another gift from Nigel — and two papaya trees, gifts from Stanley.

Until now everything had thrived, although two lime trees had never borne fruit. Asked why, and what to do about it, Mr. Flowers said, "you mussy beat them." He regarded them sternly, wiggling them back and forth as if to test their strength.

"With what?" my husband said, somewhat taken aback.

"Some t'ing heavy. Like a two-by-four."

"Why do that?"

" `Cuz then those trees know who's boss an' they goin' to grow like you say."

Feeling this was too drastic a measure, even for a tree, we asked Christine Rolle who, having put together a small booklet on the subject of island folk medicine and herbs, was considered an authority. We found her putting tins of tomato paste on the shelves at *Christine's Friendly Store* in Farmer's Hill. This day, instead of one of her remarkable hats she was wearing a gypsy kerchief knotted tightly around her head.

"Best thing to do," she said, "is drive an iron spike into them. That'll feed them the iron they need to grow strong."

When I mentioned this piece of alternate advice to Mr. Flowers, he snorted. "Miss Christine doesn't know every t'ing," he said. "Beatin' the tree is what'll do it."

I remarked that it seemed like cruel and unusual punishment for something that couldn't fight back.

"It fightin' now `cause you ain' show it who's boss."

"How can you say that?"

"You eat any o' it fruit yet?"

As usual, I couldn't argue with him. He grinned smugly. He liked winning.

We decided to make one last effort to get advice before "beatin' on the tree." In the one-street settlement of Moss Town, at the shop of Mrs. Musgrove — the person everyone agreed has the greenest thumb on the island — I met a portly lady well into her seventies. She and her farmer husband were admired island-wide for their green thumbs. Mr. Musgrove, as usual, was at his nearby farm/orchard working but Mrs. Musgrove was seated on the cement slab behind her little grocery store carefully planting hibiscus cuttings in empty coffee cans.

Beyond her stretched a hillside full of plants, a jungle of cuttings potted in all kinds of containers: rusted cans, glass jars, plastic bleach bottles, plastic dishpans, broken boxes, coconut halves, cups, old bedpans, dishes and refrigerator trays. Some of the plants reached six or seven feet into the air, twisted around each another, draped themselves in among the trees overhead, crawled along the ground, fell down dead, or, like a scene from Tarzan, tangled in a wild confusion of vines hanging from the trees. Those she doesn't sell, this sweet, generous woman gives away.

Mrs. Musgrove scrubbed the dirt off her hands in a bucket of water, shook my hand, and offered me a metal folding chair. I sat down and asked her how it was that so many things grew so well for her when many people on the island had a struggle just to keep things alive. What was her secret?

"Why, I don't know why, chile." She gave a gentle smile, "but I thanks the Lord every night and every morning that they do." It seemed very likely that was her secret. "Things grow along at their own time," she said, "you can't hurry them." What a sensible approach, I thought. I told her about our lime trees.

"Why, those trees bin thirsty a while now. They jus' needs some of God's sweet rain."

"But we've been watering them for two years now."

"Ain' the same water. That water from the well ain' got God's blessing in it."

When we told this to an American friend he related a similar experience. One spring, before he returned to the States for the summer, he put in some tomato plants and fruit trees, had a well dug, and hooked up an elaborate watering system to keep the new orchard irrigated. When he returned in December all was sere and dead. "What happened?" he asked the man who looked after his garden. "Didn't rain," was the unembellished reply.

"But I had a special well dug."

"That's artificial water. Can't use it. Things won't grow less they get rain."

By now everything on the island was drying up. Grog Pond and the other rain lakes were as low as anyone could remember. Catchments were dangerously low and daily the islanders watched for a northeasterly front to come through, their clouds heavy and sweet with rain. They didn't come. Or if they loomed on the horizon early in the morning by late afternoon they had passed on by, grumbling on southwards to dump their load of precious water on some lucky island in the Caribbean.

Instead we had days of endless sunshine and azure skies, great for tourism, devastating for island farmers and their economy. The island was hurting. At the Government Packing House Birdie Mae Musgrove, (Mrs. Musgrove's niece,) Kerlene Nixon and Alsaida Ferguson were temporarily laid off, and up and down the island people's wells were getting low.

My husband talked again of digging a rain catchment, saying that though it was estimated to cost as much as eight thousand dollars to construct, he and Stanley and Mr. Flowers could probably do it for three hundred dollars. If, as he believed, and as environmentalists who predict a global warming trend fear, this drought was a harbinger of things to come, a catchment would be a wise investment. Most Bahamian homes already had one; they knew about drought.

In time, tempers, my own included, were becoming as fragile as the thirsty plants. Never had the sun felt so hot, never was my skin so dry. I felt desiccated. Gobs of different face creams, each making varying promises of protection, preservation, repair, renewal, and regeneration, appeared not to help. My white hair, dried out and limp, looked like a string mop.

Because it felt like my whole body was slowly drying up I stayed indoors most of the day, daydreaming, writing, thinking, drinking quarts of iced tea, and reading — particularly about the island's link to American history.

Oddly enough, you'd think it would be inextricably bound to the sea and its winds but when the early Loyalist settlers came here from America, they concentrated not on the sea but on farming the land because it was what they knew. Without doubt, it must have been difficult for them, settled so far from the kind of gracious life they'd known, so far from the rich soil and soft green fields of Virginia, the Carolinas, and Georgia.

We decided to drive to a place almost at the end of Little Exuma called *The Hermitage*, the last intact plantation house remaining from those forlorn Loyalist years.

Lignum Vitae

20

Scoured by the weather as it is, vulnerable to the sun and the winds, an island existence often seems especially fragile and transitory, surviving only by a tenacious determination to struggle on and cling to life in the face of formidable odds.

Several plantation ruins still existed on the island, but the most intact was *The Hermitage* in Williams Town, on the southernmost tip of Little Exuma. Here, in the mid-1700's, lived the Kelsall family. Their history could be found in the George Town library in a collection of Kelsall family letters, assembled in a folio titled *Henrietta, My Daughter*, by Mary K. Armbrister, a Kelsall descendant.

A former wealthy landowner in America, merchant Roger Kelsall and his daughter Anne emigrated to Exuma from Georgia in 1776 where he built *The Hermitage*. There was no mention of his wife following later, but his son John and wife Lucretia, and their four children, did come later. They lived in the house until Lucretia, as so many women were to do, took the children to England and never came back.

A story similar to that of these Loyalist settlers can be found in the novel *Wind From The Carolinas*, Robert Wilder's fictional account of the Camerons, a Loyalist family of the late 1700's who, at the close of the American Revolution, chose to remain loyal to the British Crown. Though based on fact, the island life of the time was highly romanticised.

A more factual, better-researched book is titled *Exuma: The Loyalist Years, 1783-1834*, written in 1988 by Exuma winter resident W. H. "Tex" James. It reports the history of Exuma's early plantation owners, real life men and women who abhorred the American Revolutionary War, longed to remain British, and wanted no part of the plebeian rule of the newly-formed American states.

With the help of the British Government, which promised them financial compensation, transportation to the Bahama islands in Royal Navy ships, and their choice of land, they moved their families, slaves, farm animals — and in some cases the bricks of their buildings —to the Bahamian islands, including Exuma.

Here they hoped to re-establish the vast cotton plantations they once owned in America and recreate the Colonial style of life they had formerly enjoyed. They built roomy manor houses with quarters for the slaves who performed the arduous work of clearing, planting and cultivating the new cotton fields. The nameless slaves, brought originally from Africa two or three generations before, had taken their master's name and today on Exuma there is still a predominance of contemporary British names like Brown, Clarke, Forbes, Morley and Rolle.

Unhappily, Exuma's sparse soil would not support the landowners' grand scheme and their ill-starred venture failed.

Another early settler was William Walker who came to Exuma around 1784 because he was given a Crown Grant of 147 acres a mile or so off George Town on Great Crab Cay. The ruins of the guest house, cook house, warehouse, and two-story brick manor house — an impressive dwelling with carved stonework on the entrance pillars and a wide front terrace overlooking Elizabeth Harbour — can still be seen. Included is an appliance everyone in those days required — a gun emplacement to fight off pirates.

Walker, having heard about "the pockets of good earth on the island," had an avid interest in establishing tropical plants in the Bahamas and planted extensive gardens on Crab Cay. In a two acre walled garden beside the cook house he hoped to create a special botanical garden of plants from the South Seas.

In his book, author James quotes an article in the *Bahama Gazette* of August 15, 1789, which states that William Walker, Esq. brought to Exuma from His Majesty's Botanic Garden on the Caribbean island of St. Vincent "several curious and useful Plants, among which were Cinnamon, Sage, Gum Arabic, Chinese Tal-

low Tree, Mango, Bread Nut, Garlick Shrub, African Lily, Spanish Chestnut, and Ball Apple or Water Melon."

The *Gazette* article records that Walker expected soon
*"the Arrival of a Ship from Otaheite (Tahiti) with a Quan-
tity of the Bread Fruit Tree, of which he (Captain Bligh)
was so good as to promise me a Part to introduce into the
Bahamas. This Tree agreeing well with a dry Soil, I expect
it will be a most valuable Acquisition to our Planters... and
will feed them in time of drought."*

Walker, James wrote, had great hopes for the Bread Fruit
tree. In a 1798 letter which the planter wrote to a friend in Nassau, he stated: *I have long conceived that many Exotics ... would thrive
here, and be of infinite advantage to the Inhabitants, in particular, the
Bread Fruit... the Bread-fruit tree at my little Key in Exuma Harbour
has been in bearing for some time, and it is not five years since sent.*

(Ironically, today there are few breadfruit trees on the island and, according to our garden consultant Nigel Minns, few
Exumians will eat the fruit.)

Hoping to cultivate other "exotics," Walker planted sage,
garlic and thyme, and a variety of fruit trees — mango, sweet
apple, guavas, and sapodilla — and a wide range of lilies, nut
trees, groundnuts and pineapples. Few survived.

For 15 years or so — from the mid-1780's to 1800 — the
cotton planters flourished and Exuma prospered. The pioneers
built homes, a church, a school, a road and, beginning in the
year 1793, started settling a town they named George Town. The
village soon became a bustling port, with ships departing regularly for London and Liverpool, loaded with cotton and passengers.

The Loyalists' venture ended badly, however, as it did for
many of their slaves. At the beginning of the 19th Century the
cotton crops failed, the slash and burn method of clearing having exhausted the land of its thin layer of topsoil in which the
crops grew. When the deadly chenille bug attacked the weak-
ened plants, the crops died.

The final blow came in 1836 with the emancipation of the
slaves. With no free labor to work the fields, the owners abandoned their land and left the island for good, some going to Eng-

land, some staying on in Nassau, some returning to the United States. The Rolle land, for example, was divided up into five estates — Steventon, Ramsey, Mount Thompson, Rolleville and Rolletown — was left to the freed slaves and their descendants in perpetuity — though whether or not they actually left it to their former slaves is still being argued. Worse yet, however, the Loyalists abandoned their slaves, who had relied on them for survival.

These poor people, primarily farm workers, unskilled in any other trade, with few tools and even fewer resources, were now expected to fend for themselves on this stripped-bare island. Without support, without funds, without food, without skills, they struggled to survive as best they could.

One can feel sympathy for those settlers and their lost dreams — so many hopes dashed, so many grand plans blown away by the hot island winds in a searing drought that may well have lasted for years — but the abandoned slaves lost most. They were now not only poor but stateless, farming cotton the only skill they knew, their support from the Colonial government in Nassau or London minimal, they were forced by this great injustice to eke out a living on worn-out land as best they could.

As James wrote:
It is indeed a tribute to the strength and fortitude of those early Exumians who persisted during the next century, raising families and supporting themselves with a minimum of aid and support from the colonial government... Not until World War II and the years that followed, did tourism begin to provide some measure of prosperity for the island. As more and more people from the United States and Europe came to appreciate Exuma's beauty and advantages, tourism, yachting enthusiasts, and winter residents began to contribute to the economy. Jobs were created, local enterprises started up, and a new era of growth began.

We reached *The Hermitage* — often called *The Cotton House* — and parked the car on the main road at the base of the small rise on which the main house is located. Wading through a front yard of uncut weeds, long grass, and hard ground purpled with small flowers, we reached the house. Somehow, the walls had, through centuries of wind and rain, remained intact.

By no means palatial, it would nonetheless have been a comfortable home with wide views of the sea and the surrounding fields. At some point someone had restored the shingled roof and it was more or less solid, but the rooms stood empty, the windows gaping open, the plaster walls, lashed by the wind and weather of two and a half centuries, dark with age and stained by mildew. Mice scuttled underfoot as we made our way through the abandoned rooms. A sea wind that sighed through the open windows sounded like voices whispering from the past.

On a front lawn overlooking the sea we spread out our picnic cloth and ate our chicken salad sandwiches. It was the usual beautiful day — multicolored sea, high blue sky pocked with fluffy clouds — but it felt eerie. Above us the wind rustled in the tall casuarina trees, surf broke rhythmically on the rocks below the cliff, the smell of the sea mixed with wild thyme strengthened the air — and yet... and yet... there was that whisper of long ago voices in the mist... .

According to the existing Kelsall papers, on this 970 acre estate there were once great hopes for the future. Kitchen gardens thrived, pure-bred stock imported from Jamaica and England grazed, lumbering went on in the nearby woods, a sawmill, a tannery and a blacksmith shop provided needed services. Small luxuries arrived periodically from England by ship, a multitude of servants ran about, and though life was hard, the owners strove to live like they always had — English landed gentry.

Yet despite its gracious aspects, its slaves and its beautiful location, it must have been a hard and lonely life. The house lacked electricity and running water, of course, and there was no doctor, no dentist or other medical help, no radio or telephone, only one road dirt track and no near neighbors. There were two small stores in George Town. Mail, tools, supplies, household belongings, building materials, personal luxuries, farm equipment, chickens, ducks, and livestock were shipped from England to this remote island every two to three months by sailing ship — some of which didn't survive the storms at sea.

Nor was it a life of equality. The work was done by slaves. A census of the time compiled by the Anglican missionary Reverend Daniel Warner Rose in 1803, states that on Exuma the number of souls was 1,253. Of those, 140 were whites and 1,078 were slaves. One hundred and thirty of the whites attended Church of England, nine went to the Church of Scotland, and there was one lone Methodist. There were 4,656 acres under cultivation, 166 horses, 849 horned cattle, and 2,188 sheep. Staples were poultry, fish, and corn, and slave labor yearly produced between twelve and fifteen thousand bushels of salt.

In a letter to a relative in England, Mrs. Kelsall described their life. Her daughters, she wrote, "rode out" on their horses every morning, after which they studied French and geography, played the piano forte, did their fine embroidery in the afternoons, and read quietly in the evenings. It sounds a genteel life suitable to women of the times but throughout the letters there is a strong undercurrent of yearning for England.

The sons were sent to school there. For the daughters, an education at home was considered adequate. Removed from the educational opportunities and girlish pleasures they could only read about, these young women dreamed of opportunities to meet and engage male company of their own kind and persuasion so they could marry them and move away — to England.

Driving home late that afternoon, still haunted by the ghosts of *The Hermitage*, was a good time to silently ponder this island life of ours and I did so during our thirty-mile trip along the Queen's Highway. As we passed the color-splashed Bahamian homes of the Forbes Hill settlement, the derelict hotel at Pretty Molly Bay, Gloria's *Tara*, the new *La Shante* and *Blue Hole* restaurants, the homes of winter residents from the U.S., Canada, Britain and Sweden — it seemed as if all of us were merely the latest in a long line of ephemeral dream-bearers on this island. Someday, like *The Hermitage*, would our homes stand empty and open to the sky, the sea winds whispering through their gaping windows, the rain beating in on the mice scuttling across the floors?

It was a melancholy thought, one that, on this tiny sea-girt speck in the vast ocean, emphasized the impermanence of life, and I was suddenly struck by how much of a complete world all of us islanders — Bahamian and non-Bahamian alike — must create for ourselves. Somehow, on this tiny drop of land amid the wide ocean, we must fashion a life that isn't confined or circumscribed by the small space. Our needs and wants were similar to those in countries everywhere, but on an island, fulfillment of them had to be simpler. Or perhaps living on an island one actually learned to want and need less?

If the drought continued, if it went into a second year — and there were Exumians who predicted that like the Biblical drought it would continue for the full "seven years of lean" — we would all have to learn how to get along with less.

21

By the following October when we returned the drought had worsened. Ye Gods, how hot that sun! How we sweated! How everything thirsted for rain! The island baked under a sun that was like a roaring flame in the sky. We expected hot dry weather this year — Stanley had warned us — but not this, not weather that attacked and dried up the human spirit even more than the body's juices.

It wasn't supposed to be this way. Exuma's average winter temperature range is 75 to 82 degrees; by last April of this year it had been in the 90's. This made us wonder if this was just an unusual freak of nature or, as many scientists now believe, was the result of the ozone layer thinning. Was the warming of the planet already in full swing?

For days the island lay burning in never-ending sunny weather, days so bright the glare made it difficult to see anything clearly without squinting — let alone where the sea ended and the sky began. The world shrank to the shaded living room where life went on in a perpetual half-light, submerged in a shadowy coolth that helped soothe the sting of the sun.

Going outside, it was necessary to swathe oneself in cotton clothing, and put on a wide-brimmed hat, dark glasses, and sunscreen lotion, all of which caused sweat to pour out of the skin and engender a constant need for a shower — but the instant you dried off and stepped from the shower the heavy sweating resumed.

The air felt brittle. Building plans were on hold; too hot to continue work. Grog Pond was almost dry, revealing little hummocky islands never seen before. On the newly-revealed expanse of rippled sand, herons perched on long legs, necks extended, to peck about among the mangroves for morsels of fish and bivalves.

Maybe it was the heat, maybe not, but things between my

husband and me were changing. We didn't talk as much as before so I no longer knew what he was thinking — or feeling. We no longer had anything in common — but probably that's just as well because I was beginning to feel we lived in each other's pocket — too close, too much togetherness. Too stifling. A retirement wife's nightmare — for better or worse but not for lunch?

Our separateness depressed me. The island was erecting a wall between us. Most nights now I went to bed before him and managed to feign sleep when he got there.

The island and the heat were controlling our lives. Not only was too much being demanded from our marriage, the heat dictated what we wore, what we did, and, sometimes, where we went. Because of the need to conserve water, it even dictated how often we showered and how long we stayed there. The heat kept us indoors and decreed which garden plants would thrive and which wouldn't.

The sapodilla, or "dilly," sapling we'd planted in the back garden our first spring was stalled at three feet. It's glossy, dark green leaves, (from which chicle for chewing gum is extracted,) drooped. Its wood was legendary; according to archeologists remnants of ancient Mayan temples in Guatemala have been found in which the sapodilla wood was still as good as new after 500 years, but even a historically significant tree needs water.

We planted it not for posterity but for its fruit, even though at first encounter we thought it bland and insipid. It was soft, browny gold, looked like a raw potato and tasted like one. Then one day Rosemary Minns, Miss Edith's daughter, brought us a jar of her home-made sapodilla cream. This is made by whipping together the pulp of the fruit with lime juice and real cream. The taste was exotic — thick, rich and velvety smooth, both tart and sweet, and smelling faintly of flowers. When drizzled over canned fruit or rum cake it created ambrosia. It had decided us to plant a "dilly" tree.

The banana sapling Nigel gave us had also stopped growing. When planted the year before in the banana hole at the bottom of the garden it had begun sprouting after only two weeks and grew about two inches a day; now, upon reaching four feet, the drought had stopped its race to the sky. When Nigel was told this he said, "don't worry. It's just resting through the drought. It'll grow again soon as it rains."

By now the sea grape tree on the northeast corner of the house had grown sufficiently and produced enough shade so that we could place under it a small round table and three lounge chairs. The tree's broad flat leaves, shaped somewhat like a large rose petal, gave a wide-spreading shade that created a dappled green world underneath where reading or dozing was a pleasure. Mr. Flowers liked to sit there on a hot day. But this year all was brown and leathery, the leaves falling off the tree months early in drifts of dry brown petals that when you walked over them crackled like parchment.

Even the precious papaya tree thirsted. Several years earlier it surprised us, appearing out of nowhere on the north side of the front deck. It produced no fruit that first year — because, according to Nigel, it was sensitive to the north side's "chilly" weather! — but the next year, even after being constantly subjected to the sea wind and its salt, and after a full year of weathering several "northers," it decided for some reason known only to itself, to blossom.

Though small, the blossoms were lovely, fragrant and waxy white with a yellow center. They appeared on the trunk at the top of the leaf crown and before drying and dropping off, showed three minuscule green melons. As the fruit developed, new blossoms kept forming at the top, making it possible to have ripening fruit, partly-ripening fruit, and blossoms all on the same single trunk at the same time.

Since the main trunk was hollow and too slim and fragile to bear the weight of all this munificence, it had to be supported by slinging around it a rubber tube which was fastened to the deck. Now the trunk, too, was wilting in the heat.

The four coconut palms, however, thrived in the drought and it was not hard to see why people who live in the tropics value these versatile trees. Not only do they provide instant and easily replaceable roofing and building materials, as well as usable utensils and tools, they could feed and sustain a body in dire conditions.

A special fondness for these trees came from my childhood when my heroes were not *Little Women* or the pretty blond girls in the frilly dresses, but the far more admirable Robinson Crusoe. When I played "make believe" underneath the dining room table I imagined myself as that ingenious castaway living in his palm-thatched hut, eating fish from a palm leaf, and drinking from half a coconut.

(It was consoling to know that if a hurricane ever did hit and the worst came to the worst, we could, as he did, use the shells for cups and bowls, the milk to drink, the meat to eat and the fronds to build a shelter — but the hurricane would have to wait because it was going to take six more years before our coconut trees bore coconuts.)

Already, though, their fronds had proved useful. Because of the relentless heat, a place outdoors was needed in which to store the young plant cuttings we potted each year. But where to put the tender young cuttings so they would be out of the sun but still able to catch the rain?

Said Nigel: "Use your palm fronds to build a lean-to at the back of the house." He quickly sketched out a plan on an old envelope. "See, all you have to do is put in two uprights, lay a board from one to the other, nail a board across the back wall of the house, lay a couple of planks from that to the uprights, and cover it with palm fronds. Done!"

Wouldn't it fall down without some side bracing?

"It's only a temporary structure and no, it won't fall down right away. If it does, you can always build another one next year. There's lots of palm fronds. Just make sure you lay them loosely enough on the roof so if it does rain the water can get through to your cuttings — but not enough to drown them."

The wild things in the garden weren't minding the dryness or the heat. They thrived. Despite the drought the jumbay trees were growing two feet a month. (They were, of course, non-edible except to Mr.Flower's goats, who gobbled truckloads of branches on which they continued to grow fat and sassy.)

The hedge of casuarinas along the road in front of the house was shooting spikes six feet high and by now had created a fine lacy screen. From the front deck you could still see over the tops of them to the Farmer's Hill lights, and this was a fine solution for a privacy screen — until the day Christine stopped by and advised: "Burn 'em down!" The reason, she said, is that once the trees got that high their roots would work their way into the well and choke it off. "Next thing you know your water pump will seize up on you for good!"

Water pumps were the bane of every islander's existence. If they didn't break down they leaked, if they didn't leak they got corroded by the salt and seized up, and if they didn't corrode and seize up it was likely they would need priming. Since they were usually outside a house there was also a good chance they would be "borrowed" — a Bahamian euphemism for sharing something while you're away and obviously don't need it.

Christine was really at the house because she needed to fix the water pump at one of her houses and wanted my husband's help. He told her what he thought might have gone wrong with it and, knowing the answer, asked if she had the tools she'd need.

"I got a hammer and a screwdriver in the van." She gave him an artful grin. "That do?"

"Hardly."

Chris's eyes widened and she wiped the sweat off her brow. "Well, I know that, but I also know you got the right tools and I don't." She pushed back her hat. Today she was wearing a stiff-peaked army officer's cap — the one she wore when she filled her role as a tour conductor of *Christine Rolle's Island Tours*.

They went off to fix the pump and I retreated to the dimness of the bedroom. It was too hot to do anything so I lay down to read *Out Island Doctor*, the story of an American teacher back in the forties who came out to the islands and because he had some knowledge of medicines, and no one else did, he traveled around the islands helping with medical problems.

Bahamians do not hold superstitions as do the people of the West Indian islands farther south. There are some ancient tales told by the elders about *obeah* (black magic) and "the Chick Charneys", mischievous little fellows who seemingly delight in pranks and general mayhem, but there are no major, all-pervasive beliefs like Voodoo. So we were intrigued when we heard about the abandoned village of Richmond Hill which rumor had it, was haunted.

To find out we joined four friends on a picnic outing to the settlement. With a lunch of hard-boiled eggs, roasted peppers, pasta salad, fresh tomatoes, a "hand" of ripe bananas, and some chilled white wine stashed in the cold box, six of us went in search of the resident ghosts — if any.

Accompanying us were Eunice and Rand Johnson, Linda Galvin, a petite French Canadian who was now a permanent island resident, and her gentle, soft-spoken Bahamian companion, Lloyd Symonette. A yoga teacher and landscape gardener of considerable knowledge about the island's flora, Lloyd was born on Exuma but had never been to Richmond Hill. From boyhood he had heard it was "haunted."

We drove from our house across the island to the heavily wooded south side and entered the dense bush by a dusty road that was little-traveled — except, perhaps, by midnight drug runners seeking to evade the law. Apart from a wild sea meadow reclaimed naturally over time from a mangrove swamp, and walls of impenetrable growth lining the road, there was nothing to see but bush. The directions we had been given were none too clear, undoubtedly because in this deep bush there were no landmarks. Several times we got lost and ended up in some squatter's vegetable patch. After an hour, still no Richmond Hill. Maybe the encircling bush, like an advancing army, had marched right over it, swallowing it up without a trace.

Eventually the road turned away from the sea, swung around a curve, and opened out onto a wider road where, to our amazement, we found ourselves on a double lane road with a boulevard down the middle! This was part of a land development scheme, now abandoned, that an enterprising land developer began some twenty-five years ago. Like so many of its kind, the grandiose plans had never materialised and the roads so hopefully carved out of the bush were mere grassy lanes, leading nowhere.

Another mile or so and, almost by accident, we came upon Richmond Hill, almost submerged by trees and vines. On either side of what must have once been the settlement's main street and was now merely a grass-covered alley through the woods, towering trees arched overhead, all but obscuring the sky.

About eight houses lined the street on either side. Thatched with palm fronds, their wooden shutters hanging drunkenly askew, their two or three rooms open to the wind and rain, to insects, snakes, and a host of other creatures, the ruined houses sat forlornly amid their tattered overgrown gardens.

At opposite ends of the settlement two churches stood empty, one for the Baptists the other for members of The Church Of God Of Prophecy. Buildings which must have once measured out the settlement's days and seasons in regular sacraments no longer resounded to a chorus of hymns or a preacher's words. Their pews were riddled with termite holes, their frayed altar banners flapped desolately in the sea wind, their roofs were rent by gaping holes.

Lloyd remarked sadly that in his mother's day Richmond Hill was considered the garden spot of the island. Now the fruit and flowers that once grew here in abundance had gone completely wild. Guava, orange, grapefruit and lime trees struggled up through the encircling bush to arch overhead. Old bougainvillea vines, running rampant, sent scarlet spires skyward. A yellow elder tree, the national flower of the Bahamas, blazed forth in yellow fluted cups. The succulent green leaves and red spikes of a love vine filled an entire garden, smothering the picket fence in front, the house, the outhouse, and the surrounding bushes.

A view through the house windows and doors showed furniture still filling the rooms. Tables, chairs, chests of drawers, mattresses, rusted bed springs, kitchen utensils, and in some cases clothes on hangers and curtains at the windows, gave an eerie feeling that one day, years before, someone had suddenly said, "let's all go to Nassau," and the whole village rose up as one and left. Did violence disrupt them? Did poverty overtake them? Or did the young people move away leaving only old people who eventually sickened and died?

Later inquiry into the Richmond Hill mystery revealed that, as often happens in the islands, the younger people had moved away from the settlement to find jobs and the old folks gradually died off until only one man was left, Reverend Curtis, the preacher at The Church Of God Of Prophecy church. He lived alone in the settlement for several years, a solitary verger caring for the church, until, finally, he, too, moved on, to Farmer's Hill.

That was several years ago. By now vines had crept through the windows of the houses and across the rotting floors. Behind one house some tall bamboo laced through the bush. My husband and Rand, deciding to explore, entered a house and we could hear them knocking about, tapping floors and banging on walls. "Look out!" Lloyd called, "watch out for snakes!"

It was almost as if he had some precognition for just then we heard my husband call out a warning: "Rand! — snake!"

As far as anyone knows the Bahamas have no poisonous snakes, only those belonging to the harmless boa constrictor family, so when the two men approached — Rand with the snake, an eight foot boa of considerable girth gripped just behind its head — no one was too worried. The rest of the snake, however, in a single quick movement, wrapped itself tightly around Rand's arm from wrist to shoulder. As if on cue, we let out a communal gasp.

We were all pretty sure — but not certain — that it was a species of harmless boa constrictor — it might hug Rand to death but would not give him a venomous bite. On the other hand it might, for all we knew, be a new breed of island reptile, one with a venomous bite. If it should sink its fangs into Rand's skin, none of us would have the slightest idea of the correct antidote. And we were miles out in the bush.

It was, in truth, an elegant creature; silvery grey and black with a faint pattern mottling its skin, and glittering black eyes. After we had admired the color and design, Rand knelt down and lowered his arm to ground level. Everyone stepped back. Once the head was released would the creature turn and bite? Or slither away. Rand let go the head. Quickly the snake glided into the undergrowth.

What did not leave as quickly was its strong and foul odor, an overwhelmingly powerful smell that clung to Rand's clothing and skin despite a scrubbing with leaves, a sponging with the rest of our drinking water, or a washing with club soda. Upon his return home he had to burn his clothes.

"I wonder if that is why Exumians call this place haunted," Lloyd mused, giving a slight shudder. "If there is one of those big guys here there's bound to be a lot of others."

22

However peripherally, sharing an experience with others brings home how we, like every other human being, are subject to the vagaries of the forces of nature. Though we did not lose crops, water wells, or money as the Exumians did, sharing this drought formed a bond, one that would not soon be forgotten. We now had a new appreciation of what the islanders sometimes faced.

As the drought dragged on, continuing to fray the nerves, everyone, especially the farmers, longed for rain. Bugs abounded. On the dot of sunset, with no tradewinds to keep them down, the mosquitoes and no-see-ums swarmed up from the grass, the bushes, the trees and from out of the soil. The vapors off Grog Pond, made up of decomposing plant life and millions of tiny decaying crustaceans, invaded the night air, redolent with the smell of moldering fish and rotten eggs — The Great Swamp Smell.

On the hottest, stillest night so far we were invited to have drinks with some winter residents at the nearby house they were renting. It was a large place, obviously constructed by a contractor in a hurry, or by someone who didn't know the island well. The first principle of tropical island construction, is: *always build to capture the prevailing winds.*

In the old days island houses were often built by shipwrights in the eminently practical, early Bahamian style — steep roof, high ceilings, a wide, covered wraparound porch, and louvred windows oriented to the north and east trade winds.

In the house rented by our host and hostess, the north windows were fixed. There were no eastern-facing windows at all, and a thick privacy hedge of silver buttonwood and casuarina trees cut off whatever breeze might have been enjoyed. How the inhabitants got fresh air was a mystery. Perhaps all the rooms were air conditioned?

The owners were a Massachusetts' couple who seldom stayed there but frequently rented it or lent it to friends. The current friends were three couples, one of which we'd met on the beach and who had invited us over for drinks. We assumed it would be in the usual island style, a casual pre-dinner drink and some light conversation. So because it was a hot, still night, we dressed accordingly in clean shorts, shirts and sandals, and slathered on a thick coating of insect repellent — the perfume of choice for most evenings this season.

The sun was blood red, sinking fast below the horizon. There was not a hint of wind. As soon as the sun plunged the island into dusk, the odor off Grog Pond — rank, fetid, powerful — would be smelling up the air in all directions with a sulfurous miasma that was as potent as the odor off a septic tank.

We walked down the road to the house. Lights illuminated the front drive and blazed from all the windows. On the deck and across the front lawn torches flickered. Pavarotti's rich voice spilled from the open door. Men in jackets and women in tinselly silks sipped cocktails on the front deck. It was a set for *Lifestyles of the Rich and Famous*, and we were drastically under-dressed.

"We'd better go home and change," I said to my husband in a low voice. Conscious of my unpainted toenails, pulled-back hair, sunburnt nose and lack of make-up I felt the need to whisper so as not to draw attention to myself.

"If I go home I'm not coming back," he said.

We went in.

The scene could have been in Bar Harbor, Kennebunkport, The Hamptons, or Boston. Our host, who, except for the lack of a yachting cap, looked every inch the yachtsman in white denims, navy blue blazer, and silk ascot, greeted us sweating profusely.

"Hot night. Glad you could make it." He led us to the bar. "Get yourself a cold drink and come and meet people. More friends flew in this afternoon from New York."

Hot it certainly was. We accepted glasses of chilled white wine, picked up a limp biscuit with goat cheese on it, and made our way to the deck through air strengthened with *Arpege, Obsession*, and *Giorgio*. Outside it wasn't much cooler.

"Hot night." A man looking miserable in a white jacket and Bermuda shorts, nodded to us. "Is it always this hot?"

"Only when the wind dies," my husband said. "And that's usually just before a front moves through."

"A front?"

A front, I explained, proud to sound like an islander and willing to show off my local savvy, was a storm system that came in usually from the west or the north. Sometimes there was a violent storm, with spectacular thunder and lightning shows; sometimes the front moved on south, missing this island entirely. Almost always it was preceded by a dead calm, such as the one we were now experiencing.

"Dead calm, eh." He wiped his brow with a paisley silk handkerchief. "I heard this island is a little paradise."

"It all depends on who's defining paradise," I said, grateful we had stayed in our sandals and shorts.

Beside him a woman in a fashionably brief strapless cotton sheath slapped at her bare legs and arms and looked vainly to see what she was hitting.

"Mosquitoes?" she asked.

"Probably. Or no-see-ums. Or sandfleas," I said. "They come out in force when the wind is down."

"Fleas!" The woman gave a small shriek, and fled indoors before we could explain that no-see-ums are not a true flea but a minuscule sandfly.

By now others on the deck were beginning to madly search and slap. The hostess, elegantly coiffed and wisely wearing a flowing cotton caftan, drifted up to us. Leaning close in a cloud of *Eau de Joy* she whispered in my ear, "I wonder, could you tell me if that smell comes from the house drains?"

"H_2S — hydrogen sulfide," I said, smiling, feeling like The Compleat Island Dweller. "Comes off Grog Pond when the wind is down. Happens several times a year."

She paled. "H_2 - what?"

"Rotten eggs," I elaborated helpfully. "From decaying shell fish." Her hand covered her heart, then went to her throat. It was hard to tell whether this was a gesture of despair at her party's rapidly disintegrating ambiance, or a feeling of faintness from the overpowering odor now stinking up the air.

Ever the elegant hostess, though, she rallied to the challenge. "Inside, everyone," she called gaily. "There's food and more drink." She herded everyone inside, closed the doors and windows against the bugs, and turned on the air conditioners to HIGH. It helped the smell but did nothing for the climate.

We loaded our plates with catered goodies that could only have come in that day with the guests from New York, and sat around eating the imported finger food in air reminiscent of a northern New York autumn night. Before long it was downright chilly and I was regretting wearing shorts. Others must have felt the same for soon they begin wandering outdoors again.

This time, however, the host was prepared. Armed with a spray can of OFF, he went around squirting insect repellent for those who requested it. The fragrances of expensive *parfums* and aftershave were soon replaced by the strong odor of bug spray. This helped cover up the emanations from Grog Pond. A couple from Pompano Beach sat together on a bench. Both in stark white, both blindingly blonded and deeply tanned, both were, it turned out, avid golfers. The husband asked "you golf?" and when we said no, started recounting their many triumphs on the world's golf courses.

"We've played charity golf in just about every place you can name," he said. "Palm Springs. Pebble Beach. You name it. Played with some great golfers too, Bob Hope and Jackie Gleason and Chi Chi and Arnold and Jimmy and Jack. You know Jack Nicklaus? Fine man. Fine fine people. Wouldn't even know they were so rich." It was not clear why he felt a need to impress us. We don't golf, and at the moment I probably looked like one of the worst-dressed caddies at his golf and country club.

"And would you believe, I missed a hole in one at Pebble Beach by one inch. One inch! Got one once at St. Andrews though, playing with Lord B. Biggest thrill of my life." He pummelled a mosquito on his forearm. "Too bad you don't have a course here. Big lack. You aren't going to get golfers here, you don't have a golf course." It seemed a rather obvious factoid.

Suddenly, out of the corner of my eye I saw the palm fronds begin to sway. They were always the first to catch the wind. The front was moving in. Maybe this time we'd be lucky and get rain. A feeble breeze stirred the air. "Ah-h-hhh, at last," someone said, "a nice breeze to cool things off." My husband and I regarded one another with delight as, all at once, the palms moved faster and we could feel rain on the wind. We knew what was coming.

The sky lowered, the stars went out, and a great gust from the northeast rearranged everything movable.

It lifted what remained of the cups and glasses on the deck railings and whirled them away into the night. It overturned chairs, flung pillows, and lifted skirts above the waist.

The leftover *hors d'oeuvres* became airborne. Nuts, potato chips, cheese balls, bits of carrot, goat cheese, broccoli and cauliflower all took off like confetti at a wedding. Women shrieked, pushed down their skirts with one hand, tried vainly to cover their coiffures with the other, and ran for cover amid a barrage of flying veggies.

The two golfers, perhaps afraid they might never get off the island in time for their next golf game, streaked down the drive for their rented car and headed for George Town. Unable to face the indoors again, we called goodnight and ran down the road.

Within seconds the rain started. A light spatter at first, then heavier, bigger drops, then a steady curtain, finally a niagara of water. Hair streaming, shorts and shirts sodden, we slipped off our sandals and danced down the road, shouting and singing at the top of our lungs. Open-mouthed, I let the rain fill me up. And just as Mrs. Musgrove said, this water was *sweet!*

The rain continued throughout the night, battering the roof, sending up the smell of wet earth — welcome as the most expensive perfume. I got up to see if it was coming in the screen patio doors of the bedroom, which we always left open for air and so we could be lulled to sleep by the sound of the sea.

They were partly open so I slid them closed and went to check on the others. They were all locked and the rain was sluicing down in torrents, as it was on the big windows in the Great Room. I sat on the windowseat to watch and think about Mrs. Musgrove and Nigel and all the plants and crops out there — *The Greenfolk* as Mr. Flowers called them — sitting in the dark and joyfully slurping up the water.

23

We'd been given a glimpse of the harsh side of island life, its particular vulnerability to the weather and the seas. We'd seen how islanders live close to the line of survival and now we could appreciate that in hard times it took courage to face each new day — with no certainty tomorrow would be any better. Yet face it they did, their cornucopian good humor never leaving them, their faith intact. Would their world survive? It had been two long years of drought, particularly hard on the farmers whose livelihood depended on their crops, difficult for us only because we were unused to the heat, the winds, the dryness and the dearth of produce and water.

But between us the difference was evident.

We need not stay here. We could leave, go home to the States. For Exumians, there was no choice but to stay and face whatever the weather — and adversity — brought next.

Then one morning in April I woke up to a still, calm sea, with the thermometer reading 85 degrees, and realized the cooler season had passed and summer had begun. Already the sun had an extra bite, the plants and trees were starting to leaf out, and I could feel that sense of the earth's miraculous ability to keep on renewing itself.

The spring rains returned full force. Water once more began filling Grog Pond, overflowing the catchments, flooding the rain barrels, spilling from roof gutters, sluicing away topsoil from the hilltops and into the banana holes.

The jumbay trees — members of the mimosa family — were putting forth a furry, pale yellow blossom that perfumed my early morning walks with Rita. Life in the garden resumed its attractions. The spiky white blossoms of the seagrape attracted bees and made the air hum and swell with fragrance. The tiny jewel-colored hummingbirds whizzed in and out among the garden's blossoms, two Greater Antillian bullfinches arrived, along with a pair of Scarlet Tanagers.

The mocking birds, which, because of their continuous scolding Exumians aptly call "the preacher bird," performed mating dances with great flair and acrobatics on the weathervane. Yellow butterflies flitted from bloom to bloom and once again, almost as if the rain has unblocked a torrent of words within each of us, my husband and I were able to approach each other and again live together easily.

The days got longer and the sun set well after eight in a blaze of rose, pink, peach and green. The papaya melons were ripening, growing to six or seven inches long, turning pale yellowy orange, the meat thick and juicy, tasting fruity and tart when eaten with a squeeze of lime. The two lime trees, so long dormant, produced so many limes that even after giving dozens away it still took half an hour to squeeze and store them as frozen juice. Tiring of that, and unwilling to waste a one, we threw the others into the freezer whole. Upon departure in May there were still over three dozen left.

"So much for `hittin' on the lime tree' or driving a nail into it," I said to Mr. Flowers, who had brought me a "hand" of bananas from his garden. "So much for your old Bahamian voodoo beliefs and gardening hints. So much for your old native wisdom."

"Well, now," he gave me the bananas and his most engaging grin, "God works in mysterious ways his wonders to unfold."

"Yes," I said, "*she* does."

For a moment he didn't catch it. Then he clapped his hands delightedly and nodded, laughing his rusty laugh. "Oh yeah," he chuckled, "oh *yeah*!" This was a wonderful man. I hung the bananas outside.

These Exumians! Despite their modest means so many of them were, in their own way, a generous people. In hard times they helped each other out. When one of them was needy they gave what they could — taxi drivers gave gas money to a fellow taxi driver who was in difficult straits, food was cooked and taken to the sick and to the elderly, and to the Haitian refugees who landed half-dead on these shores.

As if she didn't have enough to do, Christine Rolle, who wasn't married and had no children of her own, undertook to raise the son of a niece who had five other children to tend to. His presence in Christine's life had brought her a great deal of pleasure, as well as some headaches.

She was determined he was going to finish school and make something of himself. She treated him like a son, worried about his grades, gave him all kinds of lessons and opportunities and disciplined him, reprimanding him when needed. She saw he ate properly, dressed well, went to church regularly, and encouraged him to study hard so he could go to Nassau to attend the College of The Bahamas. Most of all she tried to keep him busy so he wouldn't get into "bad mischief."

Once or twice he had gotten in with a wild bunch of kids and wasn't doing his homework or his chores. When Chris worried he was "into trouble" she soon "got him straightened around!" She forbade him the use of the phone or his radio for two weeks, and it worked.

In general, Exumians attach little or no stigma to children such as this boy, born out-of-wedlock, or any child born that way. They are never referred to as "illegitimate" but as "outside" children. Except in the case of inheritance their out-of-wedlock status within the community is not considered important. The Bahamas has no state orphanage. Every child born is accepted and cared for by someone, often joyfully, and if there is no immediate family nearby, the child is often taken in by someone in the community.

Unfortunately, on Exuma, as in so many places, there is the problem of too many teenagers having out-of-wedlock babies, but as with the problem of AIDS, the government is addressing this in newspapers, health clinics, speeches and posters; only time will tell whether Exumians will continue to look upon their out-of-wedlock children as they do now — with acceptance and without condemnation.

In small settlements like Farmer's Hill children run in and out of the houses as if the whole village was one vast play-yard. They might eat breakfast at "auntie's," take a short nap at a married sister's house, play in the yard of another "auntie" and sleep the night at "mummy's" or grandmother's house — with any one of these places being not a relative, but merely a neighbor or a friend.

The grandmothers of the islands have long been the mainstay of the Bahamian family. Traditionally, they have taken the grandchildren so the mother and father — better educated, more skilled — can earn a living for the extended family. Or, if there is no father present, which is often the case, the grandmothers offer valuable support to their daughters and their children. The children are well-kept, well-dressed, and well cared for, but not indulged. Even the youngest is expected to carry out certain household chores and the older children are expected to help care for the younger ones.

Stanley's wife, Miss Corinne, was looking after two of her son's children full-time, and two of her daughter's children during the day. It never seemed to occur to her, as it certainly would to me and, I suspect, to most of today's American women, to say, "but I don't want to do this! I have my own life to live! Please raise your kids yourself."

Up to now a grandmother's care has proven to be an admirable and practical system, one that has worked well — providing, of course, the fathers also contribute to the children's welfare (some do and some don't.) And providing there are no modern grandmothers who want to work outside the home. Increasingly, now, this is the case. It is one of the new Exumian facts of life that the Bahamas, like other nations around the globe, will have to deal with the new emphasis on women's self-identity and will have to continue to do so well into the 21st century.

The Bahamas' advantage is that it has always had a core of strong, powerful women. Now they are beginning to speak out and make themselves known. They are influencing health, education and general welfare. Women doctors, lawyers, teachers, administrators, politicians, journalists and cabinet ministers are actively influencing politics and not afraid to do so on a variety of topics they feel need airing for the good of the whole country.

As elsewhere, their voices are needed because times are changing in the islands. More tourists, more contact with outside countries, more drugs, more money and more sophistication has led to greater expectations. The world is being beamed daily into the country via satellite TV. On most Exumian bars and many homes there is a satellite dish; some sit proudly in the front yard as a status symbol. Life here will never be the same.

Whether that is all to the good, or bad for everyone, cannot at this point be determined, but a psychology professor and longtime friend who came to visit, thought American TV could only be to the detriment of the peaceful island life.

"The arrival of TV with its preponderance of grim tidings, bad news, and gratuitous sex and violence is bound to have an influence even in such a remote place as this," she said one night, looking out from our deck over the tranquil view of sea, sky and palm trees. "You think the arrival of big resort development with its huge hotels and high-rise condominiums will pollute the environment — and they will — but the nightly litany of news coming in on TV is so appallingly awful it might well end up killing everyone here."

We thought that a little exaggerated.

"Well, but," she went on, "if we are what we eat, doesn't it make sense that we may also be what we see, hear and read? The daily input from TV, radio and print repeatedly shows us the world is in a sorry mess, the human race is a pretty rotten crowd, and the world is not the way it used to be —but what difference does it make? The planet is doomed anyway."

We said we didn't think things were that bad.

She shook her head. "Maybe not, but then why is one in four American families afflicted with mental health problems caused by stress, anxiety, fear and depression? How could anyone stay sane with the daily negativity that pours into our lives? It all adds greatly to our stress and makes our lives a fight against tremendous odds. Anyone trying to live a decent life, make responsible decisions, be an independent person, raise strong healthy children, or work to better the neighborhood and the community, is fighting a losing battle!"

"Unless," my husband said, "they can find input that provides life-enhancing, confidence-building support, and I'm sure there's a lot of that around."

She sighed. "Depends on how you look at it, I guess. Right now I can only see that through its TV programs the United States is contributing to the demise of our society."

It was a sobering thought on a sunny day.

24

Island living is not for everyone, as our flight over on a small nine-seater plane from Florida this year demonstrated. Because it gives such a wonderful perspective of Exuma's sixty-mile-long necklace of islands and cays, we had always considered flying to the island one of the pleasures of living there. Counted, the Exuma cays number 365 — or as Exumians say, an Exuma for every day of the year. The water is so clear the islands appear to be floating on it and because it is the color of rare jewels — jade, sapphire, amethyst and emerald — the shifting sunlight mixes and changes the sea into amazing combinations of light and shadow.

However, the flight over the cays in a small plane can be unpredictable. It's possible to set out from Miami, or Fort Lauderdale, in bright sun and encounter a rain squall half way.

To enjoy the flight you have to get used to these sudden squalls and not be unduly alarmed when suddenly, the rain strikes the plane's windows and everything disappears — islands, sea, sky, clouds — and the small plane pitches and tosses and swirls around in a race and a dance.

It was obviously not the flight of choice for two white-knuckle travelers aboard this flight.

About an hour out of Ft. Lauderdale, Jimmy, the Aero Coach pilot announced over his shoulder "Storm clouds up ahead. May get rough. Make sure your seat belts are fastened." From the seat across the aisle I heard a soft moan.

I looked over to find a rather large woman who had boarded ahead of us wearing her new Winter-In-The-Tropics clothes. Above a strapless sun dress emblazoned with bright orange and yellow daisies, her face was white. The flowered straw hat which she'd fought with the wind in Fort Lauderdale to keep on her head, had fallen to her feet and lay mashed underfoot. "It's my first time," she gasped, reaching over to clutch my arm.

The little plane hit a downdraft and dropped into an air pocket. The woman's moan grew louder. On my arm her hand jerked and tightened in a vicelike grip. Panic can be contagious. Not too concerned up until then — having gone through this kind of flight before — I began to feel my own equanimity ebbing. My stomach dropped alarmingly, my adrenalin soared.

"We're okay," I said, attempting to encourage us both. "Jimmy's a topnotch pilot." I didn't know if he was or not, or if I believed it or not. I only hoped it was so. The little plane rocked slightly, steadied, and ploughed resolutely onward, motor churning.

Her plump husband in the seat behind her, leaned forward. "I told you we shouldn't have come." He was wearing a new straw hat that sat low on his forehead, and a white overshirt with patterned inserts down the front. "There won't be anything to do on a place this size."

"I'm with Dad." Their teenage son glared at his mother from the seat in front of me. "I hope there's TV."

His sister sitting across the aisle from him looked sullen.

With this predisposed mindset what would they think when they saw the Exuma airport? The low wooden terminal building (circa 1930) was always in need of a coat of paint, but to a lot of people it was delightfully scruffy and had great charm.

It was wide open and breezy, as were the formalities. Outgoing passengers waited to do their business at two counters in the large main room which was ventilated by windows with wooden louvres. The dozen or so plastic bucket chairs were intensely uncomfortable so most people waited outside, gathering in groups to chat, or standing in the shade of the huge silk cotton tree to watch as the taxi drivers played endless games of checkers and argued loudly about their opponent's tactics and abilities. The customs and immigration men hung out over by the customs shed.

If the plane was late, as it often was, or didn't come at all, as also happened on occasion, or you had to go to town, you could leave a message with one of the taxi drivers, or with George Holland Rolle, who handled the baggage for *Bahamasair*, and ask them to keep an eye out for your incoming friends.

You could also sip a soft drink from the machine, or go out back for a cold beer at *Kermit's Airport Bar and Lounge,* a dusty wooden building painted a particularly drab shade of green. Inside were plastic-covered stools and tables, yellowing posters, and ancient signs advertising *Pauli Girl* and *Kalik* beers. It was cool and dim and if Kermit was behind the bar there'd be stories and gossip and lots of laughter.

All this was due to change within the year. The "new brand" airport now under construction at the middle of the island would take large jets and have the latest technology. This would make the airport officials better able to deal efficiently with large crowds of passengers but many islanders were going to miss the old one.

It was a *Casablanca* kind of place. You felt that if you looked over your shoulder real quick you might catch a glimpse, through the wooden louvres, of the ghosts of Humphrey Bogart and Ingrid Bergman kissing goodbye. Or Peter Lorre sealing a deal with Sydney Greenstreet. The new airport would undoubtedly be good for commerce, the tourist business, and airline schedules, but death to romance.

As Jimmy the pilot had predicted, a few minutes later the little plane emerged into the gorgeous sight of a rain-washed sky hung above a jeweled sea. The storm moved off, a rainbow arched over us and up ahead Exuma appeared, flat and long and green, set in a sea rimmed with a ruff of white surf. When the plane landed and had taxied up to the terminal the sun was shining and all along the edge of the tarmac a crowd of smiling people was gathered in front of the ramshackle airport building.

"Oh thank God we've landed." My companion released her grip. "That was terrible! I'll never go through anything like that again!" How she intended to get off the island was a mystery.

People had congregated at the terminal because, like going down to the train station in a small U.S. town, it was something to do. They drove the five miles from George Town to see who was comin' in and who was "goin' out."

Once the plane's door was opened and the stairs were let down, the taxis zoomed out to park under the wings and the people awaiting the passengers moved through the opening in the picket fence that separated the terminal from the airfield. One woman awaited her guest at the bottom of the plane steps with a bouquet of scarlet bougainvillea and orange lilies in her arms. Another found herself besieged as a toddler on the third step shouted "Grandma!" and flung herself into her grandmother's open arms.

The sullen family of four Canadians with whom we'd traveled appeared nonplussed at Exuma's airport facilities. The woman turned an ashen face to her husband and said, "if the airport looks like this what will the rest of it look like?" Her son just looked glum. Sister had a different agenda and was busy casing the boy situation at the airport. At the outdoor customs yard the family claimed a mountain of luggage.

Christine's TAXI 25, a good-sized van, was hired to transport them and their numerous bags into the *P&P*. Since it was the place where most things go on, I assumed they would have a good time and likely end up, like many tourists, falling in love with the island and buying land to build a house. In Will Nixon's blue van taxi, we headed west to our house.

By now we had started a small ritual of return which reacquainted us with the place. It included walking around and peering into closets and cupboards, as though exploring an unfamiliar house. I thought I remembered what was in the cupboards and closets but I often came across something I'd forgotten we owned — a particular item of hot weather clothing, for example, a set of blue glasses, a gaudy tablecloth, or a video that bore seeing a second or third time.

The circumambulation of the house and garden included staring out the windows at the sea, gazing long at Grog Pond and its encircling hills and checking each tree and plant. In just six months the garden had gone wild, the bougainvillea was sending shoots skyward, the weeds were rampant, and the croton was up to the deck railing. I marveled at the tenacity of this greenery. Like the tough trees on city streets they survived by thrusting their roots down through rock to whatever water source they could find and relentlessly pushing their stems and leaves up through cracks in the cement.

After my ritual circuit I stood on the deck and lifted my

arms to the breeze, thanking whatever spirit had accorded me the munificent blessing of this island and sending up a small paean of praise for the island's simple pleasures.

However, the island's climate can wreak destruction on an unattended house, so as part of the ritual, before we changed into our bathing suits, I swept the floors and did the job I hate most: cleaning out the accumulated mouse and cockroach droppings. Mice had built a nest behind the refrigerator and cockroaches had deposited their droppings in the kitchen utensil drawer. At some point termites, too, had gnawed their way into the kitchen cabinets and left their telltale trail of chewed-up sawdust. One thing about living in the tropics — something is eating something else 24 hours a day.

The cleaning done we donned our scraggly straw hats which were hanging on their nails awaiting our return, loaded books, sunscreen, sandwiches, cold lemonade, and some bananas into the picnic basket, and drove three miles to Sand Dollar Beach.

First we swam, then we wandered the shoreline searching in the clear shallows to see the fragile white sand dollars, the shell of a sea creature that is perfectly flat and the size of a beer coaster. When we found a perfect one we scooped it up to save.

Later we would write the year on it, spray it with epoxy, and add it to the others that marked another year on the island.

Lunch was eaten seated under a bank of casuarina trees on the shore while looking at the sea and listening to the wind sigh through the branches. A turquoise light, rich as the sea, filtered down on us, the air was heavy, humid, warm. It's as if it was all there, spread out in front of us: the shimmering landscape of our dreams.

We read for a while. At twilight, when the sky was turning peach and gold, we gathered up books, picnic, sand dollars and swimming gear and headed for home. The air had cooled now and the first stars were out, pale against the still-bright sky.

The mosquitoes were also out, tiny, insistent, buzzing, vicious. From the garage we raced for the house, slammed the doors against their attacks, and turned on the ceiling fans. Bugs and all, everything was as usual. A new and promising island year was beginning...

A few days later Nigel Minns came puffing up our path,

his thatch of white hair ruffled by a strong southerly wind which was unusual for October when the prevailing winds are supposed to be from the east. He was carrying a bag of new corn grits, a jar of Miss Edith's home-made guava jam, and a freshly-caught grouper.

"From Edith." He put the gifts on the dining room table. "She couldn't come today as she isn't feeling too well." Since Miss Edith was the spryest, most alert and upbeat eighty-five year-old woman in George Town, if she was not feeling well she must be really ailing. I made a mental note to visit her soon.

Nigel had the latest island news, the bad condition of the roads, who had married, lost a job, left the island for greener pastures, gone to jail, built a house, or died. Because many of Exuma's population is aging, each winter there was usually a new death.

Favoring his right leg, Nigel limped over to the window seat in the Great Room. "I'm not too energetic myself." He eased himself onto the cushions. "South wind today. Humid. Bad for my arthritis. Feels like hurricane weather." Nigel's engaging smile and kind eyes seemed to have been given tolerance by years of hard work and hard living. Over coffee we talked about winds and weather, and the possibility that this new season might still send a hurricane boiling up from the southeast.

Hurricanes were still of concern, particularly to us because we have no hurricane insurance — undoubtedly a foolish economy on our part but done because the insurance is so vastly expensive we simply can't afford it. Of course we're taking a chance and could lose everything. The fact that there hasn't been a really serious hurricane on Exuma for more than 30 years meant nothing; one could blow in at any time, more than likely when we were off-island and unable to take suitable precautions. If one hit we might even have to leave the island.

Exumians, he said, have had their share of hurricanes but they seldom move someplace else after a disaster. "Many have seen other countries" he said, "and like their own country better."

A number of Exumians have lived in the U.S., particularly Florida, and most have visited there, and almost all have relatives there, but they always want to come home to — as Will

Nixon calls it — *this sweet place.*

It was a little late for a hurricane this year but Nigel warned we should always be aware of the possibility that one could at any time strike Exuma. Old island hands, in fact, maintained that because it's been so long since we've had one we were about due to have one of the really big storms with its alphabetical name come rolling and tumbling across the Atlantic from east to west.

Simply put, the pattern is for them to start on the other side of the Atlantic, off the coast of West Africa where the ocean's heat generates an upward swirl of air. As this heated air rises, it spins upward with increasing speed and creates winds of increasing force that spiral around a central vortex.

As this moves across the Atlantic toward the Caribbean and the U.S. it picks up speed and velocity and becomes a terribly destructive force. Its landfall is unpredictable — even our U.S. National Hurricane Center with all its sophisticated technology is still unable to predict when it might suddenly change course and direction.

So, Nigel advised, we must never become complacent about hurricanes but must watch closely to see what the new hurricane season will bring. Neither of us had the slightest idea what we could do about it if one did hit Exuma — except to try and emulate the Exumians and become, as Nigel says, "faith-filled in the face of possible adversity."

A few nights later while at the *P&P* bar chatting with Lermon Rolle, who was brewing up his invention, *The Goombay Smash*: (Bacardi Rum, Galliano, pineapple juice, and ice,) *P&P* owner Stan Benjamin stopped by our bar stools. As often happened at the *P&P* we got talking about the new jet airport, promoted as the gateway for an increase of thousands more tourists.

"Well, maybe, maybe not." Stan had been an island *hotelier* for nearly thirty years. "Exuma doesn't appeal to everyone. In fact some guests checked out this morning after just two days."

We hazarded a guess. "A middle-age couple with two teen-agers?"

Stan nodded. "When they found there was no TV in the rooms they went into a depression. Wife complained about the food and the service. Kids claimed there was nothing to do and refused to talk. Man spent all his time drinking here at the bar. They headed out this morning for Miami and the shopping malls."

We ordered another of Lermon's *Goombay Smashes* and toasted the island's backward ways and bucolic charms.

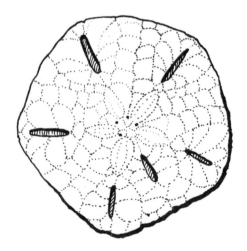

25

Social life on an island can be repetitive and boring. But I learned the hard way not to blithely write off people because of some mistaken mental image about them that I carried around with me like a stone. Casual meetings can be full of surprises.

On an island the size this is, it was possible to see the same people over and over again during the week — at bridge, at lunch, at dinner, on community picnics, at cocktail parties — all of which we seldom attended. Eventually, however, we were invited to a cocktail party at the home of the shell hobbyists and said we would go.

En route, I duly warned my husband not to be surprised if he was subjected to a display of amateur craftwork. With disdainful arrogance I suggested that, in order to remain polite in the face of what I was convinced would be some terribly inept effort, I suggested he should arrange his smile and his remarks beforehand, as I intended to do.

Once there, surrounded by a chattering crowd and while sipping my white wine, I spotted across the room an exquisite flower painting. Wandering over to have a look I found, to my surprise, it was done with shells. They ranged in size from miniscule to the diameter of a quarter, and in color from palest pink, yellow and lavender, to deepest coral, peach and brown. I had a feeling I was about to be embarrassed.

At my elbow, our host, Rodman Page, told me his wife Mary had done the shellwork and he had made the cherrywood frame.

I was sincerely impressed. "So this is the shellwork she's talked about," I said, prepared to eat crow.

"Well no. This is a sideline. Our real pleasure comes from creating — or recreating — sailors' valentines."

"Sailors' valentines?"

"Come see some." Not knowing what to expect, I accompanied him into an adjoining workroom. "They have nothing to do with Valentine's Day," he said, pointing to a shelf of octagonal boxes, "and they weren't made by sailors." He handed me one.

Arranged inside the octagonal glass-covered shadow box was a geometric design made entirely of different sized and colored shells. There were hearts and flowers, anchors and stars, diamonds and squares, compass points and other nautical motifs — in all about 2,000 shells laid out in compartments of different shapes and sizes and separated by cardboard slats.

The completed work measured about eighteen inches in diameter and the box was double-hinged so that it closed and fastened to protect the shell work and facilitate safe packing and carrying. It truly was amazing.

"Why, it's beautiful!" I said. "Like a mosaic."

"Some people do call them shell mosaics. This is one of Mary's original designs, but sometimes she copies one of the traditional antique designs used in the late 1800's."

The Page's started selective shell collecting on the beaches around their home forty years ago. Fifteen years ago, when their collection reached unmanageable numbers, they began making shell mosaics and by now are exhibiting their own designs in galleries and museums nationwide.

When, on another day, I visited Mary in her workroom I found her working on a valentine.

"Our first efforts were replications and experimentations," she said, "when we replicated the early 19th century shellcraft from the West Indies." She wiped some Elmer's Glue from her fingers. "But over the years we gradually moved into a style of our own, what I like to call a happy combination of antique and new designs."

"The antique ones were made in Barbados between 1830 and 1880 as a cottage industry and bought by sailors working on the New England whaling ships," she explained. "Those were the boom years of the New England whaling industry with Nantucket as America's whaling capital. In those days U.S. whaling ships plied the oceans of the world for up to seven years.

Away from their loved ones for a long time, when they returned the sailors presented the shell work to wife, sweetheart or mother as tokens of affection and a souvenir of the exotic lands they had visited."

She showed me photographs of several antique valentines. Some bore sentimental mottoes like *Ever Thine, Remember Me, To One I Love,* or *To My Wife,* printed out in shells; some contained a photograph, a silhouette, a lock of hair, or other personal artifact as the centerpiece. Occasionally there would be a piece of scrimshaw on which there was an etching of a mermaid, or the sailor's whaling ship.

Mary, a petite woman with a heart-shaped face, turned back to her boxes of shells. They were of every hue and shade imaginable. Carefully, she began building up layers of shells one by one; it can take her 35 to 40 to 100 hours and upwards of 2000 shells to complete a single work. Using tweezers, glue, and enormous patience and skill, she carefully glued a circle of tiny rice shells directly onto the floor of the octagonal case. Though occasionally some shells are tinted, their natural colors range from lustrous white and delicate pinks and lavenders to pale greens, purples and browns.

Her motifs were many: hearts and flowers, anchors and stars, diamonds and squares, compass points and other nautical symbols. Sometimes the shellwork is three-dimensional — roses, lilies, daisies or poppies — that spill from baskets or decorate the periphery. On others, wreaths, bouquets, or frilled and scalloped outlines surround a prized shell or a particularly lovely group of shells.

When finished, her work was displayed in one of Rod Page's octagonal shadow boxes of fine polished woods which may measure anywhere from two to twenty inches in diameter and be covered with a pane of clear glass. It may be double-sided and hinged so it can be closed and fastened for safe carrying and sometimes the cover is inlaid with marquetry of mother-of-pearl, cedar, mahogany, maple or pine.

"My hobby has always been woodworking," he explained as he worked away in his workshop across the drive from the house. He was resetting a hinge on an antique case. "Years ago I started making furniture for miniature rooms, moved on to the repair and restoration of antique furniture, especially the American Windsor chair, and now that I'm retired, achieve a lot of satisfaction making the boxes for Mary." He gave a final buff to a box of satin mahogany.

Mary and Rod also restore antique valentines. It was while restoring one of several found in the dusty attic of a Canadian home in Lyford Cay, Bahamas, that Rod removed the centerpiece and found beneath it a yellowed, handwritten note dated 1829. Penned by a homesick British soldier on duty in Barbados, then a British colony, it read:

This box of shellwork was made in Barbados in May 1829. Reader, pity the unfortunate soldier, who, after exhausting his scanty library is thus obliged to employ his time in order to avoid disapation and gambling whilst ingloriously serving his country in a sugar island between the tropics.

(Signed) James Creagh
Capt. 80th Div. Royal
County Down Reg't.

From the first day he saw it Rod wondered about the valentine's box. Of a very heavy dark mahogany, with no glass cover, but with a beautifully carved, hinged lid, it was a puzzle to him. He suspected it was English-made. "It was certainly not made in Barbados," he said, "unless the craftsman took the wood out there with him. I believe it travelled with Capt. Creagh to Barbados as a trinket or jewel box, or a stiff collar box. At one time the lid had a locking mechanism."

By now, thoroughly hooked by sailors' valentines and regretting my former arrogance and disdain, I guiltily offered to see what I could find out about the unhappy British soldier. When an English acquaintance came out from Farnborough, England, to visit friends I asked him if it was possible to track down a British officer who had served King and Empire out in the colonies 165 years ago. Was it now too long ago to trace him?

The British Government, he replied, like all governments, keeps exhaustive records and never throws anything away. When he went back he would be glad to make a search of British Army records in London's War Office Library.

After three months the documents arrived, a thick envelope with a sheaf of papers stuffed inside — copies of several relevant documents from *The Historical Records of the British Army — By Command of His late Majesty William the IVth and under the Patronage of Her Majesty the Queen.* Listed were Lt. James Creagh, along with his brothers, Lt. Jasper Creagh and Major Michael Creagh.

The record stated that they traveled out to the West Indies with the Royal County Down Regiment and concluded that *In January, 1828, the regiment... proceeded to the island of Barbadoes, where Adjutant Dolman, three serjeants, and fifty-six rank and file, died of various fevers.*

According to War Office records of *The Royal Ulster Rifles, a History prepared by Lieut.-Col M.J. P.M. Corbally,* the losses from fever among British Army servicemen serving in the Caribbean were enormous:

> "In May (1837) the service-companies arrived at Chatham (Eng.) having sustained a loss of five officers, and two hundred and ninety-nine soldiers, during the period they had been absent from Great Britain in the Indies, and bringing back four hundred and twenty four effective men."

No wonder that in the face of the death of so many of his buddies and his troops, and desperate to save his sanity, Cap't. James Creagh turned to making sailors' valentines!

The story of Captain Creagh haunted me for months. I wondered what happened to him. Did this bored and lonely officer live to return to his own country — or did he, too, die in service to the Crown while protecting commercial trade in a remote and far-off colony of the British Empire?

Said Rod, shaking his head as he fastened the last screw in the octagonal box, "unfortunately, because of thoughtless collecting and mounting ocean pollution, obtaining shells is becoming increasingly difficult."

"And," Mary added, "sad to say, though we've always been careful to take only a few at a time, beach-combing for shells as we used to do right in front of our house is not as easy as it used to be when we first came."

Rod lifted the finished shadow box from his workbench. In a stray shaft of sunlight the beautifully polished wood glowed like fine satin. "At least the mosaics will preserve the beauty of shells and people will be able to see the wonderful treasures our seas contain." He paused. "Or, if we're not all more selective when we go shelling, someday I may have to say,*used* to contain."

I stopped by to visit Miss Edith and found her not "feeling poorly" as Nigel had said, but standing tall and elegant in her kitchen cooking guava jam. Her two miniature poodles, Teddy the black one and Honey Bun the white, cavorted around her ankles.

"Nigel said you weren't feeling well."

She tossed her head. "Oh that Nigel." Down went the wooden spoon she'd been using to stir the jam. "He's always worrying about me. As you can see I'm *fine*. Let's sit down and I'll tell you what was *really* bothering me. It's nothing *he'd* ever tell."

We went into the living room and sat down on her chintz-covered couch. A few days earlier Nigel suffered a stroke, she said, nothing serious, according to the doctor, who warned him that from now on he must rest, take his medication, and not do any strenuous exercise or heavy lifting. Edith's face was serious, her eyes worried as she spoke of this event in their lives, her manner evidencing her affection and concern for her husband.

"Of course, he wouldn't tell you *that*. And well, as a result of it I did have a bad spell, oh, not because he might die — we're both prepared for that whenever it comes — after all, we are both nearing ninety — but because I'd miss him so much if I was left behind for too long." Honey Bun jumped into her lap and she stroked him with her long slim hands.

She explained that it was their belief that since death is as inevitable as birth, there was no reason to fear it, or worry about it, and so she didn't; God had promised to "take them home." She made it sound very sensible and without any anxiety. "Oh, I tell you," she gave me her sweet smile, lips turned up at the corners, and said, "I know there's nothing to be anxious about because I know Nigel will be waiting for me whenever I do get there. It's just that —" she looked away, her delicate hands stroking Honey Bun, "— we've been together 67 years and I dread him going on without me."

26

Books play a different role here from what they do in a more modern, TV-watching society. In an isolated existence a major part of life is lived through books. They not only revive memories of home, but provide learning, study, travel and opinions which tend to make the reader more grateful (or angrier, or more disgusted, or happier) than if they were read in the States where, these days, unfortunately, reading books appears to be in decline. But not in Exuma.

Though the George Town library had few resources, its quaintness, its total lack of technology, its friendly atmosphere, manageable size, varied titles, and all-volunteer staff was a delight. It was a haven and a refuge and I spent many hours browsing through the books, most of them paperbacks, some of them dusty tomes left over from the personal libraries of colonial days and smelling of damp and mildew, some of them newly-issued books on the *New York Times* bestseller list donated by generous winter residents or boaters.

As if to stave off a famine worse than mere food deprivation, I brought home armfuls of mysteries, biographies, musty classics with the covers coming off, old maps and charts, books of poems written by people long dead, leatherbound copies of Shakespeare's plays, romances, cookbooks, and trashy novels.

The small two-room library — a dingy white with faded blue trim and board shutters — was situated in the center of town across from the straw market. From its packed dirt front yard eight steps led up to a dilapidated wooden porch. It badly needed a new roof — not surprising considering it is the last vernacular building in George Town and has been many things in its long life: a private home, a schoolroom, a courtroom and a jail. As far as could be discovered, the building is almost as old as the century.

In its present role as public library it was started under the auspices of the Exuma Ladies' Club in 1972. Since no government support — other than free use of the building — has ever been accepted the library has always been staffed entirely by volunteers. Alterations and repairs have also been done by volunteers. In 1985 the back veranda was filled in and became the paperback room. The Jo Morris children's room was donated by a gracious winter resident of long-standing who dedicated herself to doing what she could to help make island life better. The room is a great favorite with the children from the pink and yellow primary school on the hill behind the library. During their morning break the various classes come in one at a time with their teacher, along with the children from the island's private school.

The unofficial head librarian is Pat Adney, a diminutive English-woman bursting with energy who came to live here twenty-seven years ago in the days when the Bahamas was still a British colony. Ken, her engineer husband, worked for the British Cable and Wireless Company laying in telephone and electric cable and supervising road building. Sometime after Bahamian Independence in 1972 the company pulled out but Ken and Pat stayed on, built a house, and have made the island their home.

She and the other women who ran the library have devoted endless hours without pay, or much support, to keeping it going. A major part of Pat's job was to persuade anyone she can to donate their new or used books. Two rooms bulging with books testify to her success. The library is open two hours a day, from 10 a.m. to noon, six days a week, and is used by Bahamians, tourists, winter residents and visiting yachters, many of whom have generously sent books upon their return to the U.S. American school librarians are among those most determined to help.

During this, our fifth winter, a volunteer position was vacated when an aging, incumbent volunteer died. Feeling somewhat like a hearse-chasing lawyer, I applied for the position and to my delight was taken on immediately. From then on, every Tuesday and Thursday morning, I bumped and jolted eleven miles over the pot-holed main highway to George Town, glad to be out of the house and in town where the action was.

By this time the little building was in better repair. Darville Lumber had donated vinyl floor tiles, some men volunteers built more shelves, and Pat and two women painted the interior. The porch still needed repair and the roof still leaked in some places, but these materials were costly and there was no money for such things so they went undone.

From the first it was a job I loved. Not only was I surrounded by books but I got to meet all kinds of people — Bahamians, winter residents, and boaters who were attracted by the swap shelf (bring one, take one.) Best of all, I met the local schoolchildren.

"Any new books today?" they invariably asked, eager to be the first to read something just in. Like American children the same age their favorites were the Berenstein Bears and Dr. Seuss, emphasizing in my mind that, indeed, there must be some really quite simple universal themes that bind all children together.

Island schools have a dress code so the children were clean, newly-brushed, and neatly dressed in school uniforms — brown and white checked shirts, with a brown tunic for the girls and brown shorts for the boys. (High school students' uniforms are red and white-checked shirts and grey tunics or trousers.) Refreshingly polite and well-mannered, the children were not without the usual childish high spirits and mischief.

One child in particular was irresistible, tiny nine-year-old Latrivia with her dimples and pink-bowed pigtails. A *gamine* with a mischievous smile and a super-quick mind, she read everything she could, grasped it immediately, understood it all, asked a hundred questions, and was completely captivating.

One day one of the boys was scolded for playing a trick on her. "Leon," said one of the volunteers, "you know she is looking for those books she's just checked out. Stop hiding them and give them to her."

Latrivia leapt to his defense. "That's all right, Ma'm. He's not hiding them. He's my boyfriend. He's holding them."

Startled that this might be some dangerous early alliance and envisioning some future teenage pregnancy or worse, the librarian said, "Latrivia! Aren't you a little young to have a boyfriend?"

"Oh, we aren't goin' to get married or anything," the *gamine* replied with cool self-assurance, "but I read better'n he does so I help him with his homework, an' he teaches me arithmetic." After that we noticed them, sitting side by side on the low stone wall of the schoolyard, heads together as they poured over a book, the *each one teach one* idea in its most basic form.

Boaters by the dozens used the library. Since George Town's Elizabeth Harbour was not only a stopping-off place for "yachties" heading south to the Caribbean and Venezuela, but a hangout for those spending the winter, by December each year it was filled up with sailboats. By mid-January well over 400 boats often lay anchored in Elizabeth harbor.

To a great extent they benefited the island economy but their presence was considered a mixed blessing. Some of them were generous. They donated books to the library, sometimes they taught classes of their particular specialty at a local school, they ran benefits, hosted a cruising regatta, and raiseed scholarship funds to send bright Exumian students to school in Nassau. This was the kind of yachter everyone liked to see drop anchor and stay awhile.

Others were not so considerate. Without thanks, or any show of gratitude, they used the library and island facilities to the utmost, littering the beaches around the harbor and cluttering them up with bits and pieces of flotsam and jetsam; on certain beaches they hung signs, painted the rocks, cut trails — and left it all behind when they sailed away. They also dumped trash in inappropriate places and polluted the harbor by emptying their sewage into the water.

But the good ones, like Jaz, were brushed by angel-dust...

27

Before Jaz breezed into the library we experienced the usual influx of boaters. It used to be assumed that all boat owners are millionaires and it takes a while to realize that the old saying *"if you have to ask how much a yacht costs you can't afford one"* — no longer applies. These days anyone can sail around in a yacht. There are big, little and medium yachts, yachts built in the backyard and palatial floating palaces of the Hollywood kind, with kitchen, single beds, wall-to-wall carpeting, wet and dry bar, TV, radar, and a patio deck. Some even carry a helicopter.

Some are sailed by their owners. Others are party boats like the huge and gleaming power yacht *Monkey Business*, the one that witnessed Senator Gary Hart's downfall. This type was chartered purely for the purpose of onboard fun and comes with or without accompanying boat bunnies, and with or without a captain and crew, at which point it is called a barebones rental.

Some boats are captained by experts, men and women long familiar with the sea. Others are sailed inexpertly by wannabees who hope to learn the ropes while afloat. This is usually a mistake, since they are the ones who most often get hung up on a shoal somewhere and have to call for help from BASRA, the Bahamian Air-Sea Rescue fleet.

Boaters fall easily into types. *The Booze Cruisers* are easy to spot because of their bleary eyes and the ruddy complexions that have nothing to do with exposure to the sun and wind. *The Old Salts*, on the other hand, are the ones who, day and night, you can hear on the VHF radio:

"Ninja Man to Sea Dog, Ninja Man to Sea Dog, do you read me, Arnie? OVER."

"Hi there, Ninja Man, this is Born Free. Your signal is weak. Want me to raise The Dog? OVER."

"Reading you poorly, Born Free. Switch to 68. OVER."

"Hi, Born Free. Read you a strong five now. Do you read me okay? OVER."

"Ho Ninj! This is Dog. Hey Fred, where the devil are you? Where've you been? Howya doin'? Can you read me? OVER."

"Read you loud and clear, Dog. You read me Born Free? OVER."

"Yeah Turtle Man, I read you. Do you read me? "I read you. Heard from No Regrets yet?..."

Then there's The *Nouveau Adventurer* — usually a Wall Street yuppie with lots of newly-acquired disposable income from investment banking or asset management. He mostly sails around the harbor bare-chested and bronzed, with a bikini-clad companion draped across the foredeck. Or, he parades around town looking like Errol Flynn in white pants, navy blazer and a yachting cap and is fond of recounting how expertly he navigated Galliot Cut in a storm and only escaped the dangerous coral heads off Stocking Island Light by some devilishly clever maneuvering. People avoid him.

The Vagabond is immediately recognizable. His old wooden tub is one he's resurrected from some boat graveyard in Lauderdale or Savannah. He's caulked its ailing joints, patched up its creaky timbers with some two-by-fours and paint, and one fine day sailed into the sunset bent upon forever staying a free man; unfortunately for him, he hadn't counted on being tied to a boat in need of perpetual care. Only eternal patching and bailing will keep it from sinking to the bottom.

Without income, and little cash, he "borrows" to stay alive. Food, ("just a cup of sugar,") tools, ("I'll bring your valve wrench right back,") sunscreen ("not much in this tube, I'll just use it up,") fuel ("I only need a gallon,") and a little hospitality ("mind if I come on home with you and have a hot shower?")

Often charming (like Pete Balloil,) sometimes a rogue or a thief, *The Vagabond* can easily be recognized by his bare feet, dirty tee shirt, sawed-off shorts, scraggy beard, unwashed hair, and a boat that looks like a peddlar's cart. Pots and pans, glass floats, fishnet, the monthly washing, driftwood, old wine bottles, plastic containers, hanks of rope, and a lot of other "found objects" litter the deck and hang like christmas tree ornaments from the stays. Sometimes he is liked, most times he is avoided.

While realizing the yachters importance to tourism, Exumians either ignore them or heartily resent this annual Invasion of The Yacht People. At the library they are gossiped about endlessly, blamed for damp books, missing books, seawater all over the floor, and, because some don't want to pay the $2 membership fee ("I'll only be here a week!") are considerd stingy.

Then one day in strolled Jaz.

He didn't fit any mold. Young, jaunty, friendly, and very self-assured, he had tanned skin, gleaming white teeth, sparkling blue eyes, and a deep cleft in his chin that made him look like the Bourbon Man. He wore a navy blue bandanna tied to one side over his curly black hair. "Hi, ladies," he said, and with his first words he set us all a-twitter.

He was the captain of a yacht owned by a wealthy businessman who left his boat tied up to the Exuma dock for the winter and flew in occasionally for the weekend. Consequently, Jaz had a lot of free time on his hands, and was sometimes bored. He looked around the library.

We watched as with undisguised curiousity he scrutinized the place, prodded various boards with his pocketknife, and finally said, "back home I restore old houses for a living. I can see you need a new roof on this building." We told him we knew that but there was no money. And that even if there was money, all our volunteers — Exumian and non-Exumian alike — had been used to the max and couldn't be asked to do yet another building job.

"The boaters can do it." he said. "I'll organize them."

It seemed unlikely he'd be able to do it and when he left we figured we'd seen the last of him. A week passed and we were too busy to think about it any more. At one point a *Vagabond Boater* wandered in — barefoot, bearded, unkempt, and dressed in the usual grotty tee shirt and sawed off jeans — and wanted to know if we could lend him — not a book or a razor — but a cupful of floor washing liquid.

He said he'd be glad to repay the loan by doing any odd jobs around the place. His cup was at the ready so Pat filled it and told him there wasn't anything to be done at present since we had no money to pay for odd jobs. He nodded and holding his cup of Mr. Clean, wandered out.

Then Jaz was back. He'd organized not only his fellow

boaters but the local merchants, some of the townspeople, the school kids, and using the VHF marine radio had announced a *Help Fix Up The Library* campaign. Promising the rewards of virtue and library memberships to all who donated money, he announced, "Twenty-five dollars will buy you a lifetime membership! And you'll feel great about yourself!"

Prompted either by his rich deep voice on the VHF radio, or his persuasive manner, boaters almost at once began stopping by to drop off checks; one was for $100. When asked if she meant to give so much, the woman said she was a former librarian in New Jersey and knew how important a library is to children. At Jaz's suggestion the donors names were posted on the library bulletin board, along with their boat's name. Over the next week the list got longer and longer.

A week later, after he'd raised over $2,500, Jazz and his volunteer crew of Bahamians and men and women boaters, swarmed over the building like pioneer farmers at a barn-raising. They pried off shingles, replaced beams, reshingled the roof. Another group, deciding on their own that the place needed painting, left $400 for paint before they sailed away. Jaz and his volunteers were not only able to repaint the outside but the inside as well.

We couldn't believe it; were these the same people who balked at paying a $2 membership fee?

Well, no; those people can be found everywhere, but as so often happens they are in the minority, and are offset by the numerous generous-hearted souls who were happy to pitch in to aid in the restoration of a neighboring country's precious resource. Many promised to send books once they'd returned home, and did.

A few days after everything was back in place the *Vagabond Boater* wandered in, full of apology.

He wasn't able to return the floor washing liquid, and had no books to swap, but if we would let him join the library and borrow books, he'd do any painting that needed to be done — providing, of course, we had the paint. Pat and I looked at one another and, much to his astonishment, burst out laughing as Pat handed him a membership card.

28

For someone used to modern urban life, living on Exuma requires invention, resourcefulness, and learning all kinds of ways to amuse and engage your energy. Some people paint, some write, many of the men fish, some women sew or play bridge, others are happy plying a craft, doing handwork, gardening, letter-writing, journal-keeping, or stamp-collecting. Carpentry and puttering occupy others. Resourcefulness is all — especially when you invite guests and things go wrong, as they are bound to do.

Inviting friends for a sunny vacation away from their winter weather is one of the pleasures of living here. But because it is an island, with not a lot of amusements, you have to be careful whom you invite. Two weeks can be a long time to be with bored or restless guests, all the time cooking and cleaning and finding amusing things for them to do... for that matter, one week can be a long time under those circumstances.

Never had I so eagerly anticipated houseguests. I intended to make a houseparty to end all houseparties. I was busy for weeks ahead preparing the house, the beds, the food and the entertainment. What I was not prepared for was that it could all go wrong.

Four women, my oldest friends, were coming to visit. We'd known one another almost all our lives. The four attended kindergarten together; they called themselves the Kinder Garden Babies, or the KGB. Two of them, born next door to each other, had shared a playpen. All married, all with adult children, they still lived within a few miles of one another and saw one another frequently.

I didn't come into the group until grade eight but was accepted, loved, and eventually became the wandering member, the one who came and went, who worked as a journalist in exotic countries like Ethiopia, Lebanon, Sierra Leone, Saudi Arabia and the Bahamas. Always, they were there for me, to bid me goodbye with presents and good wishes, to welcome me back with hugs and parties and the latest gossip.

We'd gone together through school, summer camp, teenage dating, broken romances, broken hearts, and stood up at one another's weddings. We'd since attended one another's children's weddings, and commiserated and laughed and cried over aging parents, greying hair, deepening wrinkles and mannerless grandchildren. Barb the beauty, Katie the irrepressible, Joyce the graceful and Pat the quiet one; I loved them equally.

I had planned their visit down to the last detail — the food we'd eat, the places we'd go, the videos we'd watch, the conversations we'd have, the picnic spots we'd visit, the fun it would all be. I made lists, and lists of lists; nothing was over-looked or left to chance. Everything was going to be perfect, run on time, and conform to my master plan. It would be the houseparty they'd never forget. A rerun of High School Daze.

Obviously I had preplanned a disaster. I'd orchestrated the impossible: the Perfect Vacation. Everything that could go wrong, would. And did.

On the afternoon of their arrival a festive but simple dinner was ready to go into the oven — succulent chops, baked potatoes and baked Exuma squash, with a tossed salad, wine and lemon souffle. Perfect.

In case the plane was late, which it often was, I wouldn't turn on the oven until we returned from the airport. While dinner cooked we'd drink a welcoming glass of champagne to our longtime friendship. I grew maudlin at the very thought of our joy. My dear, darling childhood friends... who, if I was to be honest, I not only loved but hoped to impress with our island lifestyle.

The plane *was* late so it was after seven o'clock by the time we reached the house. They were tired, hungry, and travel-weary. I was elated to have us together again. "You get yourselves settled in," I told them gaily, flying around like a Tupperware hostess, "and I'll get supper started and open the champagne." I loaded dinner into the stove and turned it on. Nothing happened.

No gas.

At this hour? On a weekend? How long would it take to find a propane tank at this hour? I hadn't the wit to calculate.

In the first of several crisis-saving acts that week, my husband got in the car and sought Christine. Though she was already dressed to attend Wednesday night prayer meeting, she obligingly changed from her black pumps and wide-brimmed straw hat with the roses on it to her workboots and baseball cap. She drove the van to one of her rental houses and let him borrow the propane tank.

At ten-thirty, as we finally sat down to dinner, there was a downpour. The electricity went off. The bugs arrived in force. I'd forgotten to buy OFF! That night one of the four friends, exhausted from her day, snored so loudly it shook the house and kept everyone awake.

The unplanned events were only the first of a series.

The sunny days were an aphrodisiac to our KGB guests and from the time of their arrival they understandably wanted to spend as much as possible of the day outdoors. Despite our warnings about the heat, the glare, and the bite of the near-equatorial sun, they jumped out of bed, raced to the sea, and for the rest of the day dressed as scantily as was decent.

But the rule of a tropical sun is — seek shade! Coolth is all! (As well as resourcefulness.) Forget the sun's danger at your peril! When you forget any or all of this wisdom sunburn is inevitable!

So on the second day their burned skin fired up in a fine example of skin-blistering. This, for a while, meant no more beaching, swimming or sun. Pat, fairest of all, was burned most and had to stay out of the sea, go around sweating in slacks, dark glasses, a wide-brimmed sun hat, and one of my husband's long sleeved shirts buttoned to the neck. Not a lot of fun.

We stayed indoors more than I'd planned. Nor was it just the sun... city dwellers all, they are somewhat fearful of the insects, the garden bugs, and all the other winged and crawling things outside, especially the lizards. When I reminded them of our indifference to the snakes and bugs of our summer weeks at girls' camp, they shuddered. That was different. Then we were young.

One day, we all flocked to the car and had started on our

way to town when we realized we were missing Joyce. My husband, happy to see my old friends — and my enjoyment of them — found it difficult to keep track of one woman let alone five, and had accidently locked Joyce in the house. Another time he drove off from town leaving Kay. "You married a saint," Barb said. "My husband would never put up with this."

When Mr.Flowers came by he marveled. "Wince, you're one lucky man. Call me if you need help."

Worn out by the day's sun and fresh air, my friends fell asleep early, leaving me with the day's plan incomplete, the witty conversations unsaid, the videos unviewed and the resulting weighty discussions unexpressed.

For their last night I'd planned a sumptuous dinner as a farewell. Halfway through, it was still going well. Well-primed by lots of wine, we sat reminiscing around the table in the Great Room; Kay was leaning back against the small wooden buffet which formed one end of the windowseat. At a particularly funny memory we all laughed uproariously, my husband too, but none of us has ever laughed like Kay.

Flinging herself exuberantly back against the wooden buffet, which my husband for some time had intended to fasten to the windowseat but hadn't gotten around to yet, Kay tossed back her head and *really* let go with some deep belly laughter.

From where I was sitting across from her I could see the potted plants, the blue vase and the oil lamp slowly start to disappear as they slid off the top of the tilting buffet. As its doors flew open all the plates, glasses, cups, saucers and sherbert dishes were released and smashed to the floor with a resounding CRASH! — seconds ahead of the buffet and a surprised Kay.

She was unhurt. When we extracted her from amid the shards of glass and china she was apologizing profusely while I was laughing. Wotthehell, I figured. What ever made me think I could regulate this house party? If the island and its people had taught me anything it was that life *happens*. It cannot be regulated or preplanned.

At departure all four women said they'd had a wonderful, memorable time. Waving them goodbye at the new airport I felt a wing brush of melancholy. For one moment I wished we could all be together again as those five happy carefree girls. But only for a moment. Not only does life "happen," time happens too, and we move on; fortunately, old friends and happy memories abide and endure.

That visit gave me a valuable insight. After nearly four years wintering on the island I could see that an old attitude of mine had changed. Even up until last year I would have been upset by the small disasters of the KGB visit, but I was able to shrug them off as unimportant. No doubt about it, I was getting used to the island's laid back style of living.

...which was just as well because it was going to take all our patience and resolve to get a mechanic to repair our rusting Chevy Cavalier.

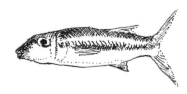

"It's not like the good ole U.S.of A.," commented a winter resident describing his problem of getting his car fixed, "there you only have to deal with cheats, liars and greed. Here you only have to worry about getting it back before you — or it — dies of old age. Basically, Bahamians aren't dishonest, just slow."

While it was true that working with island repairmen of all kinds could drive you quietly nuts, by and large they do try to do their best. Yet do-it-yourself repairs and maintenance is a fact of life on the island and those looking to live on one need to know about it. Homeowners here need to be handy at a variety of tasks, including car mechanics — unfortunately a talent my versatile husband did not possess.

So when the Chevy started acting up we took it to a smiling rogue who always greeted us with a "no prob-lem, mon, it'll be ready Wednesday" — while hoping we couldn't see the yard full of invalid cars awaiting his ministrations. He took a quick look and told us our Chevy needed a whole new muffler system. He would order it from Nassau.

Like many an island repairmen he was voluble but unskilled.

Carpenters, plumbers, mechanics — you name it — they all have accommodating smiles but only minimal training and experience. They have learned, however, to submit an itemized bill. A local plumber hired to work on our neighbor's water pump presented a bill that read:

To repaear pomp line:
$20 to go there
$20 to take pipe out the well
$20 for giving up on

Despite increasing insistence in some educational quarters to teach vocational skills, these were not being taught in Exuma's schools and could be accumulated only on the job from self-taught practitioners. If the Hubert Ingraham-led government won this year's election, this was slated to change. New vocational schools were promised.

After a three-week wait we were still waiting for our muffler. Driving without a proper muffler was a vehicle violation; we couldn't go much longer without being stopped by the George Town police. When we asked at the garage why it hadn't come we were told it was "out of stock." But no problem. "For sure" it would be on the next mailboat.

For a whole week we tried to drive quietly through town, the gears in neutral, coasting whenever we could. After a month our smiling mechanic told us the muffler would not be coming because the company had been sold.

But not to worry! He could order one from Florida or — come to think of it — he just happened to have a second-hand one in the shop which he could alter to fit our car and if we said so, would install that day. We said go ahead.

By the next day it had fallen off. He fixed it. It fell off again. He fixed it (charging us each time.) The next time it totally fell apart.

Stanley arrived. "Oh, you don't want to go to that smiling thief," he said scathingly. "You must go to Reverend Adam Brown in Farmer's Hill. He's a minister of the Baptist Church but he repairs cars on the side. Learned it in the States. He's an honest man." We took the car to Reverend Brown and within two days he had found a muffler and installed it. From then on it worked fine.

29

One of the first questions invariably asked when you meet a stranger here is always, "how did you find Exuma?" As if it was a rare jewel, which of course it is. The answers are as varied as the people, often amusing, and sometimes surprising.

Like us, few winter residents actually planned ahead to buy a house here. Blanche Frenning was one of the exceptions. Now a doughty ninety year-old of New England stock, she had never let her two artificial knees or her heart problem prevent her from spending every October to May on the island. The doctors at Mass General told her they couldn't repair her heart because they "couldn't sew eggshells" but if she would take life easy and swallow three kinds of pills every day she could live as long as she wanted.

Four years ago they figured she had one year, two years max. Little did they know this feisty lady who preferred to be called Inchie. It suited her because she was only five feet tall.

"One year, two years — pah!" she was fond of saying. "They live in Boston. They don't know Exuma."

She told them she couldn't die yet. She had too much left to do: great-grandchildren to see into adulthood, trees to plant, *Chaos* to read and understand, more study to do on her theory of negative gravity, and a new word processor to learn. She informed the doctors that more than their expert advice she needed to return to Exuma, and had done so every winter since.

Inchie's early homesteading on Exuma was a planned affair. A determined woman, with architectural training and a flair for design, she knew exactly the kind of house and the location she wanted and for many years had searched for the right spot. In 1962, then in her late fifties, she and her husband sailed into Elizabeth Harbour on a friend's yacht. Seeing George Town she announced "this is it!" From then on her life revolved around designing and building the Exuma house, a feat not without a mountain of problems.

Not the least of these was the formidable job of building on the small cay she'd chosen a few hundred yards off the main island shore. It was about two miles outside George Town, was without a causeway, a road, water or electricity. Rounding up workmen, she had the causeway built, and a road, and a dock to handle the building supplies being shipped in from Florida. Those challenges, plus sitting out a hurricane or two, didn't daunt her one bit and today her lovely house stands witness to this doughty lady's courage and determination. (More about Inchie later.) But for most of us, coming to live on Exuma happened unexpectedly, or, as with us, gradually. Planning ahead as Inchie did was not how most of us got here. In fact, that subject, too, was a favorite topic of conversation.

Even those early settlers, the American Loyalists, didn't plan to move here but were opting out of a democracy they were convinced would be ruled by the rabble. They probably got directed here by some eighteenth century British travel agent working for George the Third — who likely thought it a good commercial investment to have Brits living here so when Spanish ships sailed by they could be enticed by lights onto the offshore shoals. Once there, a party of brigand Englishmen would "save" the ship and its treasures for the king.

Stories of how we non-Bahamian winter residents got here vary. One man, a fellow writer, admitted he came because he drinks and writes. "There are those who drink, and there are decent people," he says. "There are those who write, and there are decent people. I live here because I'm not decent on either count and here nobody cares."

Another said, "I found this was the only place I sleep all day and still sleep soundly at night." One resident came because of the gardening, another the superb bonefishing, still another for the quiet. Said one honest man, "I made a bundle on junk bonds and I needed to stash it in a place where the IRS won't find it." (He's probably going to regret it because since then the U.S. and Bahamian governments have worked out a deal whereby, if the IRS requests it, any offshore U.S. funds above

$10,000 deposited in a Bahamian bank must be reported if just cause is shown.)

Often tourists will come and become so enamored of the place on their first visit they immediately buy a house. Big mistake. Only after at least two or three visits should one buy, four or five visits is better — and then only after having spent more than a week at a local hotel and talked to homeowners. Not every foreigner can live on the island, and the longer you live here the more you appreciate that fact.

For example, if you enjoy dining out Exuma is not the place to come for gourmet food. The conversation is usually interesting, though, and sometimes confrontational.

Until the early 1990's dining out on the island was mostly a matter of eating plain fare, usually peas and rice and fried chicken with fresh cole slaw or conch salad; sometimes hamburgers or conchburgers, occasionally freshly-caught fish. While tasty, it could never be considered gourmet food. One American travel magazine called island food "fatty, fried and monotonous," which was a little unfair, and which you can be sure did the tourist trade no good.

It was really not that bad, though. Bahamians are tolerably good cooks but native Bahamain food, though often tasty, is seldom varied. There were few trained chefs, and because the island is so remote all foodstuffs have to come by plane or mailboat, so much of it is not fresh. New York it's not, nor Rome nor Paris. Not even Nassau which has a fine array of topnotch restaurants.

The formerly-elegant *Out Island Inn*, and the once-attractive *Pieces of Eight Hotel* were closed along with their restaurants. A couple of local eateries existed — in particular Iva Bowe's, a Bahamian cafe where the decor is minimal and the food excellent. But fine dining as it is thought of stateside is found only at the *P&P*, its sister hotel *The Beach Inn*, or the charming, new *Coconut Cove*. All three have pretty dining rooms overlooking the water, serve a variety of American and Bahamian dishes, and some respectable wines.

Operating any restaurant on a tiny out island is, of course, a risk. Tourism is seasonal — six months at best — so going into the restaurant business here is optimistic. More than the desire to make money it's an act of devotion to good food, hard work, and the hope of benefitting the community. And when all food is prepared fresh on the premises every day it is a miracle.

Gemelli's the newly-opened Italian cafe, located on the main street across from John Marshall's Liquor Store, was a welcome addition to George Town's culinary scene and a place where, because the owners themselves had a stormy relationship, the talk was lively.

On a warm starry night soon after it opened we drove into town to try the food. Light spilled from the wide windows and splashed across the small cement terrace bordering the sidewalk. Boaters and islanders sat talking and laughing on the low cinder block wall that separated the terrace from the roadway, and that in itself was encouraging in a town where after-dark conviviality on a Saturday night sometimes revolved around drunken boaters and tourists, and rowdy, beer-drinking Exumian youths.

The cafe was decorated in Italian flag colors with bright green shutters, red trim around the door and whitewashed walls. The big airy room inside had an open kitchen along one side with a counter top displaying bowls of fresh fruit, pies and cakes under glass domes, and baskets of fresh tomatoes, peppers, garlic, onions, and eggplant. Several flats of growing herbs — parsley, sweet basil, thyme — filled the air with good smells. Red geraniums trailed from windowboxes and through an open rear door facing the harbor wafted a warm sea breeze. The place felt cosy, friendly and welcoming.

The Bahamian owner said he and his Sicilian wife had considered opening an Italian restaurant in Miami but decided that wouldn't bring any jobs or benefits to the island people, so instead they did it here on the island where the Bahamian member of the partnership was born.

His wife appeared from the kitchen side of the counter with a big scarlet apron around her waist and asked what we'd like to eat. We asked to see the menu. "You don't need a menu," she said, "I'll fix you something good. It'll take a while so have a coffee." She headed for the kitchen behind the counter and our host fetched coffee.

So far, they were doing all right, he said. His wife was a superb cook. People liked the food and the atmosphere. The school kids came in to buy a pizza slice for lunch — good nutritious food. "I tell you," his chest went out, "when a group of Italian tourists were here last week they ate here every night and said the food was terrific. Now THAT'S Italian!"

Eventually, we were served a medium pizza, two house salads of fresh greens shining with olive oil and vinegar — and some *focaccia* a light crusty hotbread drizzled with olive oil, Italian seasonings and spices.

"Did my husband tell you why we opened this year?" his wife asked. "Because when the ghost of Columbus comes back to the Bahamas for his 500th Anniversary next year he'll be able to get a real Italian pizza instead of Bahamian peas and rice." Along with the pizza she set down a basket of fresh bread, and a small dish of tortellini. "It was left over from an earlier order of *small* eaters," she said, her disdain for small eaters evident, the curl of her lip making delicate appetites sound like a crime.

Four boaters arrived and pushed two tables together. Two Bahamian couples came in. The owner went and sat with them. They ordered *Kalik* (Bahamian-made beer,) and pizza from Debbie, the waitress. The boaters ordered pizzas. The owner teased one of the Bahamians about his loud shirt. Quips and jokes flew. Suddenly it became a party as the whole place got caught up in a friendly crossfire about clothes, money, politics, feminism, and island living. Then one of the boaters who turned out to be a Canadian journalist, turned to us and brought up the subject of race relations. Subtly, the mood shifted.

"You ever think there'll come a day when this third world Country won't want you here?" he asked in a loud voice. "You ever consider you might lose everything? Let's face it, it's the rich versus the poor these days, isn't it? The *haves* versus the *have-nots*. On this island you're one of the *haves*. Doesn't that worry you?"

Our host frowned but held his peace and said nothing. The other Bahamians looked away in — embarrassment? — but appeared to be listening.

Actually, it was hard to know how to reply to this kind of remark. To protest or contradict it seems defensive and unecessary. The words *haves* and *have-nots* are a catch-phrase, as is *third world country*; both neatly categorize two-thirds of the world's population into a manageable mass that allows us to forget it's composed of our fellow mortals, each of whom has his, or her, own needs and wants, weaknesses and strengths.

Finally my husband said "it's the Bahamians' country and maybe someday they'll want us to leave, but so far it hasn't happened." The Canadian came in on another tack.

"You like being the minority race here?"

"It's an enlightening position to be in for a change," I said.

"Doesn't it bother you?"

"No. We never notice it, or think about it."

"That's hard to believe."

I could feel my ire rising at this bumptious man, my face flushing. I drew breath but before I could speak, the owner's wife called from the kitchen, "hey mon, once you know someone you move past skin color to character and values."

Our host got up. "You might consider us the *have-nots* but I don't think of myself that way. You, honey?" The fiery Sicilian, was coming from the kitchen with a steaming pizza on a tray and fire in her eye. We held our breath, expecting fireworks.

"You ever look around this island, mon?" She thumped down the steaming pizza in front of the Canadian. Hands on hips she confronted him. "You see any have-nots here? Any third world? Any homeless? Any hungry kids? Homeless kids? Mean streets where you can't walk at night? Rat-infested tenements? Dope dens? Shoot-outs, daily killings, old ladies being mugged?"

"Well I..."

"And you won't." She flourished a sharp knife and attacked the pizza with a deft hand. "You think we're have-nots? Well, mister, on this island we live better than most. Maybe we don't have big cars and fancy homes but what we have is better'n that."

One eye on the pizza knife, the man hastily apologized.

Not everyone who "finds" Exuma is made welcome.

30

lthough the Columbus Quincentennial Year was still eleven months away, on the island it was a hot topic. A yacht race from Columbus's starting point in Spain was going to end up in Exuma and the place was already gearing up for the second Columbus landing on Bahamas' shores.

One man kept wandering into the library day after day so that I wondered what he was up to. He'd walk in out of the rain each time, dripping water from his yellow sou'wester onto the floor, a small wiry man in his fifties with long red-blond hair and a rusty beard. He seldom spoke and I was curious.

He looked like an 18th century sea captain, tough, craggy and weatherbeaten. Throughout a five-day stretch of rain and high winds he kept checking out books on Columbus, so many that I finally asked him if he was researching Columbus and if so, why.

"I'm going to sail to San Salvador soon as this wind lets up and do *The Columbus Thing*." Saying that, he looked somewhat embarrassed, as if he revealing a sentimental streak, or too much about himself. "Umm-mm — ah — mmm-mmm — I'm going to sail there following his log."

This meant, he said, approaching the island from the southern tip as Columbus did, finding the same anchorage, viewing the island at 2 a.m. and stepping ashore at dawn. This salty would-be Columbus was obviously reluctant to admit this to a stranger because he was obviously on some kind of personal odyssey and didn't want to talk about it. A private man. A loner.

"But you're a year early," I pointed out. "The Columbus Quincentennial is next year." He said he had to do it before the crowds arrived and the government officials and VIP's screwed up the moment. That made sense and sounded like great fun.

Since I'd also been doing some research on Columbus for a magazine piece I was working on I asked him if he was aware there was no consensus on where Columbus first set foot in the New World. As far as I could see, the great explorer may actually have gotten lost and waded ashore on any one of a number of islands in the region. Perhaps Eleuthera, or Samana Cay, or — as some historians suggested — Puerto Rico.

Yes, he was aware of that controversy — and had already discounted it. Four years earlier, at the 1987 Conference of the Ibero-American States in Puerto Rico, the Caribbean countries agreed — probably for the sake of the forthcoming Quincentennial tourism dollars — that it *was* San Salvador. So be it as far as he was concerned.

"I envy you your trip," I said as I handed him the library copy of *Admiral of the Ocean Sea* by American author Samuel Eliot Morison. While leafing through it he said nonchalantly, "you and your husband want to come along?"

Somewhat taken aback at the casualness of it, I said I thought we'd love to but that I am not much of a sailor and know very little about sailing. Have, in fact, only ever done day-sailing, and then just as a passenger.

I paused then to check out some books and this allowed me time to collect my thoughts, one of which was that I was not about to pass up this golden opportunity for adventure and was sure my husband wouldn't want to either. "I'm no sailor," I amended, "but my husband is ex-Navy and he knows all about boats. Maybe we can work something out?"

Ian Milne came to dinner at *Cinnabar* that evening, met my husband, and the three of us sat talking late into the night. The next day we lunched aboard his sailboat. A 37 foot ocean-going ketch named *Tadita*, she had clean lines, white sails, bright avocado green hull, and a center cockpit design which, Ian explained with obvious pride, was not often found on this size boat but provided needed privacy when traveling with more than one or two onboard.

The cockpit separated the skippers' aft quarters and head (toilet) from the head and forward quarters of the passengers.

Between the two was an efficient saloon/galley with some good books, ample storage, a table, an ice box, tiny sink, and a gas stove set on gimbels.

Ian was a trained civil engineer, Australian-born, raised in Scotland, and had handled boats since he was nine. Now a Canadian citizen, he was retired and living in Kingston, Ontario. With two sailing buddies he had made his way down the long inland waterway to Miami, across the Florida Straits, and on through the islands to Nassau; from there his two buddies had returned to jobs back home in Canada.

He'd brought *Tadita* to George Town from Nassau by himself and had intended to sail on to San Salvador alone but... our company would be welcome.

Over sandwiches and beer we finalized the plans. Since it might be rough going once we were out in the open Atlantic the trip might take a week to ten days. Though *Tadita* was well-designed and sturdy, she did not — by his choice — have a lot of modern gadgetry, things like Loran, an electric refrigerator, or a modern communications sytem.

"I decided to live simply once I'd retired." Ian looked at us closely to how we took this. "You know, the *less is more* idea." He looked embarrassed, as if once again he might have revealed too much about himself. He went on. "You see, I like to plot my course without a lot of electronic gear, using only maps, charts and a compass. On this trip I hope to chart my course as Columbus did, using dead reckoning as much as possible."

Our accompanying him would be a risk on both sides. We knew it, he knew it. Included in the fact that we hardly knew one another was the possibility that once underway, he might well turn out to be Captain Ahab or Captain Bligh. (I recalled the words of the drunken boat wife.) Or, he might find he disliked being in such close quarters with us, or us with him, and we'd end up flying home from San Sal on *Bahamasair* via Nassau.

And — as if I couldn't have guessed from the beginning — once again my job was to cook, not one of my best talents, and one which, when we encountered rough weather, I would undoubtedly be unable to perform because I'd be frightened as well as seasick. Besides, I was not at all sure what "dead reckoning" meant but it sounded ominous.

Still, my husband and I were curious to see San Salvador,

and the idea of going on an adventure to do "The Columbus Thing" was intriguing.

"She's a bonny boat." Ian said, showing us around. "Responsive. Easy to steer. So seaworthy, in fact, that she can roll over and still come upright." This particular feature of his "bonny boat" was not, as he'd meant it to be, in the least reassuring to me. When I learned that dead reckoning is the calculation of a ship's position without astronomical observations, using charts, dividers, parallel rulers, a compass, and the daily log to measure distance sailed, it sounded unnecessarily antiquated and in my opinion was carrying *the simple life* too far.

The plans were set. We were to set sail as soon as the weather permitted. We were to have our gear packed and ready at a moment's notice.

Four days later we set out on *Tadita*. With the barometer promising fair weather, we climbed aboard in late afternoon, our belongings carried in two large garbage bags. Ian planned to spend the night in the harbor so we could make an early departure. He gave me a tour of the galley and made sure I understood how to work the stove on gimbels. After supper my husband and I made up our bunks in the bow cabin under the for'ard deck and settled in, lying uncomfortably side by side and toe to toe in the triangular berth.

Each time he moved, I moved. I was hot. And supremely uncomfortable. I grew restless. Couldnt sleep. Couldn't get comfortable. Or settle down. Eventually, after several hours, I fell exhausted into a light doze.

Just after 10 p.m. I came abruptly awake, jolted from near-sleep by a scene behind my eyelids so real and of such devastation it brought me bolt upright. My heart beat wildly.

The vision of leaping flames and utter destruction was so vivid my throat closed and my adrenalin pumped strongly. Since I am not subject to night terrors, clairvoyance, premonitions, or prophetic dreams, nor a believer in theomancy, religious sightings, or mysticism, I was hard pressed for an explanation.

I do, however, believe in intuition, and that a web of life connects all things, so I felt strongly this might well be an intuited announcement of some terrible forthcoming disaster.

First to mind was the possibility of our children or grandchildren in some kind of jeopardy. A devastating fire. A car accident. A plane crash...

Or maybe it was a warning. Maybe we were headed for a shipwreck at sea. A hurricane — though this is not hurricane season on the Atlantic. A tropical storm.

To calm myself, rationalise my fear, and get some needed sleep, I nudged my husband awake.

Arm around my shoulders, he reassured me it was nothing more than undue apprehension at the coming voyage. He reminded me that just before retiring Ian had talked about crossing the swelling seas of a major shipping channel in the open Atlantic, out of sight of land and out of radio contact for a time — or, as he put it, "on our own for a while." Amateur sailor that I am, the prospect had undoubtedly unnerved me.

"We'll be fine," my husband promised. "Ian is a competent sailor. I can tell that from observing him." Had I remembered to bring my seasick tablets, he asked. Good. I would be fine. There was nothing to worry about. "I'm here," he counseled. I'll look after you." He meant it.

Somewhat reassured, I laid down. But even though I was rocked by the sea's gentle wave action my sleep was uneasy. Next morning, we learned the meaning of my intuited message.

At 8 a.m. still in George Town's harbor, we tuned in *Tadita's* marine radio to *Fish Hound*, the island's volunteer news and weather reporter, Rod Page. In a solemn voice he announced that the previous night at 10 p.m. (precisely the moment I was jolted awake by a vision of fire and destruction) President Bush had announced the beginning of Desert Shield, the Persian Gulf land war. Rod ended his broadcast that morning by asking us all to "say a prayer for America and for all troops everywhere."

The thought struck me then that it was not just my family in jeopardy but many members of the human family.

With our country and its allies entering a momentous conflict at that very moment, the public glued to CNN, and most of the world concerned with destruction not some historical discovery, we set sail. As we were soon to find out, it was not an auspicious beginning to our voyage.

31

Aboard *Tadita*, February 23, 1991

Ian started the motor, set it at slow ahead, asked my Navy veteran husband to haul up the bow anchor and, since we were barely moving, went below to his cabin to check the charts for dead reckoning. I was in the cockpit writing in my journal. Time slid by, unremarked, effortless, eternal.

And so, because it was not frantic or worried, just insistent, it was several seconds before I registered a distant voice saying quite matter-of-factly, "Overboard. Overboard."

Vaguely I wondered if this was something I should be paying attention to since the voice sounded a bit like my husband's. I stood up and looked around. Where was he? I couldn't see him on the bow, where he'd last been. The voice came again, closer this time but still not insistent. "Overboard. Overboard." I leaned over the port rail.

There he was, the hardened seaman, the Old Salt, the ex-Navy expert, hanging from the port gunnel. I was so amazed I didn't know what to do, or say, except to feel annoyed by such antics. I asked querulously, "what are you doing *there*?"

"I slipped." He grinned up at me. This ex-Navy man, ex-Canadian frogman, and — I now realized ex-expert on sailing — had *slipped* off the boat before we were even out of the harbor?

He explained that his foot slipped on the wet deck and he slid through the slack railing lines but on his way over was able to grab the gunnel. I hesitated to alert Ian but knew I must. "Ian," I called. "Vince has fallen overboard."

Ian jetted from his open hatchway like a gopher from a hole, switched off the engine, and ran to the rail. "Where is he?" He scanned the water fore and aft. I pointed to my husband on the gunnel off the port bow.

"Don't worry," my husband called up to us, "I'll just drop

off and swim back to the dinghy." Which he, the best and most fearless of swimmers, proceeded to do. Once aboard he and I laughed at the mishap because we both knew he was in no danger and, in fact, had been in many a tighter spot than that when scuba diving. Ian was not so amused.

"You must be more careful," he admonished my husband. And looking at me, "falling overboard is no laughing matter." I sobered at once and nodded, determined to do better. Still haunted by the previous night's scary vision I was thinking that such a beginning did not auger well for the rest of the voyage.

Ian sighed. "I'm sure we could all use a cup of tea," he said, resorting to a remedy we were soon to learn was this Canadian's way of dealing with most emergencies. Since I was the designated cook I went below, filled the kettle, and set it to boil on the gas stove while I laid out mugs and cookies. When it was ready I lifted the tea tray through the hatch, placing it carefully on the deck, and called out "tea's ready." Then I smelled gas.

Quickly I turned back to the stove. The control knob had no on-off indicator. I flipped it back and forth; still a strong smell of gas. Had I turned it off, or further on? It worked differently from my stove at home and I couldn't remember Ian's instructions for this one. But I did remember his saying that if gas vapors seeped into the bilges — which evidently it's easy for them to do — the boat could blow up.

"Ian —" I called up through the hatchway, "there's a strong smell of gas down here and I think I may have —"

"Omigod!" He flung himself down the galley hatchway, upsetting the teapot, and by hitting the ladder on his way down, skinned his ankle. He checked the stove. The gas was full on.

"You turn it off to the *left*." His jaw was set. His cheek muscles worked mightily but he showed no other sign of anger. By now I felt he'd be justified in showing outright despair, or showing us off the boat.

But that was what we were soon to learn about Ian. He did not get mad and he did not shout. And he never got fussed. Nevertheless, I could guess what must have been going through his head at that moment: *Good God! I've invited these two to spend a week or more aboard my boat? I must be crazy!*

For my part, I contemplated a wide spectrum of misfortunes ahead. In my journal entry that day I noted that this might well turn out to be a three-person Ship of Fools. The most mistaken, most ill-fated voyage since Columbus saw San Salvador and thought he'd landed in China.

If not rough seas, a broken mast, or worse, a broken arm or leg might happen. Or an engine failure in the heavily traveled shipping lane, a hurricane, a shipboard plague of some sort, or a breakdown in the captain's dead reckoning which might cause us to miss San Salvador altogether and, reversing Columbus's voyage to America, send us sailing off across the Atlantic to the Canary Islands off the coast of Africa.

Once underway and out of Elizabeth Harbour late in the afternoon of the first day, we anchored for the night in a lovely little cove on the west side of Long Island where we swam in water clear as gin. I heated up a gourmet meal of corned beef, boiled potatoes, canned peas, canned peaches and coffee and since it was a calm evening with stars dusting the sky, we sat contentedly on deck until bedtime talking about Columbus and his men.

There were 90 of them — 40 on the flagship *Santa Maria*, 26 on *Pinta*, and 24 in *Niña*. They were uneducated, semi-literate, and superstitious men who had serious doubts about their Admiral's mental stability and his mad idea of the world's roundness. You could imagine them scoffing at his theory of finding a route to China by sailing west from Spain. Many of them had signed on believing they might never again see home. Compared to that this trip, so far, was a breeze.

Ian began describing our next day's sail. Once we'd sailed north to avoid the dangerous shoals off Cape Santa Maria, we would head east, across the wide stretch of open Atlantic toward San Salvador. That was the stretch of a shipping lane used by freighters and tankers plying between South America and Europe, and the danger there was that these huge ships might not see a small sailboat if it inadvertently got in the way. They had been known to plough right over them, he said. That a behemoth of a ship the size of a forty story apartment building might run us down was one disaster I hadn't thought of, and it terrified me...

At dawn the next morning Ian and my husband set the

sails, adjusted ropes, and took *Tadita* north toward the Santa Maria shoals off the north end of Long Island. Later on Ian asked me to stand on the bow to watch out for coral heads close to the surface. Going over them Ian reefed the mainsail to reduce speed and let the boat move gently across the dangerous reefs. Looking down on them from the boat the coral heads looked like black clouds in the dark blue sky of the sea. By noon, after a sandwich lunch eaten underway, we were free of the shoals and began sailing east across the open Atlantic.

At this point the sun had disappeared under heavy clouds and the sea looked so cold, grey and menacing it was hard to believe we were in tropical waters. We were still in Bahamian waters, but the swells were now becoming deeper and higher by the minute, and the color of the water was changing from greeny-gray to the dark navy blue of the deep ocean. There was nothing to see, no land, no birds, no ships, no tree branches, and not another boat. (All sensible sailors having stayed snugly in port somewhere safe, like Cuba or Haiti.)

Ian continued to handle his boat with great flair and confidence, visibly taking pride in his ability to sail *Tadita* alone. So what if he didn't have a lot of fancy electronic gear and technical navigation equipment aboard; plotting his course according to compass and charts as Columbus did, and using sail as much as possible, must surely be the test of a *real* sailor. In this day and age that could only be considered admirable.

"Wind's picking up. Best put on our life vests," Ian announced a little later on in his usual calm manner. We did so. He then latched himself to *Tadita* with a chain harness around the wheel post. When asked why he shrugged and explained nonchalantly, "just a precaution so I won't get tossed overboard if there's a storm." A new worry alighted on my overtaxed brain.

A long way off an enormous tanker loomed on the horizon, beating its way north in the shipping lane. From *Tadita's* deck it looked as if we couldn't help but arrive at the same point at the same time. Was I worried about that? Naa—aah.

Yes I was.

As the wind picked up and whipped higher, and *Tadita's* bow dipped and rose like a gigantic bird bobbing for a fish dinner, my stomach also dipped and rose. But at least one worry was now gone. The big tanker had disappeared from sight by the time we crossed astern of its path. I took two more seasick tablets.

I didn't need to be doing this. I no longer had to prove anything to anyone. So why was I here?

Then, strangely, something happened. It felt very odd — perhaps the seasick tablets had put me in a dazed state — but after a short while I became completely calm and, if the need arose, quite resigned to dying.

Drowning, I'd heard, is a calm death, one in which your past flashes before your eyes just before the final moment. That would be nice. I'd had a wonderful life, didn't regret too much, had done some things I was not proud of but a few I was, would miss seeing our four grandchildren grow up, but regardless, they would do that anyway.

And at that moment my sympathies went out to Columbus and his men who, all those many years ago, suffered through 33 days of this rolling and tossing not knowing whether they would end up on land or at the bottom of the sea. There was also the possibility that their Admiral was a nut case who wasn't at all sure of where he'd end up, and might well get lost and lead them off the edge of the planet.

Despite that, they had braved the Atlantic in boats little larger than *Tadita*, slept crowded together on wooden shelves in cockroach-infested holds, eaten meager food that was often served cold and full of maggots, and used a crude box affair over the side for a toilet. Since their fresh water was rationed, their daily ablutions were minimal and so, by their third day out of the Canary Islands, the ship must have smelled like a goat farm. On top of it all they were poorly paid; many had signed on only because there was the promise of gold. Compared to that kind of hardship life aboard *Tadita* was a pleasant outing.

No wonder many of Columbus's crewmen were near mutiny after a couple of weeks. They were kept in check only by the Admiral's promises of the gold and jewels of the Orient, soon to be theirs. On the Thursday night, October 11, when they sighted tree branches, saw birds, and took aboard a fragment of man-made carving, they were reassured. It was then that Columbus wrote in his log, "all breathed again and rejoiced."

177

That same night Columbus recorded that about 10 p.m. a sailor aboard *Pinta* thought he saw a light. In the rough seas no one could be sure, of course, but later, about 2 a.m. Rodrigo de Triana, aboard *Pinta*, shouted "Tierra! Tierra!" Rightfully, he should have been the one to get the purse of gold coins promised to the first man who sighted land. Instead, Columbus took it for himself and the hapless Rodrigo never got a nickel.

And this time, land it was. Columbus's biographer, Father Bartolome de las Casas, wrote:

> "At two hours after midnight, the land appeared, from which they were two leagues. They lay to, waiting until daylight. Friday they arrived at a small isle of the Lucayans which was called, in the Indians' language, Guanahani, and at dawn they went ashore." (Admiral pf the Ocean Sea, S E Morison)

"Land ahead!" Ian called out to us as if on cue. It was late on the afternoon of our second day out when San Salvador rose on the horizon of the rolling Atlantic.

First to appear was a smudge of grey hills against the sky, then as we closed, some chalky patches that turned into limestone cliffs above a ribbon of white sand. As we neared I became aware of a faint fragrance — slightly sweet, earthy, lush. Ian explained that it was the particular smell you get at sea when you are nearing a tropical land mass. For some reason all of a sudden it made me acutely aware of the two companions of all travelers: loneliness and time.

Columbus must have felt them half a millenia ago as he contemplated his landfall island. No doubt finding land where he hoped it was made him jubilant. Not until months later was he aware it wasn't the continent of China which he'd hoped, prayed and dreamed he'd discover.

Ahead now colored specks became houses, their windows winking in the westering sun. A line of foam broke against some off-shore reefs, and off to the left the pastel-colored houses of Cockburn Town (pronounced Co'burntown) clustered around a small calm bay in the rosy light of sunset. It felt as if we had arrived at the edge of the world.

32

A remote island that appears to arise suddenly from the sea appears not only ephemeral but vulnerable. San Salvador looked so small and fragile against the wide stretch of sea, so alone and defenseless under the vast sky, you could only wonder what kind of tough, sturdy independent people lived here.

San Salvador, far out on the extreme eastern fringe of the Bahamas, is the outermost of all the Bahamian islands. Just twelve miles long and six miles wide, its highest point is Mt. Kerr at 140 feet; by Bahamian standards, comparatively high.

According to some historians, the land first sighted by the Columbus crew member aboard *Pinta* might have been High Cay, just off Sandy Hook at the island's southeastern tip. They speculate that the "light" Columbus described in his log could have been the brilliant moonlight illuminating the white sand beach.

To approach the island as Columbus might have, Ian set a course for Sandy Hook. Once there, he brought *Tadita* about, and with all three sails billowing in a southwest wind, we moved northward up the island's west coast. Patches of blue sky created shafts of sunlight on the water, gulls surfed the waves. We needed a calm anchorage for the night and to get to it, we needed a break in the reef to get into a small bay and a way through the dangerous coral heads surrounding it... Columbus must have been doing the same thing when he arrived...

About a mile south of Cockburn Town we spotted a narrow opening in the reef, just deep enough and wide enough for *Tadita* to get through without scraping her bottom. Ian lowered the sails, my husband took the lookout on the bow, we motored slowly through the reef which quickly shoaled to about two fathoms, or 12 feet, and moved carefully into Fernandez Bay. It was a small bay but large enough for *Tadita* — and so it would have been for those three ancient ships if, indeed, they had made this their landfall. The sun, now a red ball behind us, was about to set as we anchored and Ian declared it was time for a swim.

That evening we reorganized the boat, stowed the sails, and ate supper sitting on deck under the rising moon while talking about Columbus. What were his thoughts half a millenia ago as he contemplated the New World — wherever it was that he landed? Did he feel jubilant? Relieved? Vindicated? Proud? But trying to imagine the explorer's state of mind and that of his crew — who were seeing land where many of them believed there wasn't any — was an impossible feat for three educated, twentieth century minds at home in today's world. We could never comprehend the fears and misgivings those ancient sailors underwent, nor those of their dauntless admiral.

It is recorded in Columbus's log that upon arrival they prayed to God in gratitude for watching over their Atlantic crossing and for guiding them safely to land. God must have listened because, unknown to them, they had crossed the Atlantic during the worst month of the hurricane season without encountering one storm.

Of that long ago night of arrival Columbus also wrote in his log:

2 a.m... the moon, past full, is riding about 70 degrees high over Orion on the port quarter...

At 2 a.m. Ian roused us and he, my husband and I stood in the moonlight on deck. The wooden planks felt cool beneath my bare feet, the breeze that lifted my hair was warm and moist. In the shadows off the starboard bow it was almost possible to see the ghostly presence of the *Niña*, the *Pinta*, and the *Santa Maria* riding at anchor in the bay, and standing on the foredeck of the *Maria*, scanning the moonlit strand through his eyeglass, the Admiral of the Ocean Sea.

But — no admiral, and no ghostly galleons. Or more accurately, no Spanish *caravel* (the *Santa Maria*) and no *naos* (the *Niña* and *Pinta*.) Just *Tadita*, not quite 500 years after Columbus, rocking gently on a moon-washed sea under a full moon. The rigging creaked, a slight wind made the waves slurp and gurgle along the hull — and it was as if the technological, computerized, mechanized and industrialized world beyond this small island no longer existed.

At such a time the word *magical* comes to mind, though it seemed insufficient for the sight of San Salvador bathed in moonlight. The shore gleamed white as a wedding carpet. A silvery glow backlit the dark hills. The silhouettes of coconut palms and casuarina trees spiked a sky pale as milk. With no habitation and no stars visible, and the moon sailing a lonely course across the sky, it was as if there was no one else on earth.

We spoke little. My husband and I realized that for Ian this was a solemn moment and after a few minutes we returned to bed leaving him alone in his moonlit reverie on deck. For him, this was an interval between dream and substance.

The plan for the day was to be up again before daylight when Ian, with the Columbus log in hand, would follow in the Admiral's footsteps and step ashore at dawn.

In the pre-dawn light he arrived on deck dressed for a special occasion in clean white deck pants, a navy blue tee shirt and a dark blue peaked cap. We readied the dinghy and with my husband aboard he rowed it in, setting me ashore with the camera then laying off until the sky lightened. In the first moment after dawn, when the light was clear but held no depth, I began snapping photographs as my husband guided the dinghy onto the sand and Ian stepped ashore for the first time.

For a moment he stood looking down at the sand, then walking thoughtfully a little way up the beach to be apart from us, he knelt down on one knee, head bowed. After a minute or so of silent contemplation, he stood up.

"Hurray-y—y-y!" he shouted. "Yahoo—oo-oo!" he yelled, throwing his cap into the air. "I made it, I made it!" He repeated this over and over as he danced across the sand, executing a sailor's hornpipe jig. Obvious to both of us, this was the culmination of a long-held private dream. Perhaps a vow made to himself, or to someone he loved.

Barefoot, we wandered the early morning sands of the beach, reluctant to speak for fear of breaking the spell of the moment, feeling we were reliving history. Sadly, the world has run out of uncharted places; only by traveling across the uncharted sea can we hope to still explore "the still unfound."

Just along the beach from our landing site we discovered a completely unexpected, two-foot-high stone slab on which was carved:

Christopher Columbus landed here on this island on October 12, 1492. This monument place here by the Yawl Heloise, *Feb. 25, 1951*

Some yachters before us, almost 40 years to the day, had believed this was the spot where Columbus and his men first stepped ashore. Certainly it was a place that any experienced seaman would have chosen to land. But like the other monuments we visited later, it could never be more than guesswork.

The true location of Columbus's first landfall is still in dispute, as perhaps it always will be. With no less than six locations promoted, the actual one may never be decided to everyone's satisfaction. The other serious contender for the landfall is Samana Cay, a tiny uninhabited Bahamian island, nine miles long, about 60 miles southeast of San Salvador.

This site, put forth as Columbus's true landfall by Joseph Judge in the November, 1986 issue of *National Geographic*, was worked out by computers. It takes current and drift into consideration and does seem to fit some of the notations made in the translated copy of Columbus's log. Even so, can computers really capture the vagaries of the ocean's currents and the mind of a sea captain?

When he stepped ashore Columbus was greeted by friendly Lucayan Indians. About them, he wrote that the encounter was peaceful, the Indians were a "docile and gentle" people, unarmed, healthy, young, probably under 30, and as naked as when their mothers bore them. They were a handsome, sturdy graceful people, with wide foreheads, the result, presumably, of the Lucayan custom of head binding. Their faces, and in some cases their entire bodies, were decorated in black, white and red paint, their hair was short and coarse, worn in bangs to their eyebrows, with a few longer locks hanging down their back.

In a letter home to his Queen, Columbus wrote that *"these gentle peaceful people are very poor in everything, yet gave all with as much love as if their hearts went with it."* He suggested that several of them could accompany him to Spain so their majesties could have them in the palace — presumably, one suspects, to exhibit as proof of the New World's slave potential.

Not disclosed until this point was the information that Columbus's mission was more than pure exploration. He believed he was destined by prophecy not only to be a discoverer, but was divinely appointed for the job of carrying Christendom to the New World. To substantiate this he cited his name — Christopher (Christ Bearer) — and to back up his claim often quoted biblical scripture.

In the manner of all imperialist explorers of the time, he utterly discounted the fact that the Lucayans called their island Guanahani and had their own full scale society and culture. Ignoring all that, he arrogantly planted two Spanish flags in the sand, claimed the island for their soverign majesties, Queen Isabella and King Ferdinand of Spain, and renamed the island San Salvador. (Later, in what can only be termed poetic justice, the colonial British renamed it Watling's Island after infamous British pirate John Watling; in 1926, by an act of the Bahamian Parliament it was again named San Salvador.)

There is no way of knowing what the Lucayans thought of Columbus but one can imagine these simple people watching in amazement as the Spaniards in all their finery — leather boots, velvet breeches, hat plumes whipping in the breeze — planted the royal flag of their Royal Spanish Majesties in the sand. Unfortunately, the Lucayans had no way to foresee what it all meant.

Never suspecting their fate, the Indians gladly exchanged gifts of cassava bread, fresh fruits and fresh water for trinkets of glass beads and hawk's bells. The Spaniards learned about hammocks, tobacco, maize, yams and possibly measles; the Lucayans learned about greed and syphilis

From archeological digs, and the radio carbon dating of artifacts, it is known that the Lucayan settlements in the Bahamas date back to around 900 A.D. Their culture probably had its roots in the culture of the Arawaks, a much more warlike tribe which the Lucayans eventually escaped by canoeing north from Cuba and Hispaniola.

Lucayan life revolved around the sea, their main diet being fish. Their homes were of wood with thatch roofs, they slept in rope hammocks, ate from pottery made of local red earth tempered with broken shells, wore jewelry made from shells and bones and beads, and used as their major tool an axe made of black rock measuring three to twelve inches long. They made extensive use of the conch, using the meat as food, the shell as a hammer and a communications horn, a drinking cup and a scraping knife.

The gold-hungry Spaniards, propelled by their arrogance, lack of compassion, and greed for riches, enslaved these gentle people and transported them to their colonies in Cuba and Hispaniola to work in the silver mines. Some became indentured servants on Spanish plantations.

In 1517 the 40,000 or so Lucayans that remained were estimated to each be worth about four gold pesos. But then the Spaniards realized they were missing a bet. The Lucayans were wonderful swimmers and divers and when the Spaniards discovered the rich pearl beds off the island of Cubaqua, near Venezuela, they transported the Lucayans there as divers. The price of each Lucayan male rose to 150 pesos.

Three years later, by 1520, the treacherous waters and cruel conditions killed off the last of the Lucayans. In less than thirty years an entire population was wiped off the face of the earth. For the Lucayans the doubtful honor of being the first people in the New World to greet the explorers was replaced by the distinction of being the first West Indian culture to be eradicated by Europeans.

British historian Arnold Toynbee calls this type of event "an historical imperative," meaning that this was the conventional wisdom of the day, the way life was lived at the time, the way things were done then. The way this reasoning goes is that because in those days other values, other moralities held sway, few people, if any, considered such exploitation of "the lesser races" wrong.

It's taken 500 years but by now, one hopes, we know better.

33

San Salvador, February 24, 1991

That night it got hotter and stickier. Off to the east the Atlantic was cooking up a storm. Around 3 a.m. the wind shifted to the southwest and the heat and humidity increased. By daylight Ian was preparing to move *Tadita* out of the rising wind and into the shelter of the Riding Rock Marina, the island's only boat harbor. Navigating the narrow entrance cut through a rock wall was tricky but eventually *Tadita* was tied up alongside the other sailboats harbored there in two of the six slips.

Reverend Livingston Williams awaited us, as if he knew we were coming. A portly Bahamian in his fifties wearing reflector sunglasses and a tee shirt that read *Protect Our Children*, he greeted us while we were still tying up. Would we like to see around the island? He was the island's Baptist minister and unofficial Columbus expert, historian, and tour guide operator. As the proprietor of this latter occupation he offered a tour of the island for $50. Would $40 do? "Sold!" He slapped Ian on the back and took us away with him in his battered blue pickup.

Starting out, I was given the soft seat up front, where several things soon became apparent: the good Reverend liked to talk, enjoyed humming hymns, was a fund of island lore, and intended that we see his island in his own way at his own time.

"I'll take you first to the New World Museum." He avoided a pothole as the truck rattled along over the island's roads with him humming *Shall We Gather At The River*. Then he talked fondly of the 15 foster children he and his wife were raising, and told riveting stories about hurricanes, hidden caves, and island life. At one point he proudly indicated the site of the proposed Club Med. "A boon," he shouted above the clatter of the engine, "a great boon! It will bring jobs. Our young people will come home."

"Just imagine —" the truck jounced through the tiny

settlment of Victoria Hill — "a Club Med with 100 rooms! And
to think that as late as 1960 we used a conch shell to relay a message from Victoria Hill to the nurse in Co'burntown!" He shifted
down to avoid some goats. "But now," he added proudly, "we
have a telephone in all the main settlements, and an East Indian
doctor. And a nurse." He shook his head in amazement at the
progress this signified in the year 1991.

At the New World Museum, a dusty compound with an
arched gate, Reverend Williams explained that the large house
and its outbuildings were the estate of wealthy American widow
Ruth Wolper Melvin, who has had a lifelong interest in the Columbus saga. Purely as a labor of love she established the museum on her estate *Polaris-By-The-Sea*, and though, because of
age, she seldom visited anymore, her family did, and maintained
the museum.

Reverend Williams rousted out caretaker Bobby Benson
from his rooms adjoining the nearby *Arawak Bar and Grill*. By
now it was over ninety degrees and breathlessly hot. "Hottest
February I can remember," said the slim elderly Mr Benson. "Bad
for my arthritis, but no prob-lem. I'll be glad to show you
around."

The walled compound was filled with mature trees: almond, banana, seagrape, and palm. We walked under their welcome shade to a one-room beach rock building the size of a two-
car garage. Mr. Benson unlocked the door and ushered us inside. With meticulous attention to detail, willing and hospitable
but bothered very much by his arthritis, he shuffled painfully
around the room proudly showing off the dusty diplay cases.

Old newspaper clippings, amateur oil paintings, and several samples of dried plants and herbs shared space with skulls
and tools of dubious date. Resting amid a collection of early artifacts of a kind supposedly used at the time of Columbus were
a log canoe, a wooden mortar and pestle, some scraping shells,
and some potsherds of Palmetto Ware. We thanked Mr. Benson
for his trouble, gave him, at his request, a dollar each, signed the
guest book, and were hurried along by Reverend Williams, who
reminded us we had yet a lot of ground to cover.

Humming his favorite hymn again, he next took us further north, past walls of impenetrable bush, to see Graham's

Harbour. This wide curve of beach scooped out of the island's northwestern shore is supposedly the "spacious harbor" to which Columbus referred when he wrote in his log: *a harbour that... could hold all the ships in Christendom.* This seemed doubtful.

Still, Columbus's largest ship, the *Santa Maria*, was, after all, only about 87 feet long, little more than two and a half times longer than *Tadita*. But — *all* the ships in Christendom? One historian has figured that would be about 10,000 vessels.

Perhaps Columbus, great navigator and seaman that he undoubtedly was, did at times exaggerate. He did after all have to justify to their royal majesties the large sum of front money they'd put up to finance his voyage, which included — so the school history books tell us — Queen Isabella's jewels.

But as a chronicler of history Columbus could sometimes be inaccurate. For example: because of a lack of topsoil and limited rainfall, historians say these islands never did produce large trees, yet in his letters Columbus wrote that he saw dugouts made from trees *so big that in some came 40 or 50 men.* Though it is probably heresy to say so, it seems likely that either the great admiral and navigator stretched the truth, or it really was on another island that he landed. A pity his crews were unlettered and unable to keep notes.

How could Graham's Harbour, with its huge surge and visible coral heads, have been the Admiral's chosen anchorage? "It's possible," Reverend Williams said, "it's possible." But he was unwilling, as a historian, to commit himself to such an irrevocable fact and, as he drove on, confessed, abashedly, that he was no longer a sea man.

"I tell you, when I was boy-size I handled boats and sailed to all the islands. Now, us Bahamians, we've lost the ability of sailors, and boat-builders, and fishermen. We don't know the sea anymore — and too sad it is too." He bowed his head and shook it back and forth as if in sorrow for a great loss.

At Dixon Hill Lighthouse on the northernmost shore Mr. S. was listed as the official lighthousekeeper but Mrs. S., his wife, a robust woman with bright dark eyes but no ready smile, was the one who led us up the long spiral of 90 steps and gave out the facts.

The lighthouse, which rises 263 feet above sea level and overlooks the open Atlantic on all sides, was built by a British firm in 1856. Mrs. S. pointed above our heads even farther up the tower to a large kerosene pressure lamp centered in a circle of highly-polished, fresnel lenses. That light, she explained, beamed a 400,000 candlepower beacon out to sea in a nineteen mile radius. It required checking every two hours. Sensing there were some hidden aspects to the job, I asked her who lit the lamp at dusk and checked it throughout the night.

"I do," she said.

"You climb up here every two hours?"

"Once in a while my husband takes a shift." She shrugged, unsmiling. "Not often, though. But he's always ready to take the credit and the salary." Her disgruntlement pointed up that in the Bahamas it is still a man's world.

From up here you saw that San Salvador was a green, well-watered island. Where the sea broke against the reefs, the shore-line was rimed with white sea foam, the interior dotted with lakes, lagoons, marshes, swamps, and small ponds — all sparkling in the sun and looking highly inviting.

Sticky with saltwater after four days without a shower, it was tempting to plunge into one of the ponds when, later, we stopped by one. Herons, egrets and gulls, crabs and funny little ducks that swam with just their necks and heads above the water made the thought enticing. Did those long ago Spanish explorers perhaps come to these inland ponds to blissfully bathe and wash their clothes? We asked Reverend Williams if we could swim.

"Not now," he said, "you must see the true Columbus cross. Come." There was no use protesting we were sticky and weary; he had his own agenda.

There are three Columbus monuments on San Salvador that mark Columbus's purported landing. The first was installed in 1891 by the *Chicago Herald*. This one can be viewed only after a drive north over a bone-shaking road. It stands on a high bluff overlooking the island's reef-bound east coast below which the ocean beats itself into towers of silver spray — a most improbable place for anyone to anchor a ship, let alone come ashore. This monument could only mark Columbus's first sight of land, since only a shipwrecked sailor out of his mind would choose to land at this spot.

A few miles farther on were the ruins of Watling's Castle,

the former bastion of that rakish nineteenth century British pirate James Watling. When he was not plundering nearby seas, he made this his home.

The next monument was erected by Mexico to commemorate the arrival of the Olympic Torch on San Salvador on September 29, 1968. A Greek battleship took the Olympic torch from Greece to Spain, where it was transferred to a Spanish battleship for the trip to San Salvador. Once there, runners bearing it aloft circled the island before lighting the flame atop the monument. After a parade and speeches the torch was put aboard a Mexican warship for the journey to the 1968 Olympic Games in Mexico City.

But the real, the actual, the most likely of Columbus's landing spots, according to Reverend Williams, was the one at Long Bay — which just happened to be Reverend Williams home settlement. Arriving there he stopped his truck, addressed us firmly as we stood beneath a 15 foot white cross with a bronze plaque erected in 1956 and proclaimed, "This," — he waved an arm and stated with unarguable conviction — "is the *true* Columbus landing spot."

By now, overheated, hungry and bone sore from traveling the pot-holed roads, we accepted his dictum.

Sic gloria transit mundi, I thought. How quickly the world's glories pass away.

34

In CockburnTown, a collection of neat, brightly-painted wood houses fanned out from a giant almond tree at harborside. We walked from there through a warren of narrow streets and lanes searching for food. On the main street were two grocery stores, a small library, several bars, some offices, and a gift shop offering Columbus souvenirs, replicas of the *true* monument, his three ships, pennants, banners, tee shirts — Columbus as tourism schlock — but, no food.

Then up ahead we spied a small white-painted building, *The Three Ships Restaurant and Bar*. The Bahamian owner greeted us warmly, promised to cook up the best boiled fish dinner we'd ever eaten and proceeded to do so. It was succulent, tasty and full of wonderful flavors he said came from a personal blend of herbs and spices which he wouldn't divulge to us or anyone. With it we ate some good crusty bread, using it to mop up the savory juices.

We strolled back to the marina along the harborfront, past the government dock, the pink administration building, a post office, a clinic, a communication tower, a telephone station, the island commissioner's house, and the white Catholic Church. Next to this was the former power station, two red brick buildings newly spruced up and freshly painted; over the arched gate, a sign read COLUMBUS MUSEUM.

We tried the door. It was locked and a passerby politely told us the lady with the key had gone home to her "chil'run." Not for the first time I wondered if this island would be able to gear itself up for next year's Quincentennial onslaught of tourism. Where, for example, when the expected crowds arrive, will they put them all? Yet knowing Bahamians are relaxed and do not get stressed about such matters, I was sure it would turn out all right.

In reflection, I saw San Salvador in those days as remarkable for what it *did not* have as for what it *did*. No casinos, discos or Big Macs. No TV, neon lights or glitzy hotel-resorts. Just one small hotel and a rugged untouched beauty that, as we wandered around its beaches and hills the next day, we surmised would soon be changed forever by the forthcoming 200-room Club Med, the regular visits by tour boats, the special "fly-ins," the archeological digs, the housing estates and time-share condos. I reminded myself all this will, nonetheless, bring forth the much-anticipated jobs that will entice the island's young people to come home.

For dinner on our last night we ate at the Riding Rock Inn, the island's only hostelry. It overlooked the western shore a mile from Co'burnTown as the locals called it. A small place of 24 air-conditioned rooms, 10 villas, and eight apartments, it boasted a swimming pool, a tennis court, and rental cars, bikes and motorbikes. Sipping a pre-dinner drink at the nautical bar, we chatted with several American divers who had just come in from a night dive on one of the surrounding coral reefs.

"These reefs are the best, man." A long-haired youth with sparkling eyes and a brown muscular body set down his bottle of *Kalik* beer. "Teeming with fish. I mean *teeming!*" His bronzed college buddies nodded in agreement and started telling stories of their recent undersea exploits. We sat around comfortably, happy to be in this tropical night listening to these young Americans, pleased that in the islands age differences matter little — unlike the U.S. where fun is thought to be exclusively a matter for the young. In the islands fun is for everyone, young or old, and all ages here seem to live in the present.

The dining room, overlooking the sea, was sparse, clean and without frills. We had freshly-caught grouper, mashed potatoes, canned peas, a cole slaw in which the cabbage had a pleasant peppery taste, freshly-baked white bread, and a modest white table wine. Dessert was home-baked apple pie. Sherry, the smiling Bahamian waitress, made us feel welcome.

Returning to *Tadita* in a lavender twilight, we ambled down a stretch of quiet road, talking softly, touched by the island's serenity. I was glad we'd come early, before the Quincentennial tourists clogged the lovely beaches and crowded Bobby Benson's dusty museum. No longer was San Salvador the remote, sleepy island Columbus reportedly found, it never will be again, and for Reverend Williams and all the other 900 or so inhabitants who will prosper because of that, I was glad.

Aboard *Tadita*, feeling we knew him well enough by now, I took a chance on invading Ian's privacy and asked, "why was it so important that you make this voyage?"

He looked startled at first, and I was afraid I'd been too personal. He said nothing, remaining quiet so long I decided he was not going to answer and that I'd probably offended him. Then he looked directly at us, and smiled.

"It was a boyhood dream. I promised myself when I was nine years old that someday I'd make it come true."

Sailing home there came for me the most magical moment of all. On our first morning out, past the dangerous shipping lanes and approaching Long Island, I was sitting on the deck near the bow when I felt, rather than heard, a disturbance in the water. To my left a dolphin was gliding alongside the boat. Never before had I seen one in the wild, only at Sea World. I alerted the men but a moment later it was gone and I was left feeling cheated because it hadn't stayed around longer.

Ian, at the wheel, said, "stand up and call it back." I didn't understand. He repeated it. "Go on. Call the dolphin back. In Australia they make nothing of calling in the dolphins. Go on, give it a try. Clap your hands loudly and call them."

Feeling foolish, not sure I wasn't being made fun of, I stood up at the guard rail, clapped my hands, then cupped them into a megaphone and called loudly across the empty sea, "Dolphins! Dolphins! Come back!"

Nothing happened. I did it again. Still nothing. Ian said to call and clap louder. Feeling silly, I did so.

I could hardly believe it when, within seconds, the bow was surrounded by playing dolphins; at least a dozen, adults and young, almost close enough for me to reach down and touch. Leaping and and diving and hooting, cavorting, clowning, frisking around the bow, smiling up at us with their happy grins, they appeared to be saying "c'mon in — the water's great!"

Enchanted, I looked into their eyes and was sure I could detect intelligence. They stayed with us for about half an hour, then as quickly as they'd come they were gone. I waited and waited, but the sea was empty, the only sound the singing of the wind in the shrouds.

It was a rare moment. Forget Columbus. This for me was the highlight of the voyage; a moment out of time shared with another species, a privileged moment beyond compare.

By the time Easter arrived the house was submerged in blooms. The salmon-pink hibiscus by the garage was covered in blossoms and the magenta bougainvillea, yellow elder, and pink and white periwinkles had all responded eagerly to the spring rains. On the rocky slope that is the back yard the limes had finally decided to produce blossoms and might, for the first time in God knows how long, produce fruit. The moss rose glowed from its raised bed under one of the palm trees and the new orchid tree put out its very first snow white blossom. It smelled like vanilla beans.

We were sipping coffee under the seagrape tree on Easter Sunday when Mr. Flowers arrived with a friend, a Mr. Brown from Farmer's Hill. Mr. Flowers was toting a plastic bucket filled with half a dozen tomatoes, some green and red peppers, and a bouquet of bright orange amaryllis liles. I made more coffee and we all sat down under the tree with the morning sun slanting around us and dropping like gold coins on the ground.

Mr. Flowers ladled his usual three spoonsful of sugar into his coffee and told Mr. Brown with great pride about the new wing and, (a sly glance at my husband,) how he and Stanley built it with the help of my husband. With much cackling and chortling in the telling he related some of the construction tales which by now were legendary. We laughed all over again, which encouraged him to tell more.

Standing up, he acted out — with gestures — the story of the windy day when Stanley and my husband were trying to nail down sheets of plywood on the roof and had to cling to the rafters and one another to keep from flying off to Grog Pond. Choked with merriment, he next regaled us with an account — again with a series of wild gestures — of how every single working day he and Stanley, after the three of them had eaten lunch on the deck, had to awaken my husband from his postprandial nap.

Pointing at my husband, Mr. Flowers pillowed his head on his arm and pretended to sleep, snoring loudly. He told Mr. Brown they continually had to shame Vince into going back to work by shaking him awake and handing him his tools.

By now we were laughing even harder. I realized those arduous days of construction had been magically transformed into something special. Existence, our laughter seemed to say, is hard and difficult, but since we're all in it together we might as well do our best to enjoy it. At that moment of shared laughter I felt all our lives were invested with a nameless grace.

"Yes, mon." Mr. Flowers spread his arms wide, nodding to Mr. Brown. "For sure, this is `we' house." And though he owned his own neat home in Farmer's Hill he looked around with all the pride of ownership at the house he'd helped build.

"And I've got news for you." My husband barely contained his laughter. "My next big project is to extend the front deck beyond our bedroom and build a bathroom on to the Garden Room — provided, of course, you and Stanley think you can stand the pace."

Mr. Flowers pointed an accusatory finger at him and right there, under the seagrape tree, my husband and Mr. Flowers came together in a bear hug.

This fine day, with its trees and bushes again in full bloom, its reaffirmation of the growth of a friendship, its birth of new ideas, and its promise of more projects to come, seemed a fitting celebration of Easter.

35

That the island was changing there was no doubt. Regret it as we might, it was inevitable. If the islanders were to prosper, the Bahamas needed development — guided development. But from a certain perspective it appeared doubtful they would get the kind they needed. Like everyone else, islanders want jobs, incomes to raise families, and opportunities to learn and enrich their lives. For this to happen there has to be development. The problem is that much of the development being proposed is not being monitored and could well end up doing more harm than good to the island's best resource: it's exquisite beauty and hospitable people.

One night in George Town, while waiting for my husband I was sitting at the *P&P* bar drinking a glass of wine by myself and talking to Lermon Rolle, the bartender. I felt smart, sophisticated, expatriated and *young*. (Well, young-*ger*.)

A man sat down on the barstool next to me, his smile attractive, his large head partly balding, his dark eyes and pepper-and-salt beard slightly menacing. But his outgoing American manner was quite charming — until I heard his first words. "Hiya honey. Bud Cerranti. Houston. You visitin' the island?"

"I live here." Unfairly, perhaps, I put frost in my tone.

"You mean a house and everything? And when I nodded, "you must be seriously rich then."

"My husband and I worked hard and saved up to buy the house," I said stuffily. Why was I bothering? I didn't want to talk to him because something was telling me I wouldn't like him.

"You feel good about living here?"

"Most of the time. Are you vacationing here?"

"Developer. Flew in to see about building a golf course and some timeshare condos outside town."

"Oh? Where?"

"Well, now, nice lady, no offense, but I can't tell you that yet. We're still working on the deal, y'unnerstand?" He laughed then, a big laugh. "As you know, it's business makes the world go round. Right?" He flashed a bulging wallet. "Another white wine? I'm buying."

"No thanks. I'm waiting for my husband. I'll introduce you."

"Oh. By the way—" his voice lowered — "you and him tried to get any good stuff lately? Know where I can get some?"

Good Stuff? Did he mean drugs? I decided he did. "Good heavens, no!" Such a casual mention of drugs made the hairs on the back of my neck rise. I'd long ago absorbed the local reluctance to discuss the subject. I decided he was really a drug dealer or a buyer. Maybe a narc. Before my husband could arrive I excused myself and went to the ladies' room, relieved to escape whatever it was this man threatened.

Developers! Timeshare condos! A golf course! An open request for drugs at the *P&P* bar! No doubt about it, what he threatened was change.

Despite my liberal leanings, I have generally found a lot of "progress" unattractive and unrewarding and secretly wish some things would stay the same. If big development came to the island what would happen to all the things that make the place special?

I recalled other tropical beauty spots which had been "improved" by a developer's promises of "environmental enhancement," and jobs for everyone. They had usually resulted in monstrous confections of glass and concrete piled ten stories high, painted mauve, and circled by floodlit palm trees. Avenues were lined with flashing signs advertising sequined entertainment, gourmet food and gambling. Ecology was forgotten, as was taste and beauty. The destruction of valuable wildlife, plantlife, birdlife and delicate ecosystems was ignored because in a multi-million dollar development everything was engineered for maximum profit; nothing else counted.

Fresh air would be another loss. On Exuma it was still clean and clear since there was nothing to pollute it — no factories, no cities, few cars, and almost no dust or pollen. It abounded here because the rains cleaned it and the forest growth used up the carbon dioxide and in return produced essential oxygen. This gave us an unfailingly clear and unpolluted substance to breathe, a solacing thought when you consider that we breathe it in 15 to 18 times a minute, and that about 15,000 quarts a day of the stuff goes up our nostrils and into our lungs.

And water! Exuma's supply of fresh water was special, filtered down through layers of limestone that took out whatever impurities are in it; if development came would it remain drinkable and plentiful?

Destroying wetlands, dredging sea beds, uprooting mangrove swamps, altering the landscape or seascape, depleting the seas of certain species (like turtles,) denuding the land of its protective bush, removing huge quantities of sand from the beaches — all to build massive resorts made no sense.

One resort developer on Bimini wanted to build a 200 berth marina, dredge an 85-foot-wide channel, and construct 78 waterfront homes, 78 condominiums with the necessary roads and seawalls, a 10,000 square foot casino, a 200 room hotel-shopping complex and club house, an 18-hole golf course on fragile wetlands, a desalination plant and sewage treatment plant, channels through wetlands that feed a wide variety of wildlife — and build an airtstrip! The impact on the delicate, low-lying land can only be imagined.

With increased wealth in the world it is now easier to destroy larger segments of the environment quicker and faster than ever before. With such rapid expansion a country's way of life is always compromised. Introduced into a simple culture, change inevitably means at least two of the island's good and rare qualities — its peacefulness and serenity — will vanish. Even in the six years since we first moved here we could see the difference even minor development has made between then and now. The first indication of changing times came with the construction of Exuma's new, multi-million dollar airport in Moss Town, on the south side. Certainly, it is modern and utilitarian, built as a hub for planes flying on south, and to accommodate the anticipated influx of thousands of future tourists. But even Mrs. Musgrove's hundreds of plantings — bougainvillea and red hibiscus bushes, palm and orchid trees, croton and oleander plants — failed to tropicalize or soften it. The stone, glass and cement block building with its sharp corners, locked doors and wire mesh fences, presents an unfriendly face to the arrivee and always will.

Gone is romance and the possibility you might meet the ghosts of Lauren Bacall and Bogey; gone the days when we could wait for our visitors at Kermit's rundown *Bar and Grill*, sit under the silk cotton tree and gossip with the taxi drivers, or stand by the white picket fence to watch the plane come in, then wander up to the foot of the steps with an armful of flowers to greet an incoming guest.

Nowadays the incoming passengers were funneled off the airfield by uniformed officials while we expectant islanders stood at a distance behind a high, wire mesh fence, noses pressed against it to try and see if friends and loved ones have arrived.

For several years there had been rumors there would be a 365 acre hotel-casino complex built on the shores of The Bight, the exquisite half-moon slice of beach at Farmer's Hill. A Bahamas Hotel Corporation sign erected there proclaimed it would be coming soon, a fact which, given the island's pace, everyone thought highly unlikely, (and thus far had proven to be true.)

Some thought it would be a boon to island tourism. The citizens of Farmer's Hill, however, were divided. Because of the attached casino the oldsters in the community like Mr. Flowers thought it a bad idea, that in the long run it would be ruination of the settlement.

"I tell you," he said once in a rare pessimistic mood, "we have gamblin' people here we get no rest from trouble."

But the younger people in the settlement were all for it, even though, under Bahamian law, they would not be allowed to gamble. Zelma's three teenagers thought it would be great. "A big hotel on the Bight? Mon, I LIKE that. That means jobs, mon, *jobs*! An' a nice place with a bar, and a place to eat, with lights an' a nice place to go and talk to people — like in the cities — awRIGHT!" (High five.)

Even earlier, back in the sixties a few American developers with grandiose plans had bought, from Bahamian landowners, large tracts of land which they divided into lots and sold off piecemeal. Americans, Canadians, Swedes, Germans and Brits with a dream of paradise bought some, often sight unseen. But for a whole lot of reasons these grand schemes came to little. There were no utilities, few roads, nothing to recommend the island to potential buyers except pristine beaches, clean water and air and not everyone thought such things a reason to leave the more inhabited tropical paradises with their glitzy entertainment; besides, they were easier to reach.

But it doesn't matter if *we* don't like it; for us to hope the island won't develop is elitist, selfish, and reactionary.

It's what the islanders like or don't like, want or don't want, that is important. Many cherish the special values of their small island and say they would prefer things be left as they are.

As Bahamian geographer, and author Neil Sealey wrote:

"Our environment is the nation's resource base. Concern to manage it sensibly should be a major and highly visible component in any government's philosophy. The public also has a responsibility to support and encourage the government ... in this endeavour. We should not stand idly by and see a unique environment, created by ages of natural processes, admired by foreigners and loved by its natives, lost through ignorance and indolence."

With the advent of the Bud Cerranti's of this world it could truthfully be said that at the beginning of 1990's, the idyllic state of the island was over. His kind of developer, with their massive machinery that will carve out time-share condos, shopping complexes, marinas, casinos, resort hotels, tours, and cruise boats is going to glitterize the world, regardless of what people want, and make of it a Disneyland Park.

For, as he said, "it's business makes the world go round." Is it?

Mahoe

36

The Columbus Quincentennial Year was three-quarters gone but on Exuma we were still in a tizzy of preparation for the Columbus 500 race, the premier sailing event of the celebration. More than 120 yachts from 20 countries, carrying about 480 people would follow Columbus's route from Spain to the Canary Islands and across the Atlantic to the finish line at San Salvador. Since there was no large harbor there, they would sail on to an anchorage in George Town's Elizabeth Harbour. All had to be here by December 19.

There was a ton of organizing to be done and some were wondering if it would get done, or whether the event would be a grand catastrophe with reverberations worldwide.

But even if so many people from so many countries had never before arrived at the same time the islanders weren't worried. With their usual easy-going aplomb they said offhandedly, "no prob-lem, mon. It'll get done." They were looking forward to the invasion. As Nigel Minns commented, "we like welcoming strangers to our shores." Fine. Maybe a few at a time. But thousands all at once?

As expected, L. and his wife were around town complaining and predicting the event would be a bust. "These people aren't up to organizing such an international event," they sniffed, lifting their nostrils. "You'll see, it'll be a complete fiasco. All those people! And the world media here! Exuma will be the laughing stock of world yachting."

They predicted this even though Bahamians in Nassau and other islands had earlier arranged, and already pulled off, Quincentennial celebrations in fine style. Special shows, postage stamps, radio broadcasts, books, tourist promotions, tours, "fly-ins" to San Salvador, and gala celebrations came off without a hitch (or maybe just one or two.) On San Salvador Club

Med was completed, the tourists, VIP's, politicians, foreign press, and the PM had a good time at the official ceremonies. Everyone was already declaring the Quincentennial celebrations a success.

On Exuma, because of the island's limited resources, a certain number of glitches were, of course, inevitable. Some shortages were expected. For example, rumor had it that many of the yachters' families would fly in to greet them and spend Christmas. Everyone agreed that if that happened there might well be a lack of rooms and services and subsequent disaster. The islanders, however, came up with a practical solution: for these prospective guests we would open our homes. Thus was born the "Adopt-a-Boat" program.

Guiding sailboats through strange shoals and into a strange harbor presented another problem. It wasn't like funneling sheep into a pen, it took maps, charts, knowledge of harbor lights, warning buoys, and a sophisticated communications setup. All this information had to be collected, printed up, and forwarded beforehand to the sponsoring organization, World Cruising Ltd. in London. This was duly done. But to be absolutely sure of safe arrivals, the local committee enlisted the aid of longtime visiting cruisers to escort the racing sailors through the tricky offshore shoals and into Elizabeth Harbour.

Also helping were Nigel Minns and his brother Basil Minns who set up the America 500 Headquarters. These were in a vacant store donated by Basil located across from the *P&P*. Basil was co-chairman with Charles King, the island's senior commissioner, but it was Basil's responsibility to see that everything ran smoothly, no small job where the most prevalent attitude was always and forever a sunny optimism in the face of problems.

The chief concern was that good weather and fair winds might not hold for the sailors already on their way across the Atlantic. Hurricane weather starts in August and is not officially over until December but crossing the Atlantic at any time is dangerous. Basil, who like Nigel was an experienced sailor, explained: "It's not just hurricanes. This time of year the wind can die altogether and you can be becalmed in mid-ocean."

George Towners were pitching in to spruce up their small capital. Overnight mature palm trees sprouted in newly-dug holes around Victoria Pond. Cynics predicted they would have a half life of about two months and might not survive that long. Not to worry the advocates said, they promise greenery for the ten days of the yachter's visit.

In other bursts of civic pride George Town homes dazzled the eyes in a rainbow of fresh paint, trash pickup became regular, rusted cars disappeared overnight and flower pots appeared on porches. The rains ended, the heat lessened, and most of the bugs departed. It was like magic.

In another spurt of activity committees put together plans for a special Junkanoo parade, a Class "C" Regatta race, several church thanksgiving services for voyages safely completed, and on prize-giving night a dance at the Community Center. To get it all done in time would take another miracle and a cast of thousands.

But it was we who worried, not the Exumians. Life is to be lived, they say, not frittered away by worrying.

By early December the flags of twenty nations fluttered in the breeze on the Government Building lawn. The yacht flotilla, having started out at Palos, Spain, (Columbus's starting point,) and sailing on to the Canary Islands, (his jumping off place,) was now *en route* across the Atlantic to his landfall on San Salvador. Having crossed the finish line there, each crew member would go ashore to plant two coconut trees, a gift from the Canary Islands to the Bahamas. The yachts would then sail on to safe harbor and ten days of prize- and party-giving in George Town.

Coming in the fleet were yachts from Argentina, Austria, Australia, Canada, Croatia, Finland, France, Germany, Great Britain, Italy, Ireland, Netherlands, New Zealand, Norway, Poland, Portugal, Spain, Sweden, Venezuela and – the largest contingent — 45 from the U.S.A.

Most had left the Canaries on November 15, the earliest date on which an Atlantic crossing is considered safe. For the 3,200 mile crossing they were allotted 34 days at an average speed of four knots, or about 94 miles a day. No motoring allowed.

As they sailed across they were being monitored by Bill and Jean Schreiber aboard the yacht *Whatever*, moored in San Salvador's Long Bay. (Rev. Williams' site of the true cross and the spot where other historians are convinced Columbus made his landfall.) The Schreibers, by listening each morning on their single sideband radio to the day's roll call of yachts, were able to plot the daily location of each boat, report emergencies, and upon the yacht's arrival across the finish line, log the time, and fax this information to 500 HQ in George Town.

There were several emergencies. The Finnish boat broke a rudder but sailed on anyway (and got an award for determination.) One day out of the Canaries, Freddy Russo, captain of the French yacht *Euphore*, dislocated a hip. And, as sailors in the past have experienced before in mid-Atlantic, two of the yachts were several times "nudged" and almost tipped over by large whales.

The first — and largest — of the yachts arrived in George Town in mid-December and as planned, was welcomed at the harbor entrance by one of the regular winter boating community, guided to a mooring, offered assistance, and shown to 500 HQ which was being splendidly managed by Ministry of Tourism representative Cleo Clarke. With unflappable good nature she registered arrivals, arranged radio links and phone messages, and helped with the huge need for boat repairs and replenishment of fuel, ice and food.

Standing by in their best duds to welcome the sailors was a bevy of Exuma's beauties. They presented each captain and crew member with a basket of flowers, fruit, maps, brochures, and a a quart of Bahamian rum. Now, these men had been at sea for well over a month and to be presented with gifts by comely young women was like being invited to The Dating Game. How many succumbed was not recorded.

The winner of the Racing Division was the 39 foot Finnish vessel *Aurora*. The 32 foot Croatian boat *Runaway* took the Cruising Division prize. But the overall winner was Portugal's *Espirito de Madeira* with a crew of five unbelievably handsome men.

Dark-haired, flashing-eyed, lean, tanned and flushed with victory, they strode George Town streets like happy pirates. Wherever they went in their dark purple tee shirts, with their boat's name in white across the front, women fluttered around them like moths and offered, on the spot, to exchange tee shirts.

Under the "Adopt-a-Boat" program we met the crew of the 38 foot *Euphore*. Seventy-two year-old captain Freddy Russo, and his three friends — a paper manufacturer, a boat-builder, and a radiologist — had a combined average age of 66. Despite Freddy's dislocated hip (now located,) and his lack of sleep, ("as capitan I mus' sleep all-ways wiz one eye o-pen,") this tough, fit, feisty crew were ready to do the race all over again, even though theirs was one of the boats bunted by a whale.

"*Mon Dieu*," Freddy rolled his eyes in true Gaelic fashion, "eet was a scerry experience. *Bien sur*, he wuz jus' *curieux*, but playing wiz a 50 ton sperm whale iz not zomezing I consider fun."

On December 19 at George Town's Regatta Park the winner's cups were awarded. A souvenir plaque cast in bronze and inscribed with the boat's name went to each captain. As a permanent record of the historical event, identical plaques were to be affixed later to a specially erected monument in the park.

Prizes were given to the four women skippers and to the youngest crew member, four-year-old Andrew Canard. The Bahamas' newly elected prime minister, the Right Honorable Hubert Ingraham, who flew in from Nassau for the occasion, made a gracious speech in which he invited the visitors to return. Then islanders, boaters, racers, guests and everyone else swarmed to the Community Center to drink rum, make merry, and toast the huge success the Exumians had pulled off. (As it turned out, thousands didn't come so there was a bed for everyone.)

Before they left the Aussie crews threw a thank-you party for Exumians at the *Two Turtles Inn*. They'd shipped in enough Australian beer to float any one of the three Australian yacht entries so everyone thought it only right to help them drink it.

The night was pleasantly cool, bright with stars. The boaters had massed in the *Two T*'s courtyard. Strings of colored lights shone down. The newest crop of sea fables were about to enter into legend as the boaters told each other lies about their voyages. In the far corner under the bamboo trees some couples were boogie-ing to piped-in music. It looked as if the whole island had gathered to celebrate.

The level of talk was deafening. People used to talking to one another against the wind, I decided, or across the deck of a boat in full sail, must find it difficult to turn down the volume when on land. Very likely some clever medical scientist will one day find that in order to compete with the wind's roar sailors have developed extra large lungs.

But if strong voices come from the love of sailing, so do the boaters' skin and hair. Sun-bleached, windblown and salt scoured, their hair was the color of fresh straw, their skin wrinkled, brown and wind-roughened. One couple, well into their sixties and more unheeding than the rest, had skin the color of walnut stain. Another woman, wiggling her bottom to a fast reggae beat, perspired in a white bra and shorts that made her look like an oversized oreo cookie. Her mate, wearing rope sandals, white deck pants, a cloth headband, and a navy and white striped tee shirt, looked like an escaped French convict. It was quite obvious they were having fun growing older.

Equally obvious, was that they cared not a whit for the opinions of dermatologists, cosmetologists, hair stylists, beauticians, or any of the other counselors and beauty experts who advised about beauty and health care. I guessed their response to all the medical and cosmetologist warnings and predictions of dire results and premature aging was: so what?

The Australian beer was smooth, mellow and strong, and with a lot more kick than I was used to. After only one my tongue seemed to have put on weight. I felt the muscles of my legs weakening and told my husband I thought we should drive home while we still could. He thought that idea was one of life's great unfairnesses but agreed it was a good idea, because his head had suddenly begun to play Waltzing Matilda.

On the way out we spotted Pete Balloil with, this time, a local island beauty clamped to his chest. He waved at us with a bottle of *Kalik.*

"What happened to Patti?" I asked.

"Got religion. Went back home to Jacksonville to marry her high school sweetheart. I told her that was smart and no hard feelings between us."

"Where're you off to next?"

"Think I'll stay around here. Place gets to you, y'know? No place like it really." He glanced down at his companion. "I hear The Moorings is setting up a place on Stocking Island. Guess I'll charter out of there for a while." For once he looked as if he meant it. "I mean, it pays to know when you're well off, y'know?"

Next day we reflected on the grand event. Amazingly, just as the Exumians predicted, it was a tremendous success. They, of course, were never in doubt. In their own way, and in their own easygoing, non-hustling style, they got it all together, with only a little help from us foreigners. Just as they took us in, like families welcoming sailors home from the sea, they took in "the strangers from away."

Apart from this generous hospitality, what I remembered next best was those four retired Frenchmen off *Euphore*, all ready to do the trip again, all refusing to be limited by their age, all determined to keep their minds active and alert by going adventuring. Adventuring, I thought, what a great way to age.

Hibiscus

37

Our friend the Bird-Watcher arrived dressed like Meryl Streep in *Out of Africa* and looking like General Schwarzkopf on his way to Operation Desert Storm. "I hear there are parrots on these islands," he said when we greeted him through the chainlink fence at the airport. He had on his cork-lined pith helmet, headgear we hadn't seen since we lived in Africa in the sixties. Even then it was considered 40 years out of date.

With the Bahamas home to nearly 300 species of birds that spend their winters in the pine yards, coppices and ponds of the islands, the government, through its Ministry of Tourism, was trying hard to become a mecca for bird-lovers. By promoting bird-watching as one of the major attractions of the islands, they hoped to appeal to all bird-watchers but particularly American bird-watchers, who alone spend an estimated $4 million a year on birding gear and expeditions in search of rare birds. Exuma, and the entire Bahamas stood to benefit greatly from this birding industry if it took off. It was also good for the Ministry's efforts promoting eco-tourism.

A bird tour-guide training program was started and within three years had 37 people receiving advanced certificates and badges. Participants were put through a rigorous process aimed at teaching them to guide tours, conduct special field trips, give lectures on local plant life and environmental issues, and know their birds. This produced the first Bahamian tour guides; before this foreigners were called in to conduct nature tours. The first of its kind in the Caribbean region, the program was a joint project by the Bahamas National Trust and the Ministry of Tourism to make Bahamians aware of their environment and to introduce birding as a hobby and possible profession.

Our own experience as local bird guides hardly got off the ground. Speaking through the wire mesh to our bird-loving friend we explained that the parrots, what remained of them, were mostly on Abaco, Acklins and Great Inagua, where there were also flamingos. One parrot was sighted on Exuma and the person who saw it was keeping mum. "But we have other birds," my husband promised his old friend. "Not a lot, but some. And spring is the time to see them."

"That's why I came now," our guest said, "but what do you mean — `not a lot?' Don't you know there are 40 species of birds indigenous to the Bahamas?" We didn't, and I wondered how up-to-date his information was.

When he emerged from customs and immigration we saw that he'd brought not only his pith helmet but his khaki backpack, camera, binoculars, notebook, canvas boots, khaki field jacket, Bond's latest edition of *Birds Of The West Indies*, a rubber poncho, and his best Banana Republic safari pants with one hundred pockets, (hidden and revealed.) We envisioned him going off into the bush and being shot by Stanley or one of his friends who might think the American Marines were invading.

Our birdman could hardly wait to get started. On his first morning he was up at dawn, shaved, dressed, and five minutes later was on his way out the door. We didn't see him again until late afternoon, when he returned tired, hungry, muddy, dusty, and happy. In private, we became hysterical mimicking him in his ridiculous "Dr. Livingston I presume," pith helmet, which he insisted upon calling a *topee*.

"I'm going to get you one of those," I said to my husband, choking with laughter at the idea of him in it. "You can wear it when you're working in the garden. They say the cork lining keeps your brains from being fried."

His reply was succinct and to the point. "Don't you dare! Stanley would never let me hear the end of it, and I might get mistaken for a missionary."

Our guest was easy to entertain. He wasn't interested in swimming or snorkeling, shelling or social life. He ate little, liked whatever was put in front of him, and mostly talked birds.

He got up early and went to bed early. Every morning right after breakfast he took his field glasses, put on his *topee*, and tramped off to parts unknown, returning late to regale us with

208

excited accounts of the island's birdlife.

Did we know, he asked, perspiring heavily in his khaki field jacket, *topee* slightly askew, his heavy glasses sliding down his nose in excitement, that around Grog Pond there were snowy egret nests and dozens of those lovely birds? That a brown pelican lived at the end of the beach, a big one, quite friendly, and almost four feet long, mostly brown but with a grey back and white head? What a wonderful sight! He was thrilled.

For fear he might hate us for not stopping the practice, we didn't tell him that come autumn, Stanley and other hunters would be stalking Grog Pond for the ruddy ducks and the small Bahamian pintail ducks, which the islanders consider a delicacy. We couldn't bear to let him know they roast them with onion and tomato sauce and serve them over rice. He was in no fit mood to face such barbarism.

Instead, we made him ecstatic by telling him that the island contained wild peacocks and osprey. His excitement made him have to sit down. He dropped weakly into a chair. "I must see them," he said. "I simply must."

We told him our friend Inchie Frenning had a family of them nesting in her woods and they frequently sat atop her flagpole; I said I'd ask her if we could take him around to see them.

However, the ospreys would be secondary, we said. He was going to enjoy Inchie far more than any birds. She was unique. Now ninety-two, until two years ago she still went fishing, swam every day, and always dressed for dinner, even when dining alone. Deciding not to be left behind in the computer age she had bought a computer, taught herself to use it, and was busy writing her memoirs. We had great admiration for her and I hoped when we were her age we'd be as brave and spunky as she. I promised to phone and see if she would receive us next day for tea.

We assured him he need not go hiking to find birds. Right in our own garden he could view any number of them just by sitting quietly under the seagrape tree. Next morning we took our coffee out there and sat in the shade. The tree's long spikey blossoms were out, the air was heavy with their fragrance. Bees hummed in and out of the branches. The "mockies" sang, the "hummers" danced. From the weathervane atop the house a "mockie" scolded us. These chatty, noisy and overly-friendly grey-brown mockingbirds were the garden bullies, guarding their various territories with swoops and dives worthy of a kamikaze pilot. They woke us in the morning, chattered at us whenever we left the house, and, perched on the tip of a nearby tree, eyed us with barely contained tolerance until we went back inside. They were not colorful — really rather drab in fact — nor particularly rare, but our guest was enchanted. He ran about taking photographs.

Small brown ground doves scooted about on the ground, the yellow, black and white banana quits hovered around our homemade feeder — half a coconut shell filled with sugar and slung from the frangipani tree — and perched above them, awaiting their turn, were the greenish-grey grass quits.

To encourage these small birds, which Bahamians call "chim-chims," we had put out a bird bath — actually an old refrigerator tray — on the deck railing. They drank from it and then — after careful surveillance all around — wallowed in it, splashing and thrashing and raising a fine spray of water in all directions. Even then they keep a constant eye out for attacking "mockies."

A pair of red-crested Greater Antillian bullfinches flew in under the cabbage palm to feast on its long cascade of red berries. Our friend, holding his camera at the ready, hopped ecstatically from one bush to another like a rabbit. "Look! Look!" he cried, "the berries are the exact shade as their crests!" His camera shutter clicked madly.

Best of show that day, though, were, as usual, the "hummers," the iridescent green, ruby-throated hummingbird known as the Bahama Woodstar, and its cousin, the tiny jewel-like Cuban Emerald hummingbird. At least four of the Woodstars flitted like colored arrows from blossom to blossom; first to the pink hibiscus to sip at the back of the flower, then to the coral plant, next to the tiny red bloom of the monkey-fiddle, on to the ixora, the purple bougainvillea, the yellow elder, and back to the pink hibiscus.

I told our guest the story of the one that tried to pull some hair from my husband's scalp to weave into its nest. "Oh, oh," he crooned wistfully, obviously forgetting he is all but bald and needed every hair he could keep. "Oh, I wish one would try that on me."

That afternoon we drove to Farmer's Hill to Miss Elsie May's to phone Inchie. Yes, she would be "at home" the next afternoon and happy to have us and our guest to tea at four o'clock. We arrived at five minutes to; this diminutive New England lady, born into the Edwardian age and brought up with its formal manners, considered it bad manners to be late.

Erect, petite, her white hair crowning her head like thistledown, she greeted us graciously in her beautiful main room and asked us to sit down. Tea would arrive soon.

The long room, lit by a delicate sea light coming through glass walls, was large, spacious and cool, with a view of Elizabeth Harbour on one side and the harbor entrance on the other. She had decorated it herself in pastels to match the sea and sky colors and now they encompassed her, shimmering around her frail figure like fractured crystal.

As we knew he would be, (as everyone always was,) our friend was enchanted with Inchie and soon forgot the egrets. He was full of questions for her: how did she happen to come to Exuma so long ago? How had she built such a lovely house?

Answering politely, pouring tea, she spoke first of how she came to the Bahamas with her parents in 1909 as a child of seven. Nassau in those pre-World War I days was a small backwater colonial town under British rule and a favorite spot for American yachters. Her father, and her mother, also a sailor, taught her how to handle a boat, how to race, and "how to win."

Later, after her mother died, she often accompanied her father, whom she called Skipper, on sailing trips throughout the islands. "I was always looking," she said, "for an adventurous and out-of-the-way place to someday build a winter home."

In 1956, now married, she, her husband, and some friends sailed into Elizabeth Harbour and she knew she'd found the place.

It was then she met island resident, yacht designer, and boating writer Linton Rigg, an Englishman who also sold real estate. He suggested she and her brother and sister buy a small island at the western entrance to the harbor. They eventually did, and she set about designing and building not only her own

211

house, but those of her siblings.

By now our birdman was no longer interested in the ospreys; he wanted to hear more about Inchie and her homesteading. Telling her story, she was in turn, charming, vivacious, and witty, with a sharp tongue at times, and not above delicious gossip.

She spoke fondly of the Bahamians and her early years on Exuma when, in between days spent mixing cement and hauling blocks, she got to know the islanders. She learned what it took to build a house the Bahamian way, (slowly.) How to get a well drilled and a road made, how to tussle with unreliable electricity and unpredictable storms (and one hurricane,) how to deal with the vagaries of a series of workmen. All these things she came to know.

To get supplies and materials to the site, she had first to have a dock built, then, a few hundred yards away, a causeway from the Exuma shore. Because she believed they would thrive here, she had a place cleared for some exotic plants and fruit trees imported from Hawaii and the U.S.

Then there was the matter of barging in all the building materials from Nassau... of finding local workmen with the skills to do the masonry, plumbing, electrical work and roofing... and the matter of a water supply... and of the interior carpentry, much of which she did herself... of spending what time she could on Exuma when she could get away from her job of raising a family and running her own interior design business back in New England... .

By this time — some 37 years later — the main house had a tree-shaded central courtyard, surrounding patios, separate guest quarters, a separate master suite, a garden, and the woods where the ospreys lived.

We never did see the ospreys that afternoon — it was too dark by the time we left — but our guest was not in the least disappointed. He said earnestly, "she's worth a whole flock of ospreys." In his enthusiasm he stumbled down the woodland path from her house, causing his glasses to fall off his nose. "That magnificent house is like a Hollywood stage set. I feel as if I'd just lived through a Bette Davis movie directed by Darryl Zanuck."

On his last day the Bird Watcher still hadn't seen a night heron. In the swamp below the house he'd seen little blue herons, a white heron on Grog Pond, a brown heron on the beach — but no night herons. A great disappointment. We told him that on many nights one walks as gently as moonlight across our deck, softly sounding its "woc! woc!" call. In the morning we often saw its footprints.

"Oh! Oh!" He appeared to be in a paroxysm of longing. Would we mind if he sat up outside on the deck tonight? No? Good, good. Then that's what he was going to do.

Having gotten up at six that morning, around nine o'clock he was ready for bed. We fixed him a comfortable cot on an outdoor lounge chair and left him to it with a flashlight and a thermos of hot coffee.

Next morning I crept out to see how fared the night's Heron Watch. The thermos of coffee sat untouched and our guest was fast asleep, surrounded by heron tracks. Figuring he'd been observing herons most of the night, I left him asleep and went inside to get breakfast.

Half an hour later he came in looking crestfallen.

It was a tiring week, he explained. He hadn't realized how physically worn out he was... all that tramping through the bush...photographing... crouching beside Grog Pond... .

Last night he'd gone off to sleep almost immediately and slept soundly throughout the night. Missed the night heron.

We drove him to the airport and bid him goodbye. Peering through his thick glasses, he thanked us for a fine vacation, and added, "I hope your island never changes... I've had the most marvelous time... you've been so kind... I can never thank you enough... it's hard for me to find words to tell you... I didn't know how to thank you enough...so I've left..." he stopped, cleared his throat in embarrassment... barged on... .

"When you get home... you'll find I've left you a present." All the way home I wondered what to expect. A strange man, an oddball, someone without guile or fancy airs who, nonetheless, we were very fond of, he had probably left an extravagant gift he likely couldn't afford.

When we got home I looked around. No gift was evident. Not on the Great Room table, in the Garden (guest) Room, the kitchen, or the living room. We forgot about it.

That night when we went to bed there it was sitting on my husband's side of the bed, looking like a large mushroom: the Birdman's pith helmet.

My husband put it on and we collapsed onto the bed, laughing hysterically.

Tropical
Mockingbird

39

The Bahamian school system was still pretty much based on teaching methods inherited from 150 years of British Colonial rule, even though this had long been outdated in the "Mother Country." Some of the islands' textbooks were still British, the teaching methods tended to be those learned in colonial days, and much of the learning was by rote, all of which made education here strict, rigidly fixed and formal.

Some of the qualities learned, however, were those that in American schooling have been lost. For example, politeness and civility were emphasized in Exumian classrooms, as was respect for the teacher. When addressing a teacher or an older person the children, and even some adults, still used ma'am and sir. It made for public civility.

Pride in their country and its diverse racial mix were taught in schools and promoted by the central government's program of *One Bahamas*. Self-esteem and pride in themselves was taught outside the schools and tended to be church-related.

When our neighbors Kenneth and Ruby Thompson invited us to attend the finals of the Youth Oratorical Contest we were pleased to accept. The event was part of the annual National Baptist Convention weekend, held this year at the Mount Ebenezer Baptist Church in Farmer's Hill.

Everyone would be there, Ruby assured us, because one of the three semi-finalists was an Exumian twelve-year-old girl, Danica Pintard. Hopes were high that she would win over the others, a boy from nearby Long Island, and another boy from Nassau.

The church, a long, low white building set on the side of a hill just below the telephone relay towers, was lit up as for a carnival; we could see the lights from afar as we drove along the Queen's Highway. It was a warm night with a million stars lighting up the great nighttime bowl of the universe and the silver crescent of the new moon perched saucily in the lap of the old. Though we were early, the place was rapidly filling up, with everyone in their best and ladies' hats rampant. We sat down next to Miss Elsie May and two of her "grans," one three-year-old, the other five.

By seven-thirty the place was packed; we estimated nearly five hundred people. Children sat on laps, people stood along the sides fanning themselves, a choir of faces peered in the open windows. The overflow stood on the porch. Ceiling fans churned the air. Humming around the big room was a buzz of excitement. Exumians were out to cheer on one of their own.

Danica, a comely junior high school student, member of the Mt. Sinai Baptist Church in nearby Stuart Manor, sat primly on a straight chair at the front between the two male contestants.

After much greeting and hand-shaking, kissing and hugging, the five-man electronic combo *The New Direction* got down to the serious business of providing music with a hundred-decibel rendition of *All Hail The Power of Jesus' Name*. There were no hymnals because, presumably, everyone knew the words. We sang, clapped in time to the music, all swayed. Miss Elsie sang when she wasn't chastising one of her grans into good behavior.

The choir, in their blue-and-white robes, marched singing from the back of the church and took their place stage-front where, without a pause for breath they launched into a lusty version of *How Firm A Foundation*. The fans whirred, Louis Rolle made the old piano talk, the drums matched the piano beat, the guitar sounded the harmony, and the electronic keyboard belted out the tune. The congregation loved it. Heads back, throats opened to full throttle, we made that church jump.

After several renditions by the choir and a solo or two, the contest started. A polite silence reigned.

The topic was not one you'd expect any youngster to embrace enthusiastically: *The Baptist Union, Past, Present and Future*. This was serious business. Rules were: the ten-minute speech must be written by the speaker, be original, factual, organized and imaginative. Points would be given for originality, delivery, deportment, composure, self-confidence and overall speaking ability. A formidable challenge for three so young.

First one up was the teenage lad from Nassau.

Speaking with one hand relaxedly in his jacket pocket, he gave the Baptist Union a competent appraisal. In both speech and demeanour he was impressively at ease and sure of himself, his head high, his words clear and precise. In his mind at least, he was a sure winner over these "out-island" bumpkins, the Bahamian "out-islands" being on a par with Iowa's corn belt.

Up next was the Long Island lad, also a teenager. He was somewhat less sure of himself but, eyes alight, voice vibrant, he spoke of the Baptist Union in a voice filled with passion. Without too much difficulty you could detect the future minister in his soul.

Both received loud, appreciative and well-deserved applause.

Next came Danica. Our Exuma star.

Throughout the two previous speeches she had sat quietly, head bent, eyes downcast, hands clasped in her lap, her manner serious. Was it shyness that caused her downcast eyes? Modesty? Or nervousness? The room waited. And hoped.

When called, she arose from her chair gracefully, carefully smoothed down her pink dress, adjusted her pink tulle-and-pearl hair ornament, and walked to the lectern. Against her dark skin a pearl necklace gleamed, tiny pearl earrings pierced her earlobes.

Reverend Irwin Clarke lowered the lectern to accomodate her four feet five inches, and stepped back, giving her a nod of encouragement.

Poised and self-assured, she began. Her challenge, as it was for the other two, was not only to make the ten-minute speech interesting and deliver it in a way that generated excitement and attention, but to do that better than the two male speakers, both of whom were older by several years.

She spoke easily, winningly. Crying babies, whirring fans, or the loud voices of the louts in the parking lot didn't faze her. At times she extended her hands to make a point, or to embrace all 500 of us in the church, drawing us along with her as she explored her subject — which was carefully crafted in her own words. Big words. Sophisticatd words. Words used correctly and effectively and strung together in fine sentences.

For a twelve-year-old it was an impressive presentation. When finished, she gave a little bow, sat down daintily, arranged her skirt, crossed her ankles, and folded her hands in her lap.

The five judges retired to a distant room. Louis Rolle and *The New Direction* struck up *O God Our Help in Ages Past*, the choir sang and swayed, the speakers blared. When the adjudicators returned, the lead judge, a woman of Amazonian stature who was here from Nassau's radio station ZNS, took the podium. A hush fell upon us.

Solemnly she announced that she would designate the winners in beauty contest fashion, with the second runner-up named first. People shuffled their feet, sighed, whether in annoyance or impatience it was hard to tell. There was no doubt in any of our minds who had won.

"And the second runner up is....."

It was the cocky and very disappointed young man from Nassau.

He got a smattering of polite applause.

Then the lady judge played with us. She knew, as did we all, that once she announced the next runner-up — second place — we would immediately know the winner. Carefully, without denoting gender, she reminded us of the rules and judging criteria: the speech must be original, factual, organized and imaginative. Points were given for originality, delivery, deportment, composure, self-confidence and overall speaking ability. The audience stirred restlessly. You could feel the overall impatience she'd aroused with her temporizing.

She cleared her throat importantly. The room grew completely silent. Even Miss Elsie's grans, guessing something was up, stayed quiet.

"And the first runner-up is... " She paused... "the young man from Long Island!... and the winner is —"

Long before she said Danica's name the room erupted. The drummer drummed, the choir sang, the keyboard wailed, and the audience cried with joy, hugged, kissed chanted, sang, clapped and danced in the aisles.

From the back of the church Mrs. Izona Rolle, the grandmother with whom Danica lived, sashayed down the aisle in her purple dress and hat, smiling ecstatically, kissing and shaking hands, acknowledging kudos with all the aplomb of a reigning queen. Once up front she danced a little samba and bowed to the crowd. This was her day too and everybody there knew it.

Danica, meanwhile, sat smiling demurely — until Mrs. Rolle, her position established as the winner's proud grandmother, shouted above the din, "she's the *best!*" Then twirling her plump figure around in a 90 degree turn she raised up this special child from her chair, this small, prize-winning speaker, and in a giant bear hug of pride and approval pressed Danica to her ample bosom.

We all cheered then, clapped, cried, and got up to dance in the aisles.

Sweet Exuma had won over sophisticated Nassau.

We concurred this year that we were getting somewhat tired of houseguests. We'd had six, two couples back to back, and though they were fun and interesting, it was also tiring. Shopping, planning meals and cooking them, and entertaining guests when you have an established and successful rhythm of your own, can prove wearying.

So when our friend The Corporate Executive wrote that he wanted to come for some R & R, we were reluctant. A man who already owned all the "boy toys" anyone could use or want, he said he was exhausted and needed some down time. We deliberated. Yes, or no?

Eventually we decided on yes; after all, it seemed selfish not to share our good fortune. Island life had renewed us, why not him?

When we met his incoming plane he certainly looked jaded. Grey skin, baggy eyes, lusterless hair. Living on the fast track, he told us on the way home, was challenging and mostly he enjoyed it but every now and then he had to get away, give up shaving and wearing a tie, sink to the slob stage, and just "veg" out. We were to plan nothing for him. He just wanted to sleep late, swim, walk the beaches, and not give a thought to making money.

Okay, we said, you're on your own.

His second day here he returned with a story to tell:

He'd walked as far as Steventon, the settlement of pink and green houses nestled among a palm grove a few miles west of Farmer's Hill. The mile-long beach was like few others he had ever seen; pristine and exquisite, covered in pure white sand, lined with palm trees, and with easy access into the azure water.

Arrested by the sheer loveliness of it, he sat down on the sand to drink it all in. A lad from the village came up, a youngster of twelve or thirteen with a spearfishing rod over his shoulder, and hailed him in a friendly manner. Our friend asked him to sit down a minute and tell him about the island.

The youngster laid down his fishing spear and sat down beside him on the sand. They talked about the island, the settlement, the boy's school. The boy said he didn't particularly like school and would rather go spearfishing or sail his dinghy.

Our friend, thinking to do a good deed that day, talked at length about the value of education and the importance of staying in school and studying hard to become a success in life.

"If you stay in school and get a diploma, or a college degree it will insure you a good job where you can make a lot of money like I do."

"What do you do with all your money?"

"You can do lots of things. Buy a house, a car, some nice clothes, a boat, and take a vacation to a place like this."

"I don't need a vacation." The kid rose from the sand, picked up his fishing spear. "I live here. I fish and swim everyday. And we have a boat. I'm going to be a fisherman."

When our friend related this story at dinner we all had a good laugh. Still, it makes one wonder. Why is running on the fast track our American view of success? Must we all rush around and compete and strive to amass great wealth? If living well is the best revenge, isn't it smart to know when you're living well?

The island youngster certainly knew that.

When our friend Dorcas Rolle Shuttleworth, the dedicated principal of the elemtary school in The Forest heard this story she commented, "you can't fool children. They are born paying attention to their inner life. Born knowing what makes them happiest."

This dedicated and respected teacher, loved by all her students, believes that when a child is educated away from that inner knowledge, or bent, in a direction they are not prepared to go, a part of them dies, a part that is essential to their becoming a fully realized person.

"That youngster knows he wants to live on his home island and fish," Dorcas said, "and I feel it would be a mistake to try and make him a teacher or a scientist in Nassau. Let those who want that, do that. What's wrong with letting this boy be a fisherman? In our society we are in desperate need of people who want to make fishing a gainful employment."

It seems increasingly clear that one important step toward educating a happy and contented human being is to correct the conventional way our high-tech society measures a successful life. Education that both directs and disciplines, while allowing the child to pursue his or her inner bent, inner knowing and inner direction, is of inestimable value. We need indicators that register not wealth and the accumulation of the things it will buy, but self-worth and service.

November, 1994. This year we planned a special Exuma Thanksgiving. Fourteen of us, Bahamians and non-Bahamians, planned to celebrate the island as well as give thanks for our many blessings. For our special dinner we divided up the cooking, used foods found only on Exuma, and created our own praise in the form of poems, prose and song.

On Thanksgiving Day Nan and Rich roasted the two freshly-caught grouper in brown paper, I made the salads, Eunice the breads, Linda the dessert fruit platter, Bobby and Phil Rubin provided the wine, Inchie the paper cups and plates, Posy and Bailey and a visiting cousin prepared the rice and hosted the gathering at their home on a ridge overlooking Moriah Harbour Cay.

We arrived there at 5 p.m. bearing food. Already the house was full of exotic smells, festive with flowers and greens, full of the reassuring sounds of friends greeting friends. The food, when arranged on a buffet, looked superb. The grouper rested in its brown paper nest, the rice steamed in a large wooden bowl, Linda's huge bamboo tray of Exuma's fruits was a masterpiece of color and texture: guavas, oranges, watermelon, grapefruit, papaya, bananas, sapodilla, limes, and sugar apples shone forth from a background of dark green leaves.

We held hands around the table while Lloyd gave the blessing. "Food is sacred," he said as he blessed the splendid array and it occured to me that one way of healing our neglected and desecrated earth was to first heal intercultural and interpersonal wounds, and that one of the most powerful ways to do that was to share food.

Seated around the large table we ate slowly, languidly, talking, laughing, telling stories, relating anecdotes.

Over coffee we made our spiritual contributions to the moment. Lloyd gave us a yoga chant, Nan an original poem, Inchie read two pages from her memoirs of the island, Eunice told an amusing anecdote about flying to the island. I read the chapter from this book about Danica winning the oratorical contest, Bobby told us a story, Linda gave a closing prayer by St. Francis of Assisi. It was a true thanks-giving.

I looked around at these friends, three races, four nationalities — American, British, Canadian and Bahamian — their faces glowing with good will and fondness for one another, and never had the island looked more beautiful.

39

Every year George Town rocked along sleepily for about 338 days of the year, a picture of peace and tranquility. Then in mid-April — two weeks before Regatta — The Fever broke out. What it generated was awesome.

The early symptoms were simmering anticipation tinged with rising excitement and a rash of unlikley exertion. For two months the "yachties" and Exumians had been holding cookouts, fairs, raffles and tee shirt sales to help pay for the grand inter-island event.

By the second week in April, as the three-day blowout neared, the whole island got infected, the results of which was a rash of frenzied activity. Zelma cooked up a freezerful of fried chicken, Miss Freda baked a mountain of sticky buns, and restaurants ordered cases of beer and soft drinks and made gallons of conch chowder. Shelves at Minns Exuma Market and John Marshall's bulged with groceries we hadn't seen for months, exotic things like Brie and smoked salmon paté, fresh grapes and mulligatawny soup, tiny frozen shrimp and pressed turkey, all at three times Stateside prices.

The Anglican church on the hill arranged a White Elephant sale, the Baptists held a Food Fair, another group called the Regatta Entertainment Committee organized a fashion show, a Little Miss Regatta contest for girls under twelve, and a variety of games, parades, cookouts, and sports events, including the much-appreciated wet tee shirt contest. Some island girls fixed dates for their wedding.

Regatta fever is not fatal, of course, but it afflicted almost everyone, islander, visitor and winter residents alike. I, for one — never a good sailor and often seasick — could fully appreciate and enjoy the beauty of the Bahamian wooden work boats in full sail. Like everyone else, I found myself cheering for my favorite as the graceful hand-hewn boats raced down the length of Elizabeth Harbour, sails billowing, crew leaning out precipitously above the water on the pry board. It was a thrilling sight.

As far as anyone knows, the Family Island Regatta is the only sailing race of its kind, a display of the last remaining, wind-driven, working fleet in the world. The yearly pageant of boats, sailed by the men who made them, attracted people from all over because it offered not only seamanship at its best but three days of revelry, heavy betting, eating, drinking, talking, dancing, and a veritable flood of implausible stories.

Mostly, though, people came because the three days of races display seamanship at its best. The fleet of wooden workboats, with their loose-footed high-flying mainsails, open fish wells, and dozen or so crew members, represented the centuries-old skills of sailors who knew the reefs and cays and currents as intimately as you or I know our way to work.

In a final spurt of zeal that bordered on the miraculous, Exumians geared up for the year's crop of visiting family, friends, yachters, tourists, and fellow Bahamians from the other islands. It was a time when friendships were renewed, the year's crop of boat entrants discussed, and people argued endlessly about the merits of their favorite boat. Regatta was the ultimate test of island hospitality — and *braggadocio*.

Before the final invasion George Town's Regatta Park was a-twinkle with strings of lights. And much to the disapproval of those winter visitors who liked the island to be neat, tidy and picturesque at all times, wooden food shacks along the government dock were being slap-dashed together. Zelma and her brood erected a shack to sell beer and fried chicken, and Darleen's sister planned to sell native shell jewelry (made in the Philippines.)

The sleek power yachts and sailboats of visiting yachstmen began arriving in Elizabeth Harbour. Other visitors flew in or arrived on the *Grand Master*. Large boats were chartered for the occasion and, as we knew from our earlier experience when we stayed with John Marshall, every available room in town would have been booked for months. Sailboat mania was in full swing.

At the beginning of Regatta Week we sat on our deck each morning drinking coffee and watching as boats from other islands sailed past our beach. There were sloops, dinghies and smacks from Andros, Long Island, the Exumas, Ragged Island, Eleuthera, Abaco and New Providence. All were harkening to the age-old siren song of *"Sail 'er Down To George Town, Mon!"*, a sea shanty that has now resounded around the Bahamas every April for 42 years.

For the captains and their crews, this was the culmination of months, sometimes years, of skilled work and practice to be the "best they can be." And their best as seamen was formidable.

Having received a magazine assignment to write about Regatta, and needing some history and background of the event, I looked up Howland Bottomley, the Regatta race commissioner and commodore. I knew him, though not well. No one did that.

A gruff, taciturn, rumpled sort of man now in his sixties, he was considered an island "character," (one of many.) A sailor's sailor, he was much liked by the Regatta boat captains and crews who considered him a fair and honest man and referred to him fondly as "Bottom." As I was soon to find out, however, if he didn't want to see or talk to you he could be gleefully intimidating.

Every non-Bahamian who ends up here has a story. Bottomley's was that around 40 years ago, while cruising the Bahamas from his home in New Jersey, he dropped anchor in Elizabeth Harbour and, captivated by the place, never left. He built a home, raised a family, developed the Regatta Point rental apartments, later divorced, and moved to Stocking Island on the other side of George Town harbor. He now lived alone there and, some said, kept a somewhat jaundiced eye on the harbor's comings and goings from an armchair on his porch. I intended to win him with my charm.

"I'm writing about Regatta for *Islands* magazine and I've come to ask about the history," I said when we eventually met.

He eyeballed me, not speaking, looking off across the harbor as if he'd rather I wasn't there. Nervous, but determined not to be intimidated, l begin to babble. I prattled on airily about ISLANDS magazine, what a class act it is, how the photos and layout are first rate, what the editor has asked me to cover, how I plan to do it. I tell him about Darrell Jones, the world class photographer who's been hired to do the photos, about how I want lots of color and activity. Commodore Bottomley listened awhile then said, "you know anything about boats?"

I had to admit I didn't know much.

"What d'you know about sailing?"

I thought back to the San Sal trip. "Not much I'm afraid."

He's not charmed. His brows come together, his blue eyes, pocketed in skin weathered by years of squinting against a sea glare, regarded me disapprovingly. "If you don't know anything about boats, an' you don't know how to sail one, I can't see how you intend to write a story about a sailboat race."

"Oh I can learn what I need to know about the race," I said with airy self-confidence, "but I'm not writing just about the boats and the race." Once more I attempted to cajole him with my best smile, "I'm writing about Regatta in general and all the events that go on around it. Including its history, and that's why I'm here. Everyone says you are the one to tell me about that."

He grunted and reluctantly began.

The history of Regatta goes like this he said:

Between 1836 and 1860 boat-building in the Bahamas was a thriving industry. Dinghies, schooners and sloops were built for fishing, conching, turtling, sponging, "salvaging" wrecks, and transporting salt and other cargo from island to island and "down" to Nassau. For centuries, such wooden sailing vessels supported as many as six brothers and their families.

But by 1950, such working sail was fast disappearing. The Grand Banks fishing schooners were all but gone, the Chesapeake oyster dreggers were going, and Bahamian vessels still under working sail had an uncertain future. And while there had always been good-natured sailing races among these boats this, too, was becoming a thing of the past.

So in 1954 the Out Island Squadron was born. Founding members were Howland Bottomley, writer J. Linton Rigg, two American yachtsmen Ward Wheelock and Arthur Herrington, and Bahama Olympic yachtsman Robert H. "Bobby" Symonette, the son of the late Sir Roland Symonette, first premier of the Bahamas. Lending support was winter resident and intrepid yachtswoman Blanche (Inchie) Frenning. The group started a fund and arranged the first organized Out Island Regatta.

The aim was, (and still is, he emphasized,) to preserve the legendary sailing skills of the Bahamians and their traditional boat-building talents. Every possible effort was made to keep the boats closely related to their working ancestors. For centuries Bahamians had built their own boats and roamed the 100,000 square miles of the Bahamas' ocean highways as expertly as Americans drive their freeways. Without benefit of modern navigational aids, depth finders, radios or charts, these consummate sailors were able to read the wind from a quick glance at the sea's surface, judge depth by the ocean's colors, and chart a course by a familiar landmark or the twinkling of a distant star.

Nor were these boats easy to sail. The sloops had no lead ballast on the keel so they depended for stability on sacks of sand, or on huge stones stowed in the bilge.

The founders set a few basic rules. Boats had to be Bahamian designed, built, owned, skippered and crewed. They must be simply rigged, free of all expensive technological gear, and the hull, rigging and sails designed to keep costs reasonable and insure stability of design. Sails had to be made of canvas, not synthetics, and must be locally sewn.

With no other rules than that, word went out that the first annual working boat regatta was to be held in George Town, Exuma, the recognized sailing capital of the Bahamas. There would be a purse for the winners. In late April of that first year, 70 Bahamian sloops, schooners, and dinghies gathered in Elizabeth Harbour. The first Out Island Regatta (as it was then known) got underway. To run it cost around $5,000.

Bahamians love jokes on one another and over the next years, because there were few rules, some of the jokes were outrageous. One year the Rev. Wilfred Gentry McPhee, an Andros man, pastor of the Mount Calvary Baptist Church in Nassau, and skipper of *Thunderbird,* was falling behind on the last leg of a tight race. To lighten his load he ordered three crew members to dive off the stern one at a time — and sailed in first. (Howls of protest!)

One year (Shark Lady) Gloria Patience, aboard her dinghy *Barefoot Gal,* in a close final race, ordered her three-woman crew to strip off their bikini bras. Momentarily seduced by the sight of this dusky bounty, the men on the other boats paused too long to stare, and, bras waving, *Barefoot Gal* sailed over the finish line ahead of them. (Howls of *Unfair!* Protests of *Foul Play!*)

It was time, however, for some new, simple, easily understood and administered rules, so the race committee initiated about 20 more, and today it's no longer okay to striptease or drop crew overboard — you must finish fully clothed and with the same number of men you started with — though it's okay to throw over your ballast (lead bars or sandbags.)

Other rules stated that if two close-hauled boats were in danger of collision, both must tack. An overtaking boat on a run must pass the boat ahead to leeward. Buoy room must be given at a leeward mark. Colliding with a mark disqualified a boat. No sculling allowed. Boats failing to help another in distress may be disqualified.

During the next twenty years or so, as the prestige of winning the Family Island Regatta increased, and boat builders throughout the islands vied with one another to build a winner, there grew up a "boat fervor" to build a boat specifically for racing. This resulted in a gradual transition from the old work boats to out-and-out wooden racing boats, now referred to as Bahama Racing Sloops.

Since it was never the intention of the Regatta to develop racing boats, but rather to encourage the sport of racing among the old-style fleets, there had to be some tightening of eligibility rules by the racing commission.

"The race committee wasn't against encouraging orderly boat development," Bottomley said, "but we felt we had a responsibility to preserve the integrity of the Bahama racing sloop and the competitiveness of the current fleet, which has some boats more than 30 years old. It would have been a mistake to jeopardize the substantial investment they represented by allowing an attitude of 'anything goes.' That would mean a new boat is obsolete after a season or two, and winning would become a contest between checkbooks."

He paused, then added thoughtfully, "in a world dominated by rapid advances in technology and an obsession with change for change's sake, it's easy to lose a sene of value and proportion. Today to put on the Regatta it costs over $50,000. To raise that much money on an island of limited means isn't easy, so now the Ministry of Tourism kicks in some money."

Why not have commerical sponsors?

"Not a good idea. We live in a time when commercialized sports are rampant. Regatta belongs to Bahamians and it's better if the money and effort comes from them, particularly the Exumians, and not from some outside commercial source seeking only publicity and PR benefits."

You could see his point. It was not hard to imagine a large American sporting company hyping these downhome workboat races into the newest Wide World of Sports event. There would be glib sportscasters endlessly discussing the merits of Rolly Gray's *Tida Wave* versus Edgar Moxey's *Pieces of Eight* and interviewing Captain Roy Bowe about *Jiffy* and how he *really* feels about the race, and does he think he is going to win it, and how does he like Earlin Knowles saying *he* expects to win it for his daddy, and will he say Earlin is not the sailor he brags he is, and...forgetting that on Exuma what counts even today is not the prize money, which isn't much, but the honor and prestige accorded the hand-crafted boat and its crew.

I thanked Commodore Bottomley and left him gazing across the harbor.

Of all the islands, Abaco has the longest boat-building tradition, having produced Abaco smacks and dinghies for 150 years now. But Andros, too, is rooted in a fine boat-building tradition and was known for its sturdy sponging boats. Ragged Island craftsmen built large boats capable of navigating the old Bahama Channel to trade with Cuba. The largest ship ever built in the Bahamas was the *Marie J. Thompson*, a four-masted schooner of 696 tons launched at Harbour Island, Eleuthera, in 1922.

There are still skilled boat-builders on Exuma, too, and we went looking for one. Eighteen miles north, and across the causeway to Barreterre, there is a small settlement with pink, yellow and blue houses on a hill. From up there the view is straight out over a wide sweep of endless blue sky and a jade sea dotted with small green islands.

Here in this remote corner of the Exumas our search ended. We found Hughrie Lloyd — skilled boat builder *par excellence*.

40

Hughrie Lloyd's boatyard spread out from under a gigantic fig tree and covered most of his back yard. We could hear a rooster crowing, goats bleating, the whine of a crosscut saw, a child crying, and above it all, Patti Page on Radio ZNS Nassau singing *The Tennessee Waltz*. In the welcome shade of the fig tree we introduce ourselves to Hughrie, were accepted, and offered a seat on two upturned wooden boxes.

Patti Page was now singing *Amapola*, the sun dappled the ground, and the smell of fresh wood shavings spiced the air. Hughrie, a slight wiry man not given much to talking or smiling, was rigging a mast with his nine-year-old son Kasium, and his partner Ucene Burrows. When he spoke he allowed as how he — but not the other two — could stop just long enough to talk to us about his boats. He put down his planer and wiped his hands on his jeans. Kasium and Ucene Burrows went right ahead rigging the mast.

"My daddy taught me to sail and build boats just like I'm teachin' him." Hughrie nodded at nine-year-old Kasium whom you could see was listening to every word from his daddy, "and in this year's Regatta Kasium is gonna be crewing aboard my Class C, blue-and-yellow smack *Fisherman's Inn*."

We asked what wood he used and as Hughrie rhymed off his favorites I again heard a prose poem in my head: *Dogwood and cyprus, horseflesh and pine; madeira, mahogany, and cedar. Lignum vitae, heartwood, rosewood and bass.* In the old days the wood was hewn in the islands; now, with much of the Bahamas' forests cut down, most wood was imported, as were the metal fastenings and canvas.

For the framing Hughrie preferred Jamaica dogwood if he could get it. Because it was light but strong, fine-grained but easily worked, he liked native cedar for the deck beams. Using the natural bent of the wood, including the roots, he sawed, not bent them to shape. For the boat's ribbands — the lengthwise timbers used to secure the boat's ribs while the outside planking was put on — Hughrie's preference was a wood called horse-flesh, (*Lysiloma sabicu.*) This he hand-sawed, cured and spaced to complete the frame.

For keels and planking, rudders and spars, oars and decks, and the transom, he used Bahamian pine (*Pinus caribaea.*) For framing the small boats, Jamaica dogwood (*Biscidia piscipula,*) was best and native cedar (*Juniperus lucayana*) usually formed the deck beams. Using the natural bent of these also, he sawed, not bent, them to shape.

For framing the larger Class A sloops, madeira, wild tamarind (*Lysiloma bahamensis,*) or *Lignum vitae* — if he could get them were his preferred hardwoods. Stem, sternpost and keel were best made of wild tamarind or mahogany (*Swietenia mahogoni,*) though, according to Hughrie, any builder would "give 'em both a brushoff" for a "good plank of horseflesh."

With pride, he showed us how, after framing, a boat was planked. He now used pine, though in the past he had used both cypress and white cedar. The mast and boom were Canadian or American pine. Once the boat was caulked and painted, a rudder of heartwood pine was attached, the canvas sails were fixed to the boom, and she was ready for her paint job; blue and yellow, the colors of Hughrie's own fleet of four boats.

Not only was Hughrie a master builder of boats that are beautiful, clean-lined, sleek and trim, he was also a businessman. He showed us a boat he was making for an American yachtsman who wanted it as a mold for a fiberglass boat he was having built in the States. There was no formal contract and the design and costs were figured out on the back of an envelope, but it would be ready when Hughrie said it would. "I made arrangement with him," he told us, "and that can't be broke."

For the first time I was looking forward to Regatta this year. Meeting Hughrie made it more vital and interesting. These workboat races weren't the classiest races in the world, but they were watched just as eagerly, fought just as competitively, sailed just as gallantly and prized just as highly as any international high-stakes yachtsmen's race.

Though there were by now 65 winner's purses, ranging in

231

content from $400 to $1,000, it still wasn't the money that Bahamians considered important. The honor and prestige of winning was what counted.

Regatta was also a favorite time for film companies to come to the island to shoot commercials — lots of sun, activity, tanned bodies and firm flesh. Around town these days we saw film crews wielding video cameras and glamorous models leaning languorously against a palm tree, reclining provocatively over the bow of a boat, splayed on the sand, breasting against a bar, or clinging to the mast of a sailboat as if it, and they, were about to confront a hurricane.

In town I came out of the front entrance of the *P&P* and walked right into a film set-up. Shooting a thirty second beer commercial were: a producer, two cameramen, and four young models, all of them attempting to project a Hollywood image by acting like the cast from *Miami Vice.*

The models' name tags read Krystal, Tammye, Sunnie and Lyndda and each was a clone of the other: tanned, honey blond, with perfect white teeth, cute turned-up noses, blue eyes, and tee shirts that came to the tops of legs as long as doors. (The locals who had gathered kept trying to see whether or not they wore anything underneath the tee shirts.) In large green letters their beer sponsor's name bobbed enticingly across their generous bosoms.

In direct contrast to these well-endowed blonds the young

Italianate director had somehow found a large and stately Bahamian woman and her two-year-old grandchild to give a local flavor to the shot. It was anyone's guess as to what would happen with this unlikely combination of hotshot producer and formidable Bahamian matriarch with gran, but it promised to be an interesting drama.

On the island the concept of human worth did not yet confine itself to the lithe bodies and unlined faces of the young; it included the attributes of age and maturity. Grey hair, generosity, and cornucopian good humor counted for much. Even in this day and age island elders were considered valuable members of society, people to be revered and listened to for their wisdom. The grandmothers, perhaps because they raised so many of the children, had a mind of their own and would seldom take direction from anyone they considered had less knowledge and experience — which was almost everyone else. Self-possessed and authoritative, with bodies as strong as their will, Exuma's matriarchs were not about to stand for any foolishness. Especially from a wannabee Italian director...

The scene was riveting. Krystal and Tammye — or maybe it was Sunnie and Lyndda — pretended to be talking to each other but were actually striking poses for the onlookers. Hands on waist, one hip outflung, legs splayed, they jittered and twitched, smiled and gabbled, combed their hair with their fingers, all the while keeping one eye out to see what kind of impression they were making on us, the audience. Most of us stared in astonishment.

The portly grandmother, on the other hand, dressed in her Sunday go-to-church clothes and best flowered hat, leaned composedly against the stone wall with her grandchild standing atop it. The little girl, her hair plaited into corn rows and ornamented with white beads, wore a tiny black and white leotard and a dress with white lace frills at neck and wrists. She looked adorable but also slightly bewildered and hung back into the safety of her granny's arms.

Although everyone was standing within five feet of him, the producer, in best Hollywood style, rallied his cast by using a loud hailer. "This'll only take a few minutes," he shouted down his megaphone, "and we'll do a wrap. Hustle up, girls. Gather round the old lady and the kid. Be sure you show some leg and tits."

Tossing their long tresses about like horses' manes, the four blond fillies pranced up to the woman and her grandaughter, ooo-ing and coo-ing at the child. "Ooo-ooh, you're *so* adorable." Lynnda, or maybe it was Tammye, stroked the child's arm.

"I *lo-o-ove* your lacy ankle sox and your patent leather shoes," burbled another, leaning so far forward that her globular breasts nearly fell out of her bra. Lyndda — or perhaps it was Sunnie — fluttered her hands over the child's corn-row braids, fingered the tiny gold ear studs, and brushed a long red fingernail across the child's extraordinarily long eyelashes. "You're *such* a *sweetie*," she babbled — at which point the child let out a howl of terror, (or possibly fury at the invasion of her private space,) and hid her face in her grandmother's shoulder. Sobs, sniffs, and gulps came forth from the child, without her even bothering to come up for air.

The filming stopped.

"We're wasting time, dammit!" The producer called loudly to the grandmother through his megaphone. "SEE IF YOU CAN PERSUADE HER TO FACE THE CAMERA, DEAR." The grandmother tried, cajoling, talking softly. The child would have none of it.

The models, now flinging their hair about like gypsies, chimed in; using their most seductive voices they promised all kinds of rewards: soft drinks; candy; ice cream. The producer got into the act by promising a ride in his bright, red, LeBaron convertible which he'd had shipped over just for his week in the sun. The little girl's head remained buried.

The photographer offered free pictures to hang on her wall. The child dug her face even deeper into her grandmother's shoulder, refusing to have anything to do with any of them. After ten minutes of trying to entice her it became obvious the child was not going to be enticed. The producer then got angry and railed at the grandmother. "Now you listen to me, Mama. Each minute this kid delays the shoot costs me money an' you won't get paid a dime. Tell her to stop sniveling and face the camera so we can get on with this bitch of a job."

Face calm, eyes stormy, the grandmother gently shushed the child, lifted her onto a plump shoulder, and without saying another word, marched away down the street. The crowd cheered.

In fine temperamental director style, the director flung down his megaphone and yelled at everyone in a disgusted voice. "Back in the car," he commanded. "We'll do our shoot without them. Whose crazy idea was it to use them anyway?"

"*Yours*, idiot," muttered the photographer *sotto voce*.

Regatta and its various madnesses was underway. Betting and *braggadocio* filled the streets. Tomorrow the long-awaited races were due to start.

41

In front of us the sea glittered, the sky was blue, the wind brisk. As the starting gun boomed and thousands of feet of canvas unfurled against the sky, there followed some minutes of chaos. Bow men shouted, crewmen rushed to get the anchor up, boats slammed into one another, lines tangled, and men shinnied frantically up masts to disentangle them. Spectators screamed and yelled insults, encouragement, praise and advice.

The 42nd annual Family Island Regatta had begun.

The America's Cup it was not.

Since the rules decreed boats must start with anchors down and sails furled, mayhem at the start of each race was ensured. This was the first race, the prelims of the Smack class, the chunky fishing boats that are the workhorses of the Bahamas. There would be two more days of racing and mayhem before all three classes of boats were tested, the winners decided.

Once the boats were on their way down the harbor we bought a conchburger from Zelma and sat down on the seawall at Regatta Point to listen to an argument about the best boat in the BIG one: the "Class A" Sloop race.

"Money say it be *Tida Wave*, you'll see," said the Exuma man. "Ain' no boat better'n Rolly Gray's *Tida Wave*. He a twenny-one-time winnin' man, I tell you." With a gnarled hand he took out a twenty dollar bill from the pocket of his faded jeans.

"No, MON!" argued his friend, shaking a grizzled head. "You jes' wait 'til *Rupert Legend* get sail up. *Legend* gonna take *Tida Wave* down easy." He turned to us and explained that the *Legend* belonged to Earlin Knowles, whose father, renowned Long Island boat-builder Rupert Knowles, finished laying the hull last year just before he died. Now, in memory of the old man, Earlin and his son Mark wanted to take the First Place cup home to Long Island "where it belongs."

"That jes' swagger talk. Forty dollar say *Tida Wave* cross the mark firs', like always." The Exuma man held out two twenties.

"That sure be gift money," said the Long Island man, grinning at us, "and if'n I takes it, you loosin' it for sure." He pulled out another twenty, took the first man's two bills, his gleeful chortle revealing a mouth full of gold-capped teeth. He handed the money to a third man to hold.

Mr. Flowers popped up beside us. "Who you bettin' on?" He held a wad of money in his hand.

I hesitated. Though I really liked the idea of *Rupert's Legend* winning for the sake of the old daddy's memory I was, after all, from Exuma and felt the bet was a bit like defending the home baseball team; a certain loyalty was expected.

I lied and said I was putting my money on *Tida Wave*. Mr. Flowers chortled his approval and gave me a low five.

The smack race ended. Hughrie's *Fisherman's Inn II* had won. With the first "Class A" race still an hour away, we walked from Regatta Point into town along the government dock, making our way between the temporary plywood food shacks, hailing friends and acquaintances as we went. Mr. Flowers seemed to know everyone and they him. Music blared, flags fluttered, and in the middle of the road a couple danced an erotic reggae. During Regatta you make a celebration of an ordinary weekday morning. We spied Hughrie in the crowd and went over to congratulate him. Kasium stood by his side, chest puffed out. My husband stopped to talk. I walked on.

From the food shacks, vendors dispensed island folklore, beer, rum, and an array of Bahamian food: boiled fish, stew fish, cracked conch, peas and rice, stewed mutton, or conch chowder. Four dollars bought a plateful. For another dollar you could wash it down with a *Kalik* beer, brewed in Nassau, and pretty good as beer goes. Mr. Flowers bought one at Zelma's shack and offered me the same. I said I preferred coffee, so we wandered on to *Miss Freda's Fine Foods* where he bought me coffee and one of her famous sticky buns. Standing up, we drank and observed the scene.

As they did every year, Exumians had re-painted the pink Government Building, the blue, green and pink houses, the yellow elementary school and the blue and white Episcopal church.

Main street was *en fête* with flags aloft and bunting hung. From the *Two Turtles* to the *Silver Dollar Bar* the friendly streets were awash in an inter-racial sea of good-spirited people; under the three giant cotton trees that shaded the main intersection they strolled bar-hopped, gossipped danced, flirted, argued, ate, laughed, bragged, bet, and swagger-talked.

"Pretty good for Exuma," Mr. Flowers observed. I wasn't sure whether he meant the effort, the influx of tourists, the island economy, or the overall party atmosphere.

"You mean it helps the economy? Or what?"

His disgusted look told me I was way off base and didn't yet understand islanders. "No,no." He waved an arm towards the boats in the harbor, "I mean those boats from all over our country coming together here on Exuma. They our people, Aileen, they our people. We all One Bahamas together."

His pride was evident and I realized I'd missed the point entirely. The most important dimension of Regatta was that it brought Bahamians together. It was a celebration of and for *Bahamians*. For yachters and tourists it was a chance to meet and get acquainted with Bahamians and fellow boaters, have fun, watch the races, and experience a moment out of history.

But for Bahamians it was more than that. It was a once-a-year reunion with other citizens of this far-flung island country, and a chance to watch as captains and crews, descendants of a proud tradition, reaffirmed the country's link with its seafaring past. It was a yearly acting out that renewed their faith in themselves as people of competence, skill and courage.

I recalled something Howland Bottomley said: "Look at the foreign fleet of plastic high tech boats anchored in Elizabeth Harbour. The Bahamian canvas-rigged, wooden boats are beautiful because they're built not from a set of blueprints but by an artist's eye, from an inborn skill inherited from generations of practical builders."

Now, at last, I could see that. Shaped by hands from natural materials, each with its own individuality and carrying with it the spirit of a long tradition, the beauty of these vessels was unsurpassed. I saw that if for no other reason than for the benefit of generations to come, these boats deserved to be nurtured by this uniquely Bahamian event.

Saturday arrived. At two o'clock this afternoon the culmination of the three days of racing would climax with the final race of the "Class A" Sloops. *Lucayan Lady* had racked up the most overall points. *Rupert's Legend* had to win this one big if she was to cop first prize.

My husband had business in town and we agreed to meet at the *P&P* where everyone at Regatta goes to hear about the latest bets and rumors. As I entered the lobby I spotted a familiar figure. Pete Balloil was, amazingly, still in town. He sat on a wicker sofa with an arm around a lovely brunette. He greeted me jovially.

"Hey! Good to see you."

"Where've you been? We thought you were staying around."

"Cuba. Fab sailing."

"Where is your former friend?" I had trouble remembering which one that was. But no matter —

"Left her off in the Dominican Republic. She met a millionaire. This is Krystal. (I thought I recognized her. One of the beer commercial beauties.) We just met. Fab cook." Krystal — tanned, nubile, nearing twenty-one, impressively robust, and wearing a black baseball cap backwards on her blond curls — gazed adoringly up into his face and pasted herself against his chest. Insouciant as ever, Pete Balloil grinned, gave me a wink, and kissed the top of her baseball cap.

He looked fab too. Bronzed by the sun, blue eyes electric, lean, hard, cocky. He'd never change, and why should he? Nothing said there can't be modern-day adventurers who spend their life roaming the world's oceans and having a girl in every port. At one time or another it was probably every man's dream to be as free and unencumbered as Pete Balloil. I must ask my husband.

I asked how *"The Bucc"* held up to the Cuba trip.

"Sup-ah. Really su-pah. Come along with us and I'll buy you a drink and tell you about it. Your husband here?" I said I was meeting him in the bar.

The bar held the usual assortment of Regatta visitors: media celebs, adorable boat bunnies, diplomats, members of parliament, journalists and VIP's — but no Royals. Thirtysome years ago Britain's Prince Philip came out for Regatta and sailed aboard the *Lady Muriel* as honorary skipper. Talk now centered on

Earlin's chances of bringing the *Legend* in first, and whether or not the Bahamian Prime Minister, The Right Honorable Hubert Ingraham and his wife were here, were not here, will not be here, will be here as usual, would not want to miss the annual presentation of awards on the last night, including his coveted Prime Minister's Cup.

Ever-friendly, Pete Balloil struck up a conversation with some cruising yachters at a nearby table. Two were from the U.S., one from Canada, one from France, and there was a salty dog from Australia. He said he'd been sailing since he was ten, loved the sea, loved these old seahorse workboats, and in his distinctive Aussie accent, said, "I tell you, mate, to see one of these Bahamian work boats under sail is to see one of man's better creations, a boat made by his own hands, from material nature provided, powered by the wind and skimming across a turquoise sea. Now *that's* a sight!"

When my husband arrived talk turned to the cruise to Cuba.

"Superb sailing," Pete said. "Absolutely superb. I say, once Cuba opens up to tourism the Bahamas are going to have to compete for the yachting dollar. The harbors and inlets there are spectacular, deep and protected. Everything is ridiculously cheap but the towns are depressing. Nothing in the shops, electricity cables lying on the ground, roads full of potholes, broken sidewalks — and a most awful air of dejection and hopelessness. I don't know what's going to happen to those people, they're as poor as the Haitians and it's going to take years to get them back on their feet."

From behind the bar Lermon called "comin' up on two-thirty, mon. Last race. Bes' get to the boats." Everyone drank up and headed harborside. Somebody announced the PM *had* arrived.

As we waited my excitement mounted. The prelims were over now, this was the Big One. The one Earlin Knowles hoped to win for his daddy. Someone said over thirty thousand dollars had been bet on this race; I wondered how they knew.

On the water was a seaful of boats. Boston Whalers, Zodiaks, cigarette boats, sailboats and sleek power yachts. They bobbed and darted, plunged and dipped like waterfowl at a nesting site.

I began to inform my husband of my newly-found sailing

lore; (Commodore Bottomly would be proud of me.)

The course, I told him, was the classic three legs: first to windward, then a reach, then a jibe to run back to the start line. (Dinghies and smacks go once around, the "Class A" Sloops twice.) The harbor was a mile wide, five miles long, and promised to be a rugged test of stamina, strength, seamanship, and good tactics. Around us everyone speculated about *Rupert's Legend*.

The warning gun sounded — one minute to go — and sails furled, a line of fourteen "Class A" sloops took their place by dropping anchor and falling back. Eyes glued on the water, everyone waited for the starting gun.

"Wind's up," said a man standing to my right, looking out across the harbor." Chop's increased. Gonna be a fast race." The starting gun boomed.

There was the usual starting mayhem — a burst of frenzied hauling and sweating as crews raised anchor — then fourteen loose-footed white mainsails bloomed against the sky.

With canvas up and sails filled, the boats heeled sharply. Bowsprits poked into topsides, booms scraped across a competitor's bow, sails were torn, spars sprung. The crews struggled valiantly to clear their boats. Then *Legend* broke free. Cheers! Yells of encouragement. Offers of advice. *Go, Legend!*

Then began a frantic scramble for the lead. Aboard *Rupert's Legend* a sailor had reefed the mainsail, Bahamian style, by wrapping a line around the boom; now he frantically trimmed the jib as his boat surged ahead.

Sails billowing in the wind, the boats took off on the first leg of their triangular course, no longer appearing heavy and broad-beamed but looking like enormous white birds in full flight. They flew down the harbor toward the first mark. I recalled the Aussie's words: "Now *that's* a sight!"

Leaning into the wind, with masts tilted at a 45 degree angle, the crews were only able to maintain their precarious balance by dangling from the outrigged plank called "the pry." This long board extended at a 45 degree angle about three feet out from the side of the boat.

Boosted by a strong east wind on the first leg of their course, the boats veered into the wind, slim as a chalk lines against the blue sky. Captain Earlin Knowles was handling the *Legend* beau-

241

tifully, having used his first tack to put her right in line for the windward mark.

The huge canvas sails needed ballast to compensate for their size, so the crews — sometimes as many as 18 men — provided live ballast by quickly shifting from one side of the boat to the other. Anywhere from one to three of them at a time could be seen straddling the pry. The others sat along the rail, riding with one leg over the side, holding onto the shoulder of the man ahead, their bodies stretched far out to windward, inching fore and aft along the rail on the captain's command.

This was a dangerous procedure. With seven or eight men scurrying from rail to rail under the boom of a 50 foot boat, not the least of the problems was the danger of a crewman being knocked out, or thrown overboard by the boom.

We, too, were now on the water, following the racers up and down the harbor in *Coquina*, Eunice and Rand's Boston Whaler. The sea was choppy, the waves white-rimmed. We could hear the bowmen calling out wind directions and course changes. Race committee patrol boats darted about checking for rules violations and warning spectators to keep clear.

We and the other spectator boats sped up and down the course, idling just off the floating orange buoys that marked the course, watching and cheering as each boat rounded the mark before heeling into the wind to start back down the harbor. The rules dictated that if two boats met and neither could cross ahead of the other, both must tack.

On the last leg *Legend* and *Tida Wave* came flying down the course, bow to bow, sails full, crews hauling rope, heading for the last buoy. As they rounded the final mark it looked as if there must be a spill, that they must collide, couldn't help but smash up on one another's bowsprit and send splinters flying.

But with topnotch seamanship, sails billowing and the crew angled 45 degrees from the pry board, *Rupert's Legend* shot out in front and crossed the finish line first.

Earlin Knowles had brought glory to his daddy's name.

The air filled with cheers and hooting boat whistles.

In late afternoon The Royal Bahamas Police Force Band from Nassau, wearing their white uniforms, white topees, red sashes and leopard-skin vests, put on a jazzy march-past and concert in Regatta Park. After that the Junkanoo band toured the streets, drumming and chanting. People danced, drank, pounded one another on the back, congratulated one another, collected their bets, and continued arguing about the races.

Strings of lights on the Government Building, the bandstand in Regatta Park, *John Marshall's* and the *P&P*, lit up the sky. The PM presented the awards from a platform in front of the Government building. When all the prizes and trophies, the speeches and congratulations were over, a final round of celebrations burst forth, culminating in the annual dance at the St. Andrew's Community Center across from the *P&P*.

Next day Mr. Flowers came by the house. "You heard about the *Legend*?" he asked.

When I said we hadn't he smiled and shook his head. Everyone was talking about the first news item that morning on Radio ZNS Nassau.

Ervin Knowles, the former member of parliament from Cat Island and a cousin of Earlin's, had offered to buy *Rupert's Legend* for $150,000.

Earlin and Mark said no.

42

When you are fortunate enough to own a second home you must — in spite of securing the place and its contents as well as possible — expect that at some time unwelcome incursions may happen. We were still in the North Country this year when Stanley phoned to tell us the house had been broken into.

Once before this had happened and the culprits were found by the police to be three local teenagers with a history of break-ins. Few things of significance were taken and the boys were sent to Nassau to the Boys Industrial School where they would be disciplined and taught a trade.

This time however it was not prankish teenagers but an escaped convict from Nassau who was on the lam and had used our house as a hideaway. Stanley encountered him when he went to check the house and found the glass patio door to the Great Room open. Upon entering the house he met the man coming out of the back bedroom where it was later revealed he had holed up for several days. By the time Stanley got to a phone, called the police and they arrived on the scene from George Town, the escapee had long gone, taking with him two duffle bags full of my husband's clothing, our scuba gear, various household items, and a supply of dried food. He was never caught.

I've heard people say that having their house robbed gave them a feeling of vulnerability, as though they had been personally violated. It's true. The thought of a stranger's eyes and hands pawing through our belongings was chilling. I felt as if our privacy had been maliciously invaded. Though we reported the missing articles, there was nothing we could do, nothing, that is, but accept the fact.

Nonetheless that was hard and could have easily aroused anger and a desire for retribution. But the fact of the matter was that these days, no matter in what society or culture or country we lived, there would always be the poor, the needy, or the just plain wanting who would resort to thievery to get what they felt they needed or should have. It wasn't a happy thought, nor one to make anyone rest easy, but it was a fact of life in this last decade of the 20th century; best we deal with it as well as we could.

This was also the year when we learned that even in Eden one does not escape death and disease. A beloved Bahamian friend, despite her years of island living and her happy outlook on life, had died of cancer. Another friend, a kind and generous American woman, was fading slowly into the mists of Alzheimer's.

One other aspect of a perfect Eden was shattered when out of the blue one day after we'd been on the island for four months my husband suggested it might be a good idea if we made a trip to Miami, do some shopping, see a show, watch some TV, lap up a little luxury. He waved a brochure at me. A major Miami hotel was having a special getaway promotion, room rates were down, there would be new things to see and do and we could phone the kids without it costing a fortune.

Not for one moment did I disagree with him. For about a month now I felt he hadn't been himself. I didn't know why this was and if he knew why he wasn't saying. I myself had been suffering from whatever undisclosed ailment was bothering him. I'd felt myself not being myself. I was seldom even-tempered or reasonable but in the last while even to myself I seemed grouchy and unreasonable. I immediately started packing our bags. Despite the senior's discount, our hotel room on Miami Beach was no Early Bird Special. It was on the 14th floor, faced west and overlooked the pool and the ocean beyond. A beautiful room with a/c, TV, yellow flowered drapes with bedspreads to match, a fruit basket, a stocked refrigerator, flowers on the bureau, fragrant soaps and shampoos in the spotless bathroom, and pale yellow bathtowels the size of tablecloths. I executed a little two-step and hugged my husband of forty-nine years. "A romantic hideaway," I caroled, "and just the two of us to enjoy it."

"Did you pack my Athlete's Foot powder? My feet are killing me." This was not the response I desired.

That evening we took a taxi to dinner at a fancy restaurant. Traffic was heavy and once into Miami's South Beach restaurant district we had to sit and wait, getting hungrier and more impatient by the moment as we listened to the driver's long list of complaints and his cursing of everyone from the local politicians and the recent crime statistics to the pedestrians crossing the street in front of his taxi. He hated them all. Especially the "young thugs."

"You got any crime over there where you live?"

We said of course we did, there were crooks and thieves in every society and these days there probably wasn't a place on earth where there wasn't some sort of crime.

"Can't be like Miami. Here the thugs rule the streets at night. I'm thinkin' of moving me and my family out. Trouble is, I don't know where else I can go and still earn a living. They need taxi drivers over there where you live?"

We told him no dice. As a non-Bahamian he couldn't get a permit to work there. Unless, that is, he was working at something that doesn't take a job away from a Bahamian. On the island there were numerous taxi-drivers.

I thought about this as we sat stalled in traffic. While crime had been mounting in Nassau for years, partly because of drugs but also because of poverty, it had taken longer to reach the island. Only when there were break-ins and robberies such as the one we just experienced were we alerted to the fact that the island had at last caught up with today's crime.

Still, I doubted there were any more thieves, drug dealers, thugs or corrupt politicians per capita in the Bahamas than anywhere else. Fortunately, crime on Exuma was still minimal and like the teenagers who stole from us and other residents, Bahamian and non-Bahamians alike, they were generally known and soon discovered. Then their families, pastor, and community judged them.

The taxi driver was going on about firearms now, about how everyone, if he was smart, owned a gun. "Women in particular were "packing." He shook his head."Next thing you know America will be going back to the Old West when the only law is the law of the gun." Crime was obviously the subject most persistently on his mind and my husband, not usually so testy, had had enough. He leaned forward, said, "it's not far now. We'll walk."

"Better be careful." The cabbie accepted our money. "Ain't

safe to walk the streets less you stay in the lighted area and walk in the middle of the sidewalk. Don't go into any sidestreets and keep your wallet next to your skin. Have a good night."

Once out of the cab the smells of the streets hit us, a flood of gas fumes, cooking oil, human sweat, garbage, dirt, smoke and stale air. Lights everywhere. People everywhere, jamming the sidewalk, pushing in and out of the restaurants, filling the sidewalks.

So many people! More people on this one street than lived in the whole of George Town. I'd always liked city living, enjoyed city culture but now, for the first time, I was feeling culture shock in my own country. I realized two things: I was older now, and big city living was not kind to seniors.

"Let's go back." Irritably, my husband took my arm, "this is depressing. Life's too short to put up with this."

I was surprised. This was so unlike him.

Stopped by his ire, I didn't quibble. He almost never grumbled and was usually upbeat, cheerful, and reasonable. At the hotel the feeling deepened that there was something wrong, something my husband wasn't telling me.

We went to the hotel's air-conditioned dining room to eat dinner, choosing to have the salad bar with our steaks. I went first, then he walked over to the salad bar and began filling his plate. To await his return I looked around the room, finally turning my gaze back to the salad bar. I couldn't find him.

He was not among the six or seven people standing there. I decided he must have gone to the men's room — with a salad in his hand? I scanned the restaurant. He was not anywhere else in the place. Where was he? Not really worried yet, I stood up to get a better look around. Had he suddenly been taken ill? Had to rush out of the restaurant? But if so surely he would have left word?

Then I spotted him. He was one of the older men at the salad bar. Shocked, I sank back into my chair. I didn't recognize my own husband! Under the restaurant's strange orangey lights his face looked drawn and lined, his eyes puffy, his skin a bleached grey. Something *was* wrong and I was frightened.

"What's wrong?" I asked before he could even sit down.

"Nothing. Everything's fine. You having a good time?"

"Yes, of course. Wonderful." But suddenly I was not hungry any more.

We returned to our air-conditioned room to watch TV, eventually turning off the a/c when it got too chilly to be comfortable. After we talked to the kids and chatted about family matters I felt more cheerful, yet I couldn't make out why my husband lacked interest in my new lacy nightgown.

"Are you all right?" I asked him again.

"Just tired."

I felt it was more than mere tiredness. More like a deep exhaustion.

Had it been too much for him — all those years of teaching, administration, consulting, helping support a mortgage, a wife, and two kids, putting them through college? Economising, saving money to realize our retirement dreams, adding to the Exuma house — was that it? Was his heart tired and giving out? Or was it being married to me for so long ...?

The TV movie we watched was filled with young and beautiful men and women in beautiful rooms, expensive clothes, and fancy restaurants, meeting more young and handsome people driving shiny new cars and pursuing lives far removed from mine. That night, as he tossed and turned beside me, I kept wondering what signal I was not catching from him, what clue I'd missed, what significant information he was not telling me. If the news was bad I wanted to know.

In the middle of the night I woke up in a cold sweat. Suddenly the hotel's long carpeted corridors, cell-like rooms, and chilly air felt like a prison. Why had we come here? Not to eat, drink and be merry in these artifical, relentlessly impersonal, and cleanly efficient surroundings. Why then? I longed to wake him up and ask but he appeared so tired... I decided I must wait until after breakfast.

But I couldn't sleep. I woke again at 3 a.m. and got up to look out the window at the sea. The moon was partially hidden behind dark clouds but the sea still glowed a mellow gold. I watched for a long time. A car passed along a nearby road, its lights briefly illuminating a palm tree. After it passed the tree appeared to sink into darkness and with it, my heart.

He was up early, fully dressed before I got out of bed. "I have to go out," he said, not looking at me. "Should be back about noon."

"Where are you going? This is supposed to be a vacation, can't I come too?"

"It's just something I have to do while we're here. Won't take long, I promise. Meet you for lunch downstairs. We can eat by the pool if you like."

"I know there's something wrong. What is it?" This was one of the few times in this long marriage he hadn't been straight with me.

He didn't answer. Walked over to the window. Looked out at the sea. Shrugged as if making a decision. "I have to go for some tests, that's all. To the hospital. It's not far from here. As I said, I should be back by noon."

My carefully structured world splintered into a thousand pieces. I must have turned paper white because he walked over and put an arm around my shoulders.

"I'm sure it'll turn out to be nothing. The island doctor thought I should come over here and check it out."

"Check what out?

"Some dark spots on my skin."

"You mean —" I couldn't say the word melanoma.

"Lots of men my age get them. It's from the sun. Too much exposure to the sun. Guess I should've been more careful all those years ago, up there on the roof with Stanley."

I tried a smile. "You should've worn the Birdwatcher's pith helmet."

"Never!" He started for the door, turned back, grinned. "Well, maybe some times. See you later."

43

While awaiting my husband's return I sat looking out the window. This was the day I realized we might have to leave the island for good. It was also the day I realized I didn't want to. The island was no longer just a piece of geography; by now it was an idea realized from my dream-mind. Away from it, I thought of it with longing. It haunted me with memories of its shimmering landscapes and days so bright and cloudless they seemed touched with magic — but mostly I remembered its gentle friendly people and their many attributes, which before now I had taken for granted.

It was a place of peace that we were blessed to be a part of, a place where the roar of the world was not yet too loud, where the people still spoke softly, with civility, where the days were filled with artless simplicity. A place still mostly free of society's man-made clutter.

I closed my eyes, remembering our life there. Not a perfect life, lacking some things, but one that brought a keen sense of being alive. I recalled those mornings when the night's rain left everything clear and shining in the light of the rising sun, when there was birdsong, and the smell of dew and freshly-wet earth.

I thought about the wonderfully dear and funny women at the Packing House; how the produce there would change almost overnight, from squash, tomatoes and watermelon to crisp and shiny red and green peppers, fresh kale, dark green bunches of celery and large, pale green cabbages that made a superb coleslaw. I thought about the tamarisk trees along the roadsides hanging heavy with yellow, sweet-smelling blossoms that perfumed my morning walks with my neighbor Rita.

I thought about the evenings when my husband and I walked out, strolling the island's roads, listening to the sea and watching the stars come out; or the times we watched the moon rise, and now it seemed strange that we could ever have lived out of touch with these phenomena, or with indifference to the elements. Had there really been a time when we found island evenings boring and the nights long?

Nowadays when friends wrote asking "what do you *do* all day on that island? Don't you get bored?" I wrote back saying there never seemed to be enough time to do all we wanted to do and quoted Tex James: "I don't know what we do but I'm three weeks behind doing it..." Fact was, I'd gotten used to island life and its simple pleasures... .

Restless, I turned away from the view and decided to go down to the coffee shop to pass the time waiting... .

Sipping hot coffee I went back to my musing.

For one thing, the island had taught me a lot about myself and my habits. I'd learned I was more flexible than I knew, and that I could survive without a lot of the things I formerly considered necessary to my well-being.

Certainly we had, in our time, been eager members of the consumer society. We'd bought our share of "stuff" we didn't need, only to store it away in a cupboard or sell it at a garage sale. And perhaps it was elitist to now say I wanted to leave that kind of life behind, but in fact it was more correct to say that island life had cured me of it.

The "shopping till you drop" syndrome and the "buying just to be buying" mania were gone. What set island life apart for me was its simplicity and frugality. There was little more to buy than the necessities. Food, gasoline, a bottle of wine now and then, an occasional meal out, perhaps some native baskets or crafts as gifts — anything else was simply not needed... .

And another thing... .

Life's greatest pleasures for me now had to do with living simply and learning to enjoy pursuits I had formerly passed by without realizing their hidden meaning or knowing how to understand them. Such pleasures were subtle and subdued; picnics, swimming, conversations with friends of all races and persuasions, good books, a perfect sunset, the freshness of early morning air, walks with a friend through a morning scented with wild thyme, pine and honeysuckle, food eaten without regard to manners or mess, private hours in which to think and write, and at the end of each day, sleep enticed by the gentle murmur of the nearby surf.

These weren't sophisticated or smart pleasures, but something far quieter and more peaceful, and, in the final analysis, more restorative.

It had taken me years but slowly, I had begun to appreciate all this and its profound influence on my inner life. It had taken time and patience for me to learn that the lure of Paradise is its timeless quality and that it is here, not there; that all time becomes the present when you completely enter into whatever it is you're doing — watching the stars, walking on the beach, writing, working in the garden, searching for shells, beachcombing, building, birdwatching, hiking, staring at the waves, being with friends — the feeling is one of transcending time. Only the moment exists.

Restless now, I looked at my watch. Only 10 a.m. My head began to pound, my teeth were clenched. My waitress brought more hot coffee... .

The clock on the coffee shop wall read 10:30. Was that all? Should I take a walk. Go shopping? Buy a magazine? I rode the elevator back upstairs and went back to sitting at the window.

In this moment — sitting on the 14th floor of a Miami hotel while looking out the window and evaluating our lives — I realized how subtly but relentlessly the island had transformed me before I was aware of it. Its tenacity, its vulnerability, lying as it does surrounded by the powerful forces of sun, wind and sea had renewed my belief in the ultimate order of the world.

I vowed to live with ever more awareness and appreciation of our good fortune if my husband returned to me in good health.

When the plane landed at Exuma's airport two days later I unexpectedly broke into tears — not from sadness but relief. I was so happy to be back after the trying days in Miami that my emotions overcame me. Everyone we saw appeared to be smiling.

Christine was there wearing a blinding turban of pink, purple and green. She gave us a hug. Zelma Nixon was there in Will's blue taxi van to drive us home. We told her we didn't have the money to pay her right then because we'd spent all our cash in Miami. She laughed. "I've done that. No prob-lem. Pay me later."

As before, to mark our safe arrival we observed our small ritual of return, believing every special event should end with a small ceremony. We did the chores then raced for our bathing suits. Wearing our ragged old straw hats we carried sunblock oil, sandwiches, lemonade, fruit, and the current books to the old (and now rust-pitted) Chevy and headed for Sand Dollar Beach.

The water was as clear and warm as ever, the shoreline still offered up the usual white sandollars. The same turquoise light was there. It had all been here waiting for us to come back.

My husband was all right. He'd had three pre-cancerous lesions removed from his skin and from now on had to be careful, wear a wide-brimmed hat, use a number 40 sunscreen at all times, stay out of the midday sun, and check with a dermatologist once a year; other than that he was fine. We would be fine. Wiser, more cautious, not so sure, but fine. I was so glad to be back I got up and ran into the sea to lie on the water and look up at the clouds pearling the sky.

In the shade of the trees we dried off, read for a while, napped briefly on our beach towels, and at twilight, when the air was cooling and the western sky was burnished with peach and gold, we gathered up books and swimming gear and headed home.

The first star was out, shimmering palely against the lighted sky. Unfortunately, the mosquitoes were also out and as insistent and vicious as ever. From the garage we ran fast up to the house, slamming the doors against their attacks. Bugs and all, everything was as usual. That comforted me. Our long-sought, long-awaited retirement life could now begin again.

EPILOGUE

Over the years, while writing down our island experiences in my daily journal I was spurred on by the conviction that much of what I had recorded would, in time, vanish forever. As the island moves into the 21st Century, the older generation of islanders like Stanley and Miss Corrine, Nigel and Miss Edith, Will Nixon, Miss Elsie May, John Marshall, Christine and Mr. Flowers, — those with the memories of a farming and fishing society — will all be gone.

Gone, too — if development continues to move forward — the simple beauty of unspoiled beaches and starry nights, of undisturbed bushland and silent walks, and perhaps, too, the friendly people with warm smiles and generous ways who, when driving a car along the Queen's Highway, never fail to wave to oncoming drivers or pick up nine-year-old hitch-hikers.

For as the island turns to full-time tourism and real estate development I fear that politeness and tranquility, friendliness and courtesy will inevitably pay the price.

Already, over the past years things have changed. Several years ago we got not only a phone but a fax. We have a new Chevy Cavalier wagon. All the trees and bushes are at least ten feet higher than when we moved in, and there are many more of them. There is a vine-covered trellis trailing wild morning glory blossoms over the deck on the northeast side of the house. The turquoise light is still the same, though, the sea still as beautiful, the sun as warm, the stars as bright.

In October, 1996, the eye of Hurricane *Lili* roared through George Town, with the loss of four houses, and some damage to boats and roofs but — amazingly — no loss of life. We lost our garage roof and our lovely old seagrape tree fell over, but with ropes and stays and friendly help we were able to save it and once again it lends us its generous shade.

Inchie died on July 4, 1996, our dear friend Nigel died during the summer of 1997; and at 95 Miss Edith lives on in her own dream world. Will Nixon "passed over" that year too, a cancer victim.

Work on the The Bight resort project — and possibly others has begun. Someday there may be a multi-million dollar resort next to Farmer's Hill with marina, golf course, casino, condominiums and fancy houses; then Farmer's Hill will lose its sleepy fishing village quality and its people will start to hustle. Perhaps the children of the village will no longer be able to run in and out of "auntie's" and grandma's house, the oratorical contest may be deemed useless and old-fashioned, and Zelma may be too busy to write a Christmas play for The Church Of God Of Prophecy.

Having lived on the island for twelve winters, I have been able, with the help of the island and its people, and the loving help and guidance from a special circle of Bahamian and non-Bahamian friends, to develop a sense not only of the sacredness of all things, but of how everyone is connected in one vast, indivisible, web of life.

For all of this I am grateful.

Living on Exuma has given us time to slow down, draw in, and reflect not only about Exuma's fragile ecology but the fragility of the planet itself. From here the world appears to be obsessed with economic and technical growth and fast profits. The results are massive pollution of water and air, dying fish and wildlife, contamination of the atmosphere by carbon dioxide, rising world temperatures, rainforest destruction, heedless development, and the death of many fragile ecosystems. One can only conclude that our lovely planet is ill; indeed, that she may be dying and is already on her knees.

Are we on a suicide mission to kill the planet that gave us life? If so, when do we pass the point of no return? And if we do pass that point, will she simply die because of our lack of care -- and take us with her?

As my husband and I near the end of our journey on this beautiful planet we sometimes ask ourselves: When we look back on our lives will the way we live now be meaningful?

To show reverence for the earth is an act of significance. So each morning, each in our own way, we give thanks for the sun of a new day, the clean air and the life-giving sea, and for the dark and the stars and the bliss of sleep.

And because everything we do, touch, see, or feel (from cutting up vegetables to kissing our kids, hugging our friends and serving our community) has individual energy in it and contains our sorrow or joy, our misery or happiness, our anger or love, we try to extend only positive thoughts and emotions, for these, we feel, are what will ultimately sustain and heal our planet.

Exumians, flocking off the plane from Miami or Nassau with bright expectant faces and happy smiles often say, "'ain no place like this sweet island". So too, do we say upon our arrival here, "aren't we blessed to share in this sweet place?".

The planet belongs to God and it is not our property to do with as we please. It is on loan to us and we are expected to return it to the Creator in good condition. Or, quite possibly, in better condition than we found it.